Joseph Schumpeter's Two Theories of Democracy

Thomas J. Wilson Prize

The Board of Syndics of Harvard University Press
has selected this book as cowinner of the thirtieth annual
Thomas J. Wilson Prize, honoring the late director of the Press.
The prize is awarded to books chosen by the
Syndics as best first books accepted
by the Press during the calendar year.

Joseph Schumpeter's Two Theories of Democracy

John Medearis

HARVARD UNIVERSITY PRESS

Cambridge, Massachusetts

London, England

2001

To my mother,
Mary Ellen Marble Medearis,
and to the memory of my father,
Donald Norman Medearis, Jr.
(August 22, 1927–September 29, 1997)

Library of Congress Cataloging-in-Publication Data

Medearis, John.
  Joseph Schumpeter's two theories of democracy / John Medearis.
    p.   cm.
  Includes bibliographical references and index.
  ISBN 0-674-00480-9 (alk. paper)
    1. Schumpeter, Joseph Alois, 1883–1950—Contributions in political
science.   2. Democracy.   3. Elite (Social sciences)   I. Title.

JC251.S37 M43   2001
321.8—dc21   2001016577

Contents

Acknowledgments

Carole Pateman inspired me to rethink my conception of democracy in the contemporary world, and has provided invaluable guidance and criticism throughout the preparation of this book. I knew Richard Ashcraft for only a few years before his death, but in that time he continually challenged me, and helped me to hone the interpretive tools I used to uncover a different story about Joseph Schumpeter. Jeffrey C. Alexander and Eugene Victor Wolfenstein offered far more counsel and support along the way than I could have reasonably asked for. Especially in the early years of this project, a special group of friends and colleagues— Clyde Barrow, Timothy Gaffaney, Jessica Goodheart, Danise Kimball, Mike Miller, William Niemi, Daniel O'Connor, Eugene Sheppard, and Keith Topper—prodded me to refine and clarify my ideas. Eugene Goodheart commented thoroughly, sympathetically, and helpfully on a version of Chapter 3. Amy Reynolds was a superb research assistant and helped enormously in preparing the manuscript. Stephan Mayer assisted my translation of portions of "Sozialistische Möglichkeiten von heute." Ian Shapiro and Richard Swedberg very generously sent me advance copies of materials that were going to press as I finished this work. I have been lucky to find in Michael Aronson, my editor at Harvard University Press, an astute reader and an able guide to the editing and publishing process. Julie Ericksen Hagen, my copy editor, smoothed the rougher edges of my prose. The staffs of the Österreichisches Staatsarchiv in Vienna, the SOWIDOK archive of the Kammer für Arbeiter und Angestellte in Vienna, the Bundesarchiv in Potsdam, the Universitäts- und Landesbibliothek in Bonn, and the Harvard University Archives in Cambridge facilitated my research patiently and resourcefully. I would also like to thank the Harvard University Archives for permission to quote from materials in its possession. Portions of Chapters 1, 3, and 4 are drawn from my article "Schumpeter, the New Deal, and

Democracy," *American Political Science Review* 91, no. 4 (December 1997). Portions of Chapters 5 and 6 are drawn from "Ideology, Democracy, and the Limits of Equilibrium: A Schumpeterian Critique," *British Journal of Political Science* 31, no. 2 (April 2001). I would like to thank both journals for permission to incorporate materials from those articles in this book.

1

Introduction

Publicly, at least, Joseph Schumpeter disdained his own 1942 book, *Capitalism, Socialism, and Democracy*. But that cannot be said for the generations of political scientists who came of age during their discipline's crucial postwar development. The book that Schumpeter dubbed a "potboiler" has had an "extraordinary impact" on Anglo-American political science and theory during the past half century (Allen 1991, 2: 133; Held 1987, 164). In it, Schumpeter treated democracy as a form of elite political competition, and this conception of democracy deeply influenced some of the texts that have shaped political science, helping to originate a school of democratic theory that is variously labeled "contemporary," "equilibrium," "elite," or "empirical" (Ashcraft 1995, 1; Bachrach 1967, 18–22; Held 1987, 164; Macpherson 1977, 77; Pateman 1970, 3–5; Shapiro 1994, 125; Skinner 1973, 287; Swedberg 1991a, 278 n. 141). Scholars have learned from Schumpeter to define democracy as a "method" or "institutional arrangement" for arriving at political decisions, to identify democracy with "competitive leadership" and "the rule of the politician" rather than mass participation and popular rule, and to decouple the discussion of democracy from any set of ends or values, especially those associated with what he called "the classical doctrine of democracy" ([1942] 1976, 250–264, 269, 270, 282, 284, 285).

Even figures who loom large in political science in their own right have been almost eulogistic in acknowledging Schumpeter's influence. Anthony Downs wrote that Schumpeter's "profound analysis of democracy" provided the "inspiration and foundation" for the "whole thesis" of *An Economic Theory of Democracy*, and added that his "debt and grati-

1

tude" to Schumpeter were "great indeed" (Downs 1957, 29 n. 11). One of the structuring premises of Seymour Martin Lipset's influential article "Some Social Requisites of Democracy," and of his book *Political Man*, was a definition of democracy Lipset said he "abstracted" from the work of Schumpeter and Max Weber (1959, 71; 1960, 45). Decades after Lipset wrote those works, prominent political scientists continued to follow in the "tradition of Joseph A. Schumpeter" by borrowing a definition of democracy from his work (Huntington 1984, 195). Schumpeter's elite conception has even justifiably been cast as the "prototype" for works on democracy whose authors credited him less directly, such as Robert A. Dahl and Bernard R. Berelson (Berelson, Lazarsfeld, and McPhee, 1954, 305; Dahl 1956, 131 n. 12; Held 1987, 164; Macpherson 1977, 78 n. 1; Pateman 1970, 8; Skinner 1973, 287). So it should be no surprise that the authors of a recent article titled "What Democracy Is . . . and Is Not" report that to this day "the definition [of democracy] most commonly used by American social scientists is that of Joseph Schumpeter"; indeed the authors' own definition of "modern political democracy" shows clear marks of Schumpeter's influence (Schmitter and Karl 1996, 61 n. 3).

Of course, the idea that democracy is just a method or institutional arrangement has long been quite widespread outside of academia as well. Whether the subject is the power of the "oligarchs" in Russia, economic crisis in Asia, get-out-the-vote operations in Iowa, or pork-barrel politics in Washington, for the elite whose voices are heard in newspapers and on television, democracy is simply synonymous with the existence of familiar electoral and legislative institutions. Thus Schumpeter's influence has done its work in a receptive social and political environment. True, proposals for town meeting–style discussions and other devices for making American representative democracy more deliberative have received some attention in the media. And the voices of political activists who use the language of democracy to criticize American society and to describe and justify social and economic change are occasionally heard. But in general, the idea that democracy might require, entail, or imply more than elite electoral competition seems virtually lost on most of those who set the agenda for political discussion on television, radio, newspapers, and now the Internet. And, needless to say, the idea that there might be a democratic approach to trade agreements, affirmative action, or labor relations gets no hearing at all.

Yet, pervasive as it is today among professional academics and journalists, the assumption that democracy could be *just* a matter of elite competition for office within the confines of particular political institutions would have seemed strange indeed to nineteenth-century writers who tried to understand the growth of democracy in North America and Europe. We may smile at Alexis de Tocqueville's claim that "the gradual development of the principle of equality" was "a providential fact"—a sign of God's will, manifest in an "irresistible revolution that has advanced for centuries" ([1835] 1945, 6). But Tocqueville was simply expressing in the most profound terms available to him his view that to write about democracy was in part to write about the progressive spread of equality and the ways in which this could transform every aspect of social life. John Stuart Mill praised precisely this aspect of Tocqueville's work, and incorporated it in his own writings on democracy ([1835] 1973, 173–213).

I mention this not to launch a revival of Tocqueville or Mill, but rather to demonstrate that the idea of democracy as a mere method or institutional arrangement has a history, has temporal and social limits. Despite the air of self-evidence surrounding it now, it would have seemed anything but self-evident to commentators on democracy in Mill and Tocqueville's time. Often the first steps toward criticizing a pervasive idea are to cut through its pretensions to self-evidence and universality, to reveal its concrete origins and lay bare the practical and choices associated with its emergence. Surprisingly enough, Schumpeter's own writings provide the materials needed for such a critique of the elite conception of democracy with which he is so often associated.

In this study I challenge the standard view that the elite conception of democracy as a method was Schumpeter's only definitive statement on the subject. From about 1916 onward, Schumpeter actually theorized about democracy in two distinguishable ways. As is well known, he theorized about the ways that elite groups and parties may be able to preside over a formally democratic institutional arrangement, providing some measure of political competition but certainly not providing opportunities for wide participation and human development on equal terms. In *Capitalism, Socialism, and Democracy* his elite conception of democracy as a political method was the last and fullest expression of this dimension of his thought on democracy. But over the course of thirty years, and in a variety of works that include *Capitalism, Socialism, and Democracy,* Schumpeter also developed a different conception of democracy as a real historical tendency implicated in social transformation. Although both conceptions were related to his broad theory of the development from liberal capitalism to democratic socialism, there were always clear tensions between these two conceptions of democracy.

The neglected *transformative* conception of democracy—to give it a name—stressed the importance of democratic beliefs and ideology, whereas the elite conception of democracy minimized their significance. The transformative conception of democracy highlighted the radicalizing, dynamic effects of movements that attempt to realize democratic values and act on democratic ideologies, while his better-known elite model depicted democracy in static terms and as institutionally stable. And the transformative conception emphasized the social and economic implications of spreading democratic movements and practices, whereas the elite conception held that democracy was simply an arrangement of *political* institutions. Any complete interpretation of Schumpeter's democratic theory must include both of these ways of conceiving of democracy. For even his elite conception of democracy is best understood not in isolation as a complete and freestanding theory of democracy but rather in relation to his theory of liberal capitalist development. It was not merely a descriptive conception—although it reflected what he thought was a clear-eyed view of politics. It took on practical, prescriptive significance as part of a sketch of a "democratic" socialist society in which the most dangerous democratic tendencies, from Schumpeter's deeply conservative standpoint, would be curbed. It was, in short, a reactionary response to the democratic social, economic, and political tendencies that he most deplored.

Viewed in this light, Schumpeter's political thought takes its place in a tradition of conservative critiques and reconceptualizations of democracy, dating back at least to the early nineteenth century and aimed at taming democracy's transformative potential. Along with Schumpeter, some of the creators of this tradition are Alexis de Tocqueville, Max Weber, and various elite theorists, such as Vilfredo Pareto, Gaetano Mosca, Robert Michels, and Gustav LeBon.

By using the term *tradition* to link these figures, I do not mean to emphasize the conscious handing down of ideas. Members of this tradition are linked to each other not so much by lines of influence—though these exist—nor yet by awareness that they constituted a school, but rather by a common defensive posture toward the unfolding historical phenomenon of democratic change. Their precise language and conceptions of democracy differed, but all worried about the historical processes of democratization, in one way or another, and were critical of democratic societies. All were especially concerned that the masses who were empowered (or at least embraced) by democracy lacked the requisite capacities for responsible and meaningful participation in politics. In this sense, all had transformative conceptions of democracy. Yet, like Schumpeter, these conservative critics did not explicitly argue in favor of *alternatives* to democracy, such as monarchy or dictatorship. They, too, saw some form of democracy as almost inevitable. Thus they focused their energies on arguing that democracy's bad effects either could be or somehow would be ameliorated or minimized. And they expressed this common view often by redefining democracy itself to include a strong element of elite influence. Some specific attention to a few of these critics of democracy helps throw into relief the elements of Schumpeter's political thought that are most important.

Tocqueville thought the practical stakes in reaching a proper analysis of democracy in the 1830s and 1840s were quite high, especially for the kind of enlightened French conservative he represented. Revolutionary waves were washing over Europe with regularity. The spread of democracy seemed to him all but inevitable. The question was what form it would take. "The advent of democracy as a governing power in the world's affairs, universal and irresistible, was at hand," he wrote in his 1848 preface to the twelfth edition of *Democracy in America*, looking back fifteen years to the time he first published the work ([1835] 1945, ix). "Though it is no longer a question whether we shall have a monarchy or a republic in France, we are yet to learn whether we shall have a convulsed or a tranquil republic, whether it shall be regular or irregular, pacific or warlike, liberal or oppressive, a republic that menaces the sacred rights of property and family, or one that honors and protects them both" (ibid.). Tocqueville began and ultimately remained quite sympathetic to the many wealthy Americans he met, most of whom feared this "democratic tide" (Wilentz 1988, 215–216). And *Democracy in America* is accordingly peppered with critical and skeptical comments about democracy that reflect his own aristocratic biases. America's democracy tended to produce poor leaders, he argued, attributing this phenomenon to (among other things) the fact that "it is impossible, after the most strenuous exertions, to raise the intelligence of the people above a certain level" ([1835] 1945, 207). Reflecting the weaknesses of the masses, democracies were unstable, flitting from preoccupation to preoccupation and rarely placing long-term benefit ahead of short-term gratification (ibid., 219–220, 239). In a similar vein, he said democracies were excitable and, in their excitement, lavish (223–224). Their leaders were susceptible to corruption, and their citizens guided more by feeling than reason (233–234, 237). Worst of all, the unchecked power of the majority in democracies made them prone to tyranny of action and opinion (264–280). Yet Tocqueville parted from those of democracy's American critics who drew the darkest possible conclusions from such views. In particular, he believed that there was little danger that democracy in America would necessarily turn radical and challenge "property" or those classes that had it in abundance (254). This conclusion was no doubt supported by his tendency to be overly impressed by the spread of the equality of conditions in America, to downplay signs of social conflict, and to mistake his middle-class informers for the masses (Wilentz 1988, 219). But it also derived from his view that Americans ceded much of their power to and took political instruction from the legal elite ([1835] 1945, 282–290). And it resulted from his positing a fairly narrow redefinition of democracy that included such elite influence, and ignored the more radical democratic visions of people like artisan republicans (Wilentz 1988, 221, 223–225). In this sense, Tocqueville contributed to a revaluation of democracy as something even those hostile toward popular sovereignty could accept, however unhappily.

Writing seventy years later in Germany, Weber's greatest fear was that the advance of democratic mass politics—a tendency by then beyond doubt, he thought—would crowd out political judgment and the "ethic of responsibility" in politics (Weber [1919] 1946, 120). (For more on Weber and his influence on Schumpeter, see Chapter 4.) Weber shared many of Tocqueville's biases against the masses—and added a few to the list. The masses were "soulless," suffered from intellectual and psychological proletarianization, and could not take moral responsibility for acting on their values (Breiner 1996, 165). Their time in politics had come, but Weber thought that it was nearly inevitable that the masses would find themselves dominated by some kind of elite leadership. Mass politics meant elections, and elections could function only with active elites organizing and shaping the passive electorate. "It is unimaginable how in large associations elections could function at all without this managerial pattern," Weber wrote in "Politics as a Vocation," his best-known and most comprehensive statement on the subject (Weber [1919] 1946, 99). There was, then, essentially no possibility of democracy as meaningful self-organized mass political activity, no "possibility of realizing a concept of freedom as direct public participation in the common matters of political society," as one scholar puts it (Breiner 1996, 145). The choice was rather between leaderless democracy, in which unprincipled party bosses acted as generals in the electoral battle, and leadership democracy, in which politicians with a calling and a commitment to "responsibility" took charge (Weber [1919] 1946, 113, 115–120). Weber, of course, favored the latter possibility, and his "Politics as a Vocation" was intended to call attention to the need for such responsible politicians. Thus Weber's intervention to curb the excesses or dangers of democratization also entailed a reconceptualization of democracy.

The European elite theorists of democracy attempted an even sharper revaluation. (For the influence of the elite theorists on Schumpeter, see Chapter 4.) In common with Tocqueville and Weber, the elite theorists feared democratizing change. They argued further that all societies were necessarily characterized by some kind of elite-mass division, with the elites generally ruling over the rest (Bottomore 1964, 2–3; Meisel 1962, 33, 37; Pareto 1966, 155, 267–270; Michels [1915] 1962, 70, 79, 111; Nye 1977, 29–30). This contention was at least partly based on the view that the masses were irrational, subject to manipulation and suggestion, unable to follow settled plans, and easily distracted by emotion and desire (Michels [1915] 1962, 64–65, 85–89, 105, 111, 107–112; Nye 1977, 12; Pareto 1966, 111). Elites, by contrast, were constituted of those few individuals whose unusual talents fitted them for leadership. Since these claims were regarded as universally valid for all societies, no mere change in the form of government, no mere commitment to popular participation, could change them. Democracy, from this standpoint, could not be an *exception* to elite rule; rather it could only be a *special instance* of it. This was one meaning of Michels's "iron law of oligarchy," which held that even democratically inclined parties inevitably became dominated by party leaders (Michels [1915] 1962). This view was perhaps best expressed in the work of Mosca and Pareto, who insisted that democracy could at best be a kind of window dressing around elite rule, or a kind of increase in the legality and peacefulness of the methods of elite domination (Mosca 1967, 50; Pareto 1966, 270). The elite theorists' reconceptualization made democracy not just potentially controllable by elites but actually intrinsically, necessarily so dominated.

That Schumpeter belongs to this tradition will become even more clear throughout this book. Yet his contribution to it is unique for the clarity with which he laid out the possibility of both a radical form of democracy that would be transformative in its implications and a form of democracy (that he preferred) in which elites would take control. It is also unique for its influence on contemporary political science, a field in which Schumpeter is still regarded as a detached and realistic scholar, not a committed archconservative.

The general failure to understand the practical significance of Schumpeter's elite conception of democracy—its meaning as a political intervention—derives in part from the failure to perceive the transformative conception in his work at all. In this study, by contrast, it is the recognition of this transformative conception of democracy in Schumpeter's work that underpins virtually everything else. Recognizing the transformative conception, for example, opens the door to comparing Schumpeter's two conceptions of democracy and assessing their relative merits. A transformative conception of democracy acknowledges that, empirically and historically, democracy has always been an ideology, a system of beliefs, practices, and values capable of motivating political action, and not just a method or an institutional framework. Since the practical grounds and critical reach of democratic ideology cannot necessarily be limited to politics, defined narrowly, and since most liberal capitalist societies are still characterized both by political institutions that embody some degree of formal political equality and freedom, and by social and economic institutions that embody a significant measure of *in*equality, compulsion, constraint, and *non*participation, democracy in this sense is always potentially transformative. From this standpoint, a conception that eliminates these aspects of democracy a priori will always seem deficient.

Recognizing the existence of this transformative conception of democracy in Schumpeter's work also reveals puzzles and questions that would not otherwise be evident. For example, given Schumpeter's general recognition of the egalitarian, dynamic, transformative implications of democracy, what changes in emphasis were entailed in making his hierarchical, static elite conception in *Capitalism, Socialism, and Democracy* appear to be a general statement of the limits and nature of democracy? This question is not usually even asked, since Schumpeter's elite conception is assumed to stand by itself and to be grounded in nothing more than definitional fiats and hardheaded realism. The answer is that Schumpeter theorized his elite model of democracy as method on the basis of pessimistic assumptions about "human nature in politics." But the problems Schumpeter encountered in this process make it evident that no theory of democracy built on the assumption that the vast majority of people by nature lack the potential to reflect, discuss, persuade, and act in common can provide an adequate account of democratic rights to participation and expression, or distinguish convincingly between democratic and nondemocratic forms of society and politics (see Chapter 4).

Finally, explicating Schumpeter's transformative conception of democracy also sheds new light on his approach to social science, which was focused on the problem of social transformation (see Chapter 5). And an understanding of this social science project opens up even more critical possibilities—opportunities to use Schumpeter against himself. From the standpoint of what I term Schumpeter's *science of social transformation,* certain features of his elite model of democracy as a method seem clearly deficient. In particular, that elite model embodies a form of equilibrium analysis, but Schumpeter's whole economic career involved transcending equilibrium analysis. With Schumpeter's help, it is possible to see the severe limitations of equilibrium analysis for understanding democratic development and democratic ideology (see Chapter 6).

It is customary for scholars with new critical interpretations of classics in political theory to offer a schematized argument about the way their work relates to older interpretations. Throughout my study I contrast my methods, evidence, and findings with those of others who have written about Schumpeter. But the character of my intervention—what makes it new—also diminishes the importance of a sustained introductory comparison of my work with that of others. In the first place this is because my main criticism of much of the literature on Schumpeter's democratic theory concerns not what it does say but what it does not say. I do not disagree with the standard view that Schumpeter *had* an elite model of democracy as method. Rather, I argue that he *also had* what I term a transformative conception. In the second place, I argue that many interpreters have missed this transformative conception not because of the interpretive methods they articulate but because of implicit assumptions that structure their interpretations—especially assumptions about the definition of political theory, the meaning of social science, and Schumpeter's scientific and practical aims.

Virtually every work that interprets, criticizes, or incorporates Schumpeter's theory of democracy discusses only his elite model of democracy as a method, elaborated in Chapters 20 through 23 of *Capitalism, Socialism, and Democracy* ([1942] 1976). Certainly this is true when Schumpeter's particular contribution to the history of democratic theory is discussed. When David Held refers to Schumpeter's "extraordinary impact" in his comprehensive survey of democratic theory, *Models of Democracy,* there is little question that it is this model he means (Held 1987, 164). Likewise, C. B. Macpherson's oft-cited chronicle, *The Life and Times of Liberal Democracy,* explicitly refers to Schumpeter's "equilibrium" or "pluralist-elitist" model of democracy and locates it in "a few chapters" of *Capitalism, Socialism, and Democracy.* The same is true of full-length intellectual biographies of Schumpeter. Robert Loring Allen's thorough biographical study, *Opening Doors,* mentions only Schumpeter's "theory of democracy" as a "method" and naturally locates it in the same place in the same work (Allen 1991, 2: 129). Richard Swedberg, while breaking ground in the analysis of Schumpeter's economic sociology, concurs with the standard view of his democratic thought (Swedberg 1991a). Eduard März (1991) and Wolfgang F. Stolper (1994), for their part, barely discuss democracy. Furthermore, when such scholars of democracy as Anthony Downs, Seymour Martin Lipset, Samuel Huntington, and Gabriel Almond cite Schumpeter or explicitly mention his influence on their own work, they too refer to the elite model (Downs 1957, 29 n. 11; Lipset 1959, 71; Lipset 1960, 45; Huntington 1984, 195; Almond 1980, 21). Finally, it is to this elite model of democracy as a method that Schumpeter's many critics and admirers have directed their attention in a flood of monographs too large to list exhaustively (for example, Ashcraft 1995; Bachrach 1967; Bellamy 1991; Elliott 1994; Plamenatz 1973; Ricci 1970; Santoro 1993; Skinner 1973; Walker 1966; Xenos 1981). None of these works makes any mention of the transformative conception of democracy in Schumpeter's work.

One reason some interpreters have failed to grasp Schumpeter's transformative conception is that they have assumed, more or less, that he was interested in politics only as a scientist, and that his social scientific practice could be summed up in twin commitments to diligent fact collection and the ruthless purging from social science of any theoretical terms lacking empirical referents. The standard behaviorist insistence on a hard distinction between facts and values, and between the context of discovery and context of justification, has entered uninvited into interpretations of Schumpeter's work and made it difficult to sustain any inquiry into his active involvement in the social and political world. But without examining how Schumpeter viewed and responded practically to the worlds in which he moved, it is difficult to perceive the guiding thread of his work on democracy. Thus we have Allen insisting improbably that Schumpeter was "forced" to write about democracy because of "the vagueness of what people meant by democracy" (Allen 1991, 2: 129). And even a critic like Held argues that Schumpeter "sought to free thinking about the nature of public life from what he took to be excessive speculation and arbitrary normative preferences. His primary task was explanatory: to account for how actual democracies work" (Held 1987, 164). These claims capture neither Schumpeter's approach to social science nor the motives and approaches that guided his construction of a transformative conception of democracy. But these are largely isolated comments, not part of a lengthy analysis of Schumpeter's vision of social science that needs thorough examination.

Despite these problems, there is actually a wealth of work on Schumpeter from which my study has profited. Some early critical responses chose a fairly weak line of attack, arguing that Schumpeter and his intellectual heirs failed to recognize that democratic theory was meant to be inspiring. In a sense, these critics said, Schumpeterians were *too realistic* (Walker 1966). But beginning most strikingly with Carole Pateman's *Participation and Democratic Theory*, critics questioned precisely this realism, meeting Schumpeter on empirical grounds and pointing out that a case "for the retention of a participatory theory" of democracy could be made even "in the face of the facts of modern, large-scale political life" (Pateman 1970, 103). I have followed in this tradition of criticism, even using Schumpeter's own arguments and insights against him to demonstrate that his elite conception of democracy is in-sufficient—not just insufficiently inspiring. In Chapter 4 I show how many of the weaknesses of Schumpeter's conception of democracy as method, as pointed out by earlier critics, are linked to his incorporation of elite theory's assumptions about human nature.

A more recent body of literature on Schumpeter's "economic sociol-ogy" and dynamic approach to economic theory also offers important insights. This work has brought to light Schumpeter's interest in broad-ening economics to include the study of economically relevant insti-tutions, beliefs, and practices. Tom Bottomore (1992), Allen Oakley (1990), Yuichi Shionoya (1990a, 1990b, 1991, 1997) and Swedberg (1989, 1991a, 1991b) have done particularly good work that has forever changed our understanding of Schumpeter as a social scientist. Indeed, recognizing Schumpeter's overarching interest in a comprehensive sci-ence of social transformation has helped me recover the elements of his transformative conception of democracy and fit them together.

This study is not intended to be an exhaustive biography or intellec-tual portrait of Schumpeter. I have little to say here about his family, his marriage, his friendships, or even his professional relationships with other social scientists. Likewise, many of Schumpeter's most famous economics works—such as his *Theory of Economic Development* ([1911] 1934) and *Business Cycles* (1939)—figure here only as background for understanding Schumpeter's methodology and view of social science, or his theory of the development of capitalist societies.[1] Even some of his best-known sociological works, such as "Social Classes in an Eth-nically Homogenous Environment" ([1927] 1991) and "The Sociology of Imperialisms" ([1918–1919] 1991), play only supporting roles in the story I tell about Schumpeter's democratic theory.

Several biographies and broad intellectual studies of Schumpeter have appeared in the last decade, and they provide invaluable biographical in-formation and analysis for projects such as mine. Allen is exhaustive in his use of Schumpeter's diaries, making him an invaluable source on such topics as Schumpeter's Nazi sympathies (Allen 1991; see Chapter 2). Stolper, both in his biography (Stolper 1994), and in the collections of Schumpeter's early essays, speeches, letters, and memos he has helped edit (Schumpeter 1985; Schumpeter 1992; Schumpeter 1993), has pro-vided scholars with documents that are crucial to any well-informed view of Schumpeter's political thinking. Swedberg, in his intellectual biography (1991a) and in his introduction to a collection of essays by Schumpeter (1991b), weaves together a fine biographical narrative with a compelling portrait of the full range and aims of Schumpeter's extensive social science writings.

I have adopted an interpretive strategy that stresses the way in which Schumpeter's intentions, understood in historical context, structured his work. As opposed to textualist interpretive methodologies, this makes reading political theory a matter of social science, an exercise in understanding an actor's intention in writing and publishing a work. This approach is generally associated with Quentin Skinner, who has forcefully demonstrated some of the absurdities inherent in ignoring intentions, and in assuming that great political theorists talk to each other across the ages (Skinner 1988). But my view of interpretive methodology is closer to those who, while acknowledging that writing is an intentional act, have stressed the need to read political theory as ideology (Ashcraft 1975; Mannheim [1936] 1985; Shapiro 1982). The purposes of this slight modification of Skinner's approach are to emphasize even more clearly that an individual's intention is not an absolute datum requiring no further explanation; to stress the ways in which the meaning of a text can actually escape the intentions of an author; and to explicate both of these problems in terms of social structures, including discourses, that enable and constrain the act of writing a text. In lieu of any lengthier or more exhaustive discussion of my interpretive methodology at this fairly high level of abstraction, however, I will make a few more related points and then refer readers to the application of my approach in the chapters that follow.

Some may think that a historical-contextual approach involves *assuming* that every political theorist is a political activist or that historical context *determines* the content of political thought. I did not set out by assuming that because Schumpeter lived in Austria in 1919 or in the United States in the 1930s that either the postwar Austrian council movement and discussions of socialization or New Deal labor politics and policy formed the appropriate contexts for reading his work on democracy. In practice, historical and textual interpretations are not so neatly distinguished from each other. Schumpeter's own writings provide ample evidence for believing that these historical events and problems were central to the way that he thought about democracy. Having established that, I interpreted Schumpeter's work as a thinking response to his historical context.

I argue that Schumpeter's elite conception of democracy as a method has to be understood as a deeply conservative response to democratizing social tendencies in liberal capitalist societies. Thus one potential objection to my study, especially from those committed to a similar vision of democracy, might be that Schumpeter's personal motives and beliefs do not impugn those of others who support a similar vision or raise any questions about the validity or realism of that vision. Such an objection, I think, misunderstands the nature and significance of ideology critique—a point that can be explained with reference to Schumpeter's own writings on science and ideology.

From the standpoint of any social science built on a categorical distinction between facts and values, ideology critique can mean only one thing: claiming that an individual allowed his or her values to interfere with neutral procedures for collecting facts. But Schumpeter himself argued that attempts to understand the relationship between science and ideology that were based on an analytical distinction between facts and values were a dead end (see Chapter 5). All scientific investigation, like all meaningful inquiry about the social world, began, he said, with a socially conditioned vision and socially conditioned concepts and cognitive tools that directed the collection of facts. Ideology critique consciously explores the way in which these socially conditioned visions, concepts, and cognitive tools arise out of concrete social situations and how they enable and constrain one's understanding of the social world. It is undoubtedly true that we cannot directly infer from Schumpeter's conservative commitments that others who adopted his elite conception of democracy as method had the same commitments.

But ideology critique can help demonstrate something more important—that there are limitations to an elite conception of democracy, regardless of a person's values or adherence to scientific procedures. These are the limitations as to the social structures and social tendencies that can be seen and understood from the standpoint of such a conception. Above I argued that a transformative conception of democracy recognizes that, empirically and historically, democracy has always been a system of beliefs, practices, and values capable of motivating political action—and not just a method or an institutional framework. And I pointed out that, historically, the practical grounds and critical reach of democratic ideology has never been limited to politics, defined narrowly. Therefore, so long as we, like Schumpeter, continue to live in a social world characterized by structural social and economic *in*equality, compulsion, constraint, and *non*participation, democratic ideology in this sense will always be potentially transformative. And so long as this is so, an elite conception of democracy as method that ignores these aspects of democracy a priori will always have severe limitations. To connect ideas, social structures, individual intentions, and scientific investigation in this way is to engage in ideology critique.

Throughout this work, I point to contradictions in Schumpeter's thought. Many readers will be troubled by my arguing that Schumpeter held contradictory positions, contradictory views of democracy. On the whole I think that these contradictions can best be explained by saying that Schumpeter theorized an elite conception of democracy *because* he recognized the egalitarian, radicalizing potentialities of democratic ideologies and democratic movements. But recognizing this practical, political relationship between the two ways he conceived of democracy does not diminish the many logical and practical incongruities in his thought. Indeed, since Schumpeter's thought developed over time, these contradictions and tensions took on manifold shapes throughout his career. Explaining these discrepancies does not explain them away.

Some may wonder, accordingly, why I have chosen to write about a political theorist whose commitments I do not share and whose work, by my own account, embodies so many tensions and contradictions. Why not look instead for one whose political system I can elaborate sympathetically and as a cogent whole? The answer is that I think it is possible to learn a great deal from thinkers whose work displays such tensions. It may not assuage readers much to say that I think it is these unresolved disjunctures and inconsistencies that make Schumpeter interesting. My interest in inconsistency stems from a nagging suspicion that political theory that presents a perfectly consistent aspect to the world is hiding something. In any case, I have found it helpful to show that Schumpeter himself had doubts about the approach to democracy with which he is most commonly associated. I have found it revealing to use Schumpeter against himself, to demonstrate that his elite conception of democracy is incomplete from his own standpoint, and that it violates some of his own canons of social science.

*   *   *

The following six chapters trace the historical and political roots of Schumpeter's two conceptions of democracy, critique the elite conception best known to most Anglo-American readers, and examine Schumpeter's broad approach to social science. In Chapter 2, "Tory Democracy, Transformative Democracy," I take up the analysis of Schumpeter's democratic thought in political context. Both of Schumpeter's conceptions of democracy, I argue, had their origins in the years surrounding the establishment of the first Austrian republic, about 1916 to 1921. On the one hand, his elite conception of democracy stemmed from his attempt to initiate a "Tory democracy" movement of Austro-Hungarian aristocrats. A few years later, however, he advanced a transformative conception of democracy, agreeing reluctantly with Austro-Marxist theorists who held that economic democratization would build the foundation of a democratic socialist society.

After moving to the United States in 1932, Schumpeter continued to develop his transformative conception of democracy. In Chapter 3, "The New Deal and Transformative Democracy," I analyze Schumpeter's conviction that democracy was one of the tendencies propelling liberal capitalist societies toward "democratic" socialism, and demonstrate that he regarded labor politics and the reorientation of state policy in the New Deal era as evidence of these tendencies.

Schumpeter's elite conception of democracy also developed in these years, from the vision of Tory democracy in his early work into his later model of democracy as an "institutional arrangement" or a "method." In Chapter 4, "Schumpeter's Elite Conception of Democracy as Method," I show that he built his model of democracy as method around certain assumptions about "human nature in politics" that limit democratic possibilities. Resorting to these assumptions led to many of the most severe problems and contradictions in his work that have been pointed out by critics, including his intellectual undermining of freedom of expression and the right to vote, and his inability to provide credible grounds for distinguishing democracy as he described it from nondemocratic forms of society.

Chapter 5, "Schumpeter's Vision of Social Science," examines how Schumpeter started out as a proponent of neoclassical economic theory but then expanded dramatically the scope and ambition of his social science project from its early emphasis on neoclassical equilibrium models toward what could be called a science of social transformation. This vision of social science underpinned his transformative conception of democracy. In this chapter I also discuss the implications of that science of social transformation for Schumpeter's views of "methodological individualism" and rationality, entrepreneurial agency and the historical process of rationalization, and the relation between science and ideology.

Interpreters such as C. B. Macpherson (1977, 77) have rightly noted that Schumpeter's model of democracy as a method contains elements similar to neoclassical equilibrium models. In his influential *Economic Theory of Democracy* Anthony Downs (1957) developed this feature of Schumpeter's work into his own equilibrium vision of democratic politics. In Chapter 6, "Democracy and Equilibrium," I argue that despite this lineage, Schumpeter's own approach to social science makes clear the limits of equilibrium as a conceptual framework for understanding democracy. Equilibrium analysis, I contend, cannot adequately comprehend democratic ideologies, and in part for this reason, it cannot adequately grasp how such ideologies themselves can be sources of transformative change.

In the wake of communism's collapse, democracy and democratization of a sort are at one of their highest tides in history, yet it is evident today that radical forms of democracy, such as experiments with the democratization of social and economic institutions, are not being widely demanded or discussed, either in new or in long-established liberal democracies. In Chapter 7, the concluding chapter, I address this embarrassing fact for the revival of any transformative conception of democracy, and defend the relevance of such a conception for understanding recent transitions to democracy and for addressing urgent problems in liberal democracies. A "transformative" conception of democracy would emphasize two things that seem to have been crucial to at least the Eastern European transitions of 1989: the development of democratic ideologies that were responsive to the needs and problems of people living under Soviet-style communism, and the deployment of those ideologies by democratic movements. And while the Eastern European transitions have resulted in polities that look far more like Schumpeter's elite conception of democracy than his transformative one, that should not blind us to the fact that Eastern European dissidents for many years discussed conceptions of democracy that had far more room for participatory mechanisms in civil society and at work. Perhaps most important of all, however, a transformative conception of democracy is relevant today as a critique of any liberal democratic polity. The potential for freedom of action in liberal capitalist democracies continues to be unequally distributed, some people having at their disposal almost unprecedented social powers, others finding their capacities underdeveloped and their scope of activity constrained by poverty and poor jobs, historically rooted racial structures, and persistently unbalanced gender relations. So long as such conditions persist, the possibility of a democratic critique remains—and with it the transformative potential of democracy.

2

Tory Democracy, Transformative Democracy

In late May 1919 Otto Bauer, the Social Democratic foreign minister of the seven-month-old first Austrian republic, wrote to Karl Renner, its new chancellor, who was representing Austria at the peace talks in France. The fragile republic was beset by troubles. At the end of an unthinkably brutal war, Austria had endured a hard and hungry winter while still facing wartime blockades, and the state's ability to meet the people's most basic needs was in question. On the right, the conservative rural states of Austria wanted nothing to do with socialist-dominated Vienna, to the point, at times, of refusing to make agricultural shipments. On the left, communists wanted to outflank the Social Democrats and establish a soviet state. Nevertheless, Bauer told Renner, the domestic scene was pretty quiet, all things considered. Various cabinet members, he noted, seemed to be performing well. "Schumpeter, however, carries on with his intrigues," Bauer wrote (translated in März 1981, 172).[1]

Political intrigues of various kinds had in fact been a recurrent theme of Schumpeter's life since the middle of the First World War. In those declining days of the Habsburg monarchy, he labored secretly to organize a new aristocratic conservative party to aid the kaiser. After the war, while finance minister of Austria, he held unauthorized meetings with allied diplomatic representatives that threatened to undermine government policy, and conspired with counterrevolutionary Hungarian aristocrats.[2] Bauer would later accuse Schumpeter of a role in clandestine financial dealings designed to block the government's socialization plans, as well, a charge that is still debated decades later.[3] These "intrigues" took place behind the scenes of Schumpeter's more public political involvements:

first, as a member of the German Socialization Commission, then as finance minister.[4]

Contrary to the received image of Schumpeter as a detached scholar, it is this political involvement that forms the backdrop to his earliest writings on democracy. Scholarly interest has almost always focused on the elite conception of democracy as method that Schumpeter sketched in *Capitalism, Socialism, and Democracy*. But that elite conception actually originated in Schumpeter's reflections on political struggle in Austria-Hungary during the war, and in Austria after it—a time during which he also developed his transformative conception of democracy. Although there were clear tensions, even contradictions, between the two conceptions of democracy he developed throughout his life, the conceptions were also connected to each other, both practically and politically. It is because Schumpeter believed that democracy could be transformative, that it had the potential to threaten or remake the conservative institutions and hierarchies he cherished, that he theorized a form of elite-dominated democratic politics in which democratic change could be stifled. This connection stands out starkly in Schumpeter's early political writings, from 1916 to 1921, where often in the same passage he deplored democratization and extolled "Tory democracy" as a program to curb it.

Schumpeter's early writings on democracy thus responded to contemporary Austrian problems in two distinct ways. During the final war-ravaged years of the Austro-Hungarian empire, Schumpeter corresponded with aristocratic politicians about the conditions and requirements for initiating a reactionary, counterdemocratic political movement. His elite conception of democracy—the most complete version of which he presented in *Capitalism, Socialism, and Democracy*—found its first expression in this period, not as part of an academic, purely reflective enterprise, but as part of this attempt to initiate a "Tory democracy" movement and to reestablish elite control over Austria-Hungary's democratizing and fragmenting society. It began not as a general "theory of democracy" but as an argument contending that aristocratic elites, employing the right techniques, could curb democracy and national fragmentation and preserve traditional social and political hierarchies in Austria-Hungary.

It was also in this period that Schumpeter began to analyze democracy as a historical tendency that was changing and undermining Austro-

Hungarian society in ways he regarded as dangerous. Such a conception was present as the background to his early writings on Tory democracy. In the years after the First World War, after a brief public career that involved Schumpeter in official deliberations on socializing industry in Germany and Austria, his transformative conception of democracy took shape on its own. Incorporating into his own writings the view of contemporary Austro-Marxist theorists, he argued that the democratization of industry and the economy would ultimately build the foundation of a democratic socialist society within the crumbling walls of liberal capitalism.

Five broad problems characterize the literature on Schumpeter and his writings on democracy—and have prevented scholars from noting or grasping the significance of the political memos, letters, and activities that I analyze in this chapter. The first is the misconception that Schumpeter was neither very involved in nor very concerned with politics in his lifetime, or that his engagement, such as it was, was limited to a brief, exceptional attempt at a political career, a misguided effort to apply his purely scientific knowledge of the economy in a political context. Robert Loring Allen's assertion that throughout most of his life, Schumpeter "knew little of practical business and cared nothing for partisan politics" and his insistence that Schumpeter's engagement with political matters was short and ended decisively are typical expressions of this vastly overstated argument (1991, 1: 5, 149, 179). The second is the misconception that, insofar as Schumpeter was politically active or had political views, these matters can be neatly separated from his work as a social scientist. Allen's repeated and misleading claims that Schumpeter sharply severed his scientific thought from his various political views are again typical (Allen 1991, 1: 86, 144, 150, 154, 163–164; 2: 60, 155, 168–169).

A third problem—a kind of interpretive distortion—has resulted from scholars' attempts to soften Schumpeter's known and documented reactionary political statements by insisting they be read in light of sometimes unsubstantiated claims about his commitment to such things as limited, representative, constitutional government; civil rights; toleration; and free expression. This can lead to odd juxtapositions. Allen, for example, attempts to balance Schumpeter's sympathetic views about Nazism and his characterization of "the vast majority" of people as "subnormals" with the claim that Schumpeter favored "maximum personal, civil, and economic liberties for individuals" (Allen 1991, 2: 192–193).[5] Wolfgang Stolper very similarly extenuates Schumpeter's well-substantiated monarchism by attributing it to his alleged hostility to "all kinds of nationalisms and intolerances which lived by suppressing other 'different' people" (Stolper 1994, 197).[6] The fourth problem, stemming from traditional definitions of political theory, is the widespread view that certain key chapters of *Capitalism, Socialism, and Democracy* constitute "the only example we have of a study in political theory by Schumpeter," a premise that may obscure the significance of many of the letters, essays, and memos I examine in this chapter (Swedberg 1991b, 60).[7] Eliminating these from view, in turn, colors our understanding of Schumpeter's political commitments and thought. The fifth problem is that none of the recent full-length studies of Schumpeter's work integrates his political activities during this period in Austrian history with an analysis of his writings on democracy.[8]

I devote considerable attention in this chapter to analyzing part of the political terrain of late imperial Austria-Hungary and the early first Austrian republic.[9] In particular, I analyze the political stances and arguments of the Austrian Social Democratic Party (SDP) and its leading intellectual figures, the Austro-Marxists, such as Otto Bauer, as well as those of the Austrian Christian Social Party (CSP) and its most important thinkers, such as Ignaz Seipel. An analysis of their ideological positions forms—in two distinct senses—a crucial context for Schumpeter's political thought on democracy during this period. First, Schumpeter's writings and activities were frequently responses to these other major groups in Austro-Hungarian politics and society. Second, Schumpeter frequently adopted important positions and assumptions from these groups, and the significance of these borrowings becomes much clearer when their origin is made clear. The effort that is required to understand the historical context of Schumpeter's early political writings is, I hope, more than repaid.

This historical context also forms the best background for understanding Schumpeter's anti-Semitism and sympathetic attitude toward Nazism. Although Schumpeter had moved to the United States by the time of Hitler's rise to power and thus was never involved in the Nazi consolidation of power, as were some intellectuals, it is important to try to understand these things as part of an overall portrait of his political thought. Schumpeter's Nazi sympathies, though they never spurred him to practical action, should be understood, at least in part, in light of his continual search for some means of staving off what he considered the dangerous social tendencies linked to democratization.

Political Democracy and the Mobilization of Aristocratic Elites

The Austrian Social Democrats and Political Democratization

Schumpeter's advocacy of an elite democratic program he termed "Tory democracy" can best be understood in contrast to the positions advanced by the Austrian Social Democratic Party and its leading intellectual figures, the Austro-Marxists, on the question of political democracy. For it was largely the SDP's oppositional movement, along with those of the nationalist groups, that framed the political choices Schumpeter faced during the final tumultuous years of the Habsburg monarchy. Schumpeter's own hostility toward democracy stands out by comparison to the SDP's program for a thoroughgoing political democratization of Austria-Hungary. His agenda for curbing democracy was in part a specific reaction to social democracy and the threat it posed to the old order.

Alone among political groups and parties in their time, the SDP and the Austro-Marxist intellectuals who served the party both as agitators and theorists advocated a comprehensive program of economic, social, and political democratization—indeed, favored a democratic path to socialism (Bauer [1907] 1978, 112; Diamant 1960, 84, 102–103; Gulick 1948, 1; Rabinbach 1983, 2; Rabinbach 1985, 81).[10] By contrast, the kaiser and most of the Austro-Hungarian aristocracy, along with the other major German-Austrian parties in the late Habsburg empire, not only resisted democratic socialism but also opposed universal suffrage or any extension of the franchise to include more members of the poorest classes, attempted to thwart the establishment of a republic until the final weeks before the collapse of the empire, and—in the case of the Christian Socials—even mounted a comprehensive theoretical critique of political democracy.

The SDP's polemicists rarely made principled arguments on behalf of *purely political democracy*.[11] They did, however, often demand the fulfillment of the promises of liberal democracy (Rabinbach 1983, 11). From the birth of the Social Democratic movement in Austria-Hungary, the party worked to achieve political democratization, understood in the broadest sense to mean the legal protections and institutionalized practices necessary for a robust democratic politics: not just universal suffrage and free elections, but also the rights of free speech, free association, and a free press, and a justice system capable of defending such democratic rights.[12]

THE SOCIAL DEMOCRATS AND UNIVERSAL SUFFRAGE. One of the most obvious manifestations of the SDP's commitment to political democratization was its longstanding effort to extend the franchise. In addition to excluding women and poorer people from the vote, the electoral system of the late Habsburg empire was based on "curias," or bodies of voters distinguished from each other by socioeconomic class. In elections for the imperial parliament, for example, landed proprietors constituted a curia, as did large capitalists (Gulick 1948, 31–32). This curial system, which structured the voting even for cities and towns, gave greater weight to voters in the smaller, more privileged curias by assuring them a fixed percentage of representatives (Pulzer 1988, 148). In Vienna, for example, each of the three curias elected one-third of the city council (Boyer 1995, 466 n. 2).

From its birth at the Hainfeld Congress of 1888–89, the SDP determined to settle for nothing short of universal, free, and equal suffrage (Gulick 1948, 31; Rabinbach 1983, 10). Indeed when Kaiser Franz Josef I (1846–1916) and his minister Count Eduard von Taaffe proposed in 1893 to eliminate some features of Austria-Hungary's privileged voting system and to extend suffrage to literate men, twenty-four years or older, who had maintained six months' residency—while maintaining the curiae—the SDP's party congress rejected the proposal and authorized a general strike in support of universal suffrage (Gulick 1948, 31–32). A dozen years later, in November 1905, the party mobilized about a million people across Austria-Hungary—200,000 in Vienna alone, by some estimates—for marches in support of universal suffrage.[13] Although the party had—for obvious reasons—only a tiny representation in the parliament, these tactics provided the popular pressure needed to bring the last electoral reform of the empire: the establishment of male suffrage in late 1906 (Boyer 1995, 79; Gulick 1948, 33).[14] The party, however, was unable to achieve universal suffrage until after it came to power briefly with the collapse of the monarchy in 1918. In the intervening period, the onset of war brought with it an additional set of practical questions about the meaning of democracy.

THE KAISER'S WARTIME ATTACK ON DEMOCRACY. At the outset of World War I, Kaiser Franz Josef I quickly suspended the constitution, effectively eliminating parliament from any role in the state. In fact, the kaiser's minister Count Karl Stürgkh was so contemptuous of parliament that he had the parliament building—one of the few, precarious symbols of republican government in imperial Vienna—converted into a military hospital for the duration of the war (Schorske 1980, 40–43; Boyer 1995, 373). With this attack on parliament came others on civil liberties that were particularly irksome to opposition groups and to workers. Franz Josef suspended the rights to free association and assembly, and systematically violated the confidentiality of mail (Gulick 1948, 34; Hobsbawm 1992, 127). Meanwhile, a series of imperial decrees essentially established a wartime system of forced labor and removed the few protections workers enjoyed prior to the war. One measure allowed industrial concerns to be put under state "protection," while another required every male eighteen to fifty years old to perform whatever services he was capable of; under these laws, workers could be court-martialed and in some cases sent to the battle front as punishment (Gulick 1948, 34–35).

Throughout the war, Social Democrats of all stripes opposed this militarization of political and economic life under the Habsburgs and their ministers. Social Democrats continually called for the reconvening of parliament and a relaxation of censorship, protested the harsh forced labor conditions in industry, and demanded amnesty for political prisoners (Gulick 1948, 39; May 1966, 295–296).[15] In the end, the mounting war casualties, the growing sense of the war's futility, and the tremendous burdens placed on civilians strengthened the position of opponents of the kaiser's war and dictatorship.

In 1917 the Social Democrats finally won the reopening of parliament. And with the restoration of some semblance of constitutional government and protection of political action, the party emerged, relatively united, as the leading opposition to the Habsburgs' antidemocratic stance. Friederich Austerlitz, the editor of the socialist *Arbeiter Zeitung,* published in June and July 1917 a searing multipart exposé of "judicial murder" as practiced by the military courts that had been given jurisdiction over Austro-Hungarian civilians (Gulick 1948, 40; May 1966, 644).

And SDP leaders, joined by Slavic national groups in the parliament, led a legislative revolt, denying the kaiser the retroactive approval he sought for his dictatorial rule (Bauer [1925] 1970, 31; Gulick 1948, 40; May 1966, 644).

THE ESTABLISHMENT OF A DEMOCRATIC REPUBLIC. The Social Democrats, however, cannot be given all or even most of the credit for the fall of the Habsburg monarchy, which enabled the establishment of an Austrian democratic republic at the end of the war in 1918. The monarchy had been in a state of decline for decades, and its final collapse, in the wake of Germany and Austria-Hungary's military defeat, came when nation after new nation that had once been part of Austria-Hungary separated itself from the empire. After this process, the Austro-Hungarian empire had ceased to exist, geographically, demographically, and politically, and the question now was what form one part of the old empire—German Austria—would take (Gulick 1948, 62–63). But alone among the major political forces in that rump Austrian state, the Social Democrats wholeheartedly favored a democratic politics. Years after the establishment of the republic, Bauer wrote that in the last few months of the war, leading Social Democrats were determined to "utilize the revolutionary crisis" brought on by the war and nationalist movements to "overthrow the dynasty, establish a democratic republic, and begin the struggle for Socialism upon the basis of democratic institutions" (Bauer [1925] 1970, 33).

In September 1918, with the United States' entry into the war having virtually guaranteed the defeat of the central powers, and with Austrian and German lines crumbling, Kaiser Karl I initiated a series of attempts to reach an armistice with the Allies. Meanwhile, as the separatist movements of various former nationalities of the empire forced a constitutional crisis in October, the Social Democrats called for a "parliamentary revolution," by which they meant a meeting of the German-Austrian members of the parliament to discuss the future constitution (Gulick 1948, 55). At the first meeting of this "provisional assembly" on October 21, Viktor Adler called for a recognition of the right of national self-determination—in effect, no more than endorsing the ongoing dissolution of the old empire, which was actually fueled by military collapse and by the Allies—and demanded that a democratic republic be established in the remaining German portions of Austria (Gulick 1948, 53–54). Although to the very end the other parties in the assembly continued to support monarchy, the SDP reaffirmed its intention to create a democratic and socialist German-Austrian republic, and since the party effectively led the assembly (without having an actual majority of votes), it was able to have a republican constitution drawn up on October 30, and then to have the democratic republic declared just a day after Kaiser Karl's ambiguously worded "abdication" on November 11. This declaration of the republic, which established the terms for upcoming elections for the Constituent Assembly, effectively initiated true universal suffrage on the national, provincial, and local levels, and wiped away the final political remnants of feudalism (Bauer [1925] 1970, 63–64; Gulick 1948, 61).

DEMOCRACY AND NATIONALISM.   Democratization was also key to the Social Democratic Party's approach to the national question. For decades the prewar SDP, itself composed of not just German-Austrian but also Slav, Czech, and Hungarian members, had had to confront nationalism as a problem both within and without the party (Bottomore and Goode 1978, 30; Rabinbach 1983, 14). In 1899, after years of bitter disputes, the party adopted the Brünn program, which included a set of platforms designed to accommodate national ambitions and the quest for self-determination while retaining a commitment to democratic politics and social revolution. Under Brünn, the SDP proposed a federal reconfiguration of Austria-Hungary's multinational state: the transformation of Austria-Hungary into a "democratic federation of nations," with the governments of each self-administering nation elected by universal suffrage, and with protections for the rights of minorities within each nation and (concomitant to this) the rejection of the idea that a particular national group should enjoy "supremacy" within each nation (Rabinbach 1983, 14–15; Gulick 1948, 1369–1370).

In works written between 1899 and 1907, Karl Renner and Bauer developed their own theories of nationalism and how to deal with it. Although each reached different conclusions about the origins of nationalism—Renner viewing nationality as a freely chosen individual attachment and Bauer viewing it as one aspect of the historical construction of identity—they agreed on the need to subordinate nationalism to other interests (Hobsbawm 1992, 7; Bottomore and Goode 1978, 32, 109). For this reason, and because the Brünn program provided not for the complete dissolution of the supranational empire but for its democratic transformation, the Social Democratic Party and its programs came to be known, especially among nationalists, by nicknames that suggested its beholdenness to the Austro-Hungarian state and even the kaiser: "Imperial and Royal Social Democracy" and "palace socialism" (Gulick 1948, 1370; Rabinbach 1983, 15).[16]

But the hope for any such multinational federation collapsed with the tremendous strengthening of national movements during the First World War. As soon as it became clear that there would be independent Czechoslovakian, Hungarian, and Yugoslav states, the Social Democrats' practical orientation toward the question of nationalist ambitions changed. The party gave up any drive for multinationalism and became committed—Bauer, especially—to the integration of German Austria into Germany as a whole. The Social Democrats' main reasons for adopting this position, however, were economic; like so many other Austrians, they had severe doubts about the economic viability of German Austria as an independent polity (Rabinbach 1985, 21–38).[17]

The Austrian Christian Socials and Political Democratization

Schumpeter's main tie with the Austrian Christian Social Party was a shared opposition to the Social Democrats' multifaceted program of democratization. He did not write or act as a Christian Social intellectual, nor did he ever adopt the religious character of Christian Social thought. While the Christian Social movement drew its support from the lower middle class and peasantry, Schumpeter regarded himself as an adviser to aristocratic political circles. It is true that, after the fall of the Austro-Hungarian empire made his Tory democracy program virtually irrelevant, Schumpeter developed ties to the Christian Social leader Ignaz Seipel, even though he was finance minister in a predominantly SDP government at the time; and after he was dismissed as finance minister Schumpeter actually joined the CSP, aligning himself, pragmatically at least, with the only viable antidemocratic movement left in Austria in 1920 (*Arbeiter Zeitung*, 24 March 1920; Gulick 1948, 139; März 1981, 170–171; Stolper 1994, 255; Swedberg 1991a, 58).[18] Nevertheless, the Christian Socials help us understand Schumpeter by making clear the character and depth of antidemocratic and antisocialist thought in Austria-Hungary between 1910 and 1930.

The CSP was profoundly antidemocratic—perhaps even surprisingly so, for a party that owed its existence to an expansion of the suffrage, which brought lower-middle-class men into the Viennese electoral fold for municipal elections in 1882 (Gulick 1948, 26; Pauley 1972, 8; Schorske 1980, 138).[19] Before the war, Vienna's Christian Social mayor, Karl Lueger, had cobbled together a political platform appealing to the resentments and anti-Semitism of the city's lower middle class, and had carried out a popular program of so-called municipal socialism, mainly consisting of then-novel forays into city-owned utilities and services (Boyer 1981, xi, 419–421; Schorske 1980, 134–135, 142–143).

Schumpeter did not derive much direct inspiration from the intellectual sources that motivated Christian Social thinkers. Nevertheless, it is important to understand them. The Christian Socials constructed their worldview from official church doctrine regarding the political and social developments of the eighteenth and nineteenth centuries—including well-known documents such as Pope Leo XIII's encyclical *Rerum Novarum* and Pius XI's *Quadragesimo Anno*—and from the writings of Austrian romantic critics of the Enlightenment such as Adam Heinrich von Müller and Karl von Vogelsgang (Diamant 1960, 23–25, 29, 35–38, 41–48). Well into the 1930s Christian Socials and those whose work inspired them contended that civil authority was divinely granted (Diamant 1960, 10–11, 108); that, as a result, church and state should be closely united, as they had been in the Austro-Hungarian empire (Diamant 1960, 8, 46, 71); that alternative accounts of the legitimate sources of political power, especially those that referred to individual rights or to a social contract, were not merely inaccurate but dangerous (Diamant 1960, 7, 9, 11, 44, 56–57); and that even practical attempts to institutionalize a set of civil rights should be opposed or limited (Diamant 1960, 9, 11, 107–108). Politically, most Christian Socials were unwaveringly monarchist (Boyer 1995, 439; Diamant 1960, 36, 38, 43, 107), and socially they were corporatist, favoring a thoroughgoing structuring of society along medieval lines, according to hierarchical corporate bodies that would "represent" individuals in accordance with their particular place in society while enforcing a set of duties and standards derived from natural law (Diamant 1960, 12, 36–38, 44, 45, 60, 256–285).

Although Schumpeter's conservatism shared few of these particular themes, he did come to share with CSP thinkers some common views about the kind of historical challenge posed by democratization and the most practical way to respond it. These can be summed up in three points. First, Christian Socials never regarded democracy only as a political system, but believed that democracy had social and economic manifestations and implications.[20] Second, Christian Social thought treated democratization as a historical tendency characteristic of modern Western societies—one that required a response from conservatives. Third, Christian Socials, spurred by Ignaz Seipel, the most prominent Christian Social politician and ideologist of the immediate postwar period, came to accept democratization of some kind as unavoidable, and thus focused on political aims that could be accomplished in a democratizing society. (Apparently reluctant to identify himself in the first few years after the war as an opponent of democracy, Seipel advanced the same antidemocratic arguments that other Christian Socials had employed—arguments for restraining or modifying practices and tendencies that most proponents of democracy considered essential—under the cover of pleas for "true" democracy.) Schumpeter's writings on Tory democracy shared these three broad characteristics.

In practice, these strands of Christian Social thought—separated here for emphasis—were intertwined. Diamant argues that Christian Social ideology may be understood as presenting an attempt to formulate a Catholic position on two modern "secular" forces—capitalism and democracy (Diamant 1960, 6 n. 6, 9, 33). In Diamant's view, Christian Socials regarded democracy both as a social fact to be dealt with, not denied, and as something to be criticized and fought. Christian Socials, he argues, saw themselves as being nearly "helpless" in the face of a "democratic flood," a democratizing historical tendency, which had had its origins in the Enlightenment and in the early twentieth century had become a "radical democratic Zeitgeist" (ibid., 70, 84).

If the democratic "flood" that Christian Socials perceived threatened only to wash over political institutions, it would hardly have imperiled the Christian Socials' whole worldview as it did. But the Christian Socials' conception of democracy was as broad as that of the SDP; indeed it mirrored, and was in part a response to, that of the SDP (Diamant 1960, 70–72). Noting that Social Democrats tended to justify "internal political changes," change on behalf of "suppressed nationalities" as well as "social and economic revolution against established privileged groups," all in the name of democracy, Diamant writes: "The demands for democratic changes [thus] came chiefly from the opponents of political and social Catholicism . . . Catholics, therefore, opposed 'democracy'—political, social, or economic—because they associated it with these attacks on existing institutions and proposals for change" (ibid., 1960, 72).

Austrian Christian Socials were opposed to the SDP on virtually all the practical questions of democracy that arose early in the twentieth century in Austria-Hungary. The party originally opposed the establishment of manhood suffrage in 1905, and later did very little as the movement for an expanded suffrage gained power; but the CSP had to shift its position in light of the prodemocratic Social Democratic "juggernaut" (Boyer 1995, 75).[21] Karl Lueger, the Christian Social mayor of Vienna, argued that any expansion of the suffrage should be offset with measures favoring the CSP: long residency requirements to exclude the many seasonal workers who lived in Vienna, and a mandatory-voting law to compensate for the party's weaker grassroots voter-turnout organization (Boyer 1995, 74). More than a decade later the CSP, always loyal to the crown, was largely left on the sidelines during the first wartime parliamentary session; the session was dominated by the speeches of different national groups seeking radical reconstruction and by the coalition of Slavic national groups and the Social Democrats, which, as mentioned above, led the parliament in rebelling against the kaiser and his request for legislative sanction for his authoritarian wartime measures (May 1966, 640–645).

The Christian Socials' sense of resignation toward democracy was often manifest in attempts to advance Christian Social arguments under the guise of a theory of "true democracy," rather than in the form of an attack on democracy. This can best be seen in Christian Social responses to the collapse of the Habsburg monarchy. At the end of the war, Christian Socials opposed the establishment of a democratic republic in Austria as long as possible, and even denied, after the republic had been declared, that the kaiser had truly abdicated. In the Christian Social newspaper, the *Reichspost*, writers insisted as late as three days before the abdication, in response to declarations that the provisional government's power was derived from the people, that the provisional government had no right to make such declarations and could never alter the fact that the kaiser, the imperial family, and the empire persisted as the legitimate bearers of political power (*Reichspost,* 8 November 1918). Ignaz Seipel himself convinced Kaiser Karl not to use the word *abdicate,* so as to be able to claim later that he had merely withdrawn to allow the people to handle affairs for a while (Diamant 1960, 107). Thus the *Reichspost's* report on the "abdication" held that the founding of the republic rested, for its legitimacy, on the kaiser's voluntary withdrawal, not on the assertion of popular sovereignty (*Reichspost,* 13 November 1918). Throughout the period, such writers described the Christian Social posture toward the new democratic republic as one of resignation, not enthusiasm, continually reasserting longstanding arguments for the divine origin of civil authority, for the duty to obey, and for corporative rather than direct elective representation, and continually criticizing a belief in equality as a basis for democracy (Diamant 1960, 107–112; *Reichspost,* 8, 13, 21, and 27 November 1918).

Ignaz Seipel's four-part series on the new democratic republic, published in the *Reichspost* in November 1918, took a slightly different approach, weaving many of the CSP's antidemocratic themes into a position nominally in favor of what he called "correctly conceived democracy" or a "true democratic spirit" in politics (Diamant 1960, 108; *Reichspost,* 21 November 1918). Seipel did not pretend that this meant Christian Socials could support the Social Democrats' broad and egalitarian conception of democracy; in fact, Seipel implicitly acknowledged that his "true" democracy was quite different from the understanding of democracy that was important in the founding of the democratic republic. "We do not deceive ourselves in this moment," Seipel wrote,

> what a deeply meaningful difference there is between the organic state constitution and the autonomistic state constitution, from which the demand for general voting rights stems. On the contrary we hold that state to be more profound and better ordered that seeks to exist not directly from connectionless individuals, who in theory are all the same, but who in reality are unequal, but rather takes hold of its citizen indirectly through his family, professional group, and class. (*Reichspost,* 21 November 1918)

Though different in form and content, Schumpeter's own Tory democracy writings do share something with these passages: a hope of rescuing from the jaws of democratization a kind of "democratic" political life that could sustain his conservative values.

*Pan-German Nationalism and Schumpeter's Political Letters
and Memos*

Schumpeter's impulse to defend the Austro-Hungarian monarchy from
the forces threatening it was initially awakened when the ideas of a German named Friedrich Naumann, who favored the creation of a tariff alli-
ance between the German and Austro-Hungarian empires, began taking
root in Austria-Hungary. The war itself—and the attendant Allied blockades of Germany and Austria-Hungary—had already forced a high level
of economic cooperation between the two powers, and so Naumann's
plans had a certain plausibility (May 1966, 144–145). Naumann may,
according to some accounts, have had respect for non-German nationalities in Austria-Hungary, and he was mainly interested in the problem of
developing trade areas and states of sufficient size to sustain economic
health. But he had also, in wartime visits to Vienna, developed contacts
with a variety of pan-Germanic groups, many of whose members clearly
saw his book *Mitteleuropa* as aiding their plans (Boyer 1995, 381–382;
May 1966, 147; Stolper 1994, 171). Such groups had for some time been
devising lists of "war aims" that would serve the purpose of consolidating the power of Austro-Germans in the empire to the detriment of
other national groups (Boyer 1995, 381).[22] These nationalists naturally
found Naumann's economic proposals to be a convenient addition to
their war-aims propaganda. Meanwhile, the idea also caught the attention of German officials, who—no less nationalistic—showed both anti-
Slav bias and a poor understanding of the nationalities problem in poly-
glot Austria-Hungary by bluntly proposing closer economic ties and a
campaign to suppress Slav national groups in Austria-Hungary (Stolper
1994, 172–173; Swedberg 1991a, 49–50).

A staunch supporter of the Habsburg monarchy who saw its supranational character as its essence, Schumpeter was deeply suspicious of
pan-Germanism. His concern that Naumann's ideas were gaining adherents, the news that the Germans were pushing them, and his fear that
even the kaiser might not understand the dangers of greater economic
integration with the German empire spurred him to act.

Over the next few years, he wrote a series of letters and memos, some
to his former teacher Heinrich Lammasch, who had political ties to the
kaiser, and some to Count Otto Harrach, an archconservative aristocrat
and a member of the Austro-Hungarian parliament's upper chamber. Re-

gardless of the initial recipients, Schumpeter's idea was that his memos should be circulated among members of the high aristocracy in order to prompt them to action (see Stolper 1994, 170–171, 201, and Swedberg 1991a, 48–54).[23]

The main policy issue discussed in Schumpeter's first political memo was Naumann's tariff scheme, which Schumpeter vehemently opposed because it could strengthen ties between German Austrians and Germany, potentially alienating the other ethnic groups of the empire. But the aims and scope of his early political writings were far broader than this suggests. The memos and letters were a response to the entire set of problems he associated with democratization and dangers to the Habsburg monarchy, not just to the pan-German economic program. They surveyed the various nationalist forces that threatened to splinter the Austro-Hungarian empire and offered proposals for responding to them.[24] His theme of Tory democracy as a plan of action provided a unifying focus of attention.

Schumpeter and Tory Democracy

In 1916 Schumpeter was a young but highly respected economist at the University of Graz, located about one hundred miles southwest of Vienna. He was only thirty-three, and he had published his career-making *Theory of Economic Development* five years earlier. His father had been a cloth manufacturer in a town in what is now the Czech Republic, but he had died when Joseph was young. His mother had remarried, to a member of the lowest echelon of the aristocracy, Lieutenant-fieldmarshall Sigismund von Kéler, who, because of his military rank, could be admitted to the kaiser's court, unlike other lower aristocrats (Johnston 1972, 39–40). The status Schumpeter attained through his mother's remarriage may well have contributed to his strong political identification with the aristocracy.

Tory democracy—Schumpeter's conception of democracy and his political program from 1916 to 1918—was anchored by his belief that an elite aristocratic political movement could counteract the various dangers to the Habsburg empire through domination of public opinion, parliament, and the press. Such a movement, he was convinced, could both strengthen the monarchy and counter the democratizing and disintegrating tendencies in Austria-Hungary. The existence of such a conception and program is significant, because it demonstrates that the earliest roots of Schumpeter's famous elite conception of democracy *as a political method*—developed in *Capitalism, Socialism, and Democracy* (1942)—are to be found in his practical attempts to mobilize aristocratic elites and to counter more thorough democratization and fragmentation. Schumpeter's well-known conception of democracy as a method had three chief features: a focus on elite competition for mass support, the treatment of democracy as nothing more than an institutional arrangement, and the attempt to decouple democracy from values such as equality and participation. Schumpeter's conception of Tory democracy—although formulated and expressed quite differently—embodied each of these characteristics. His argument focused on *aristocratic* domination of *democratic institutions*. Thus, on the one hand, he implicitly reduced democracy to the mere existence of certain institutions, such as parliaments and parties, while he asserted not just the possibility but the necessity of elite domination of these institutions. And clearly his program not only presented a democratic politics that would minimize equality and participation but also directly rejected those traditional democratic values.

THE PRIMACY OF MONARCHY AND THE NEED FOR A CONSERVATIVE PARTY.   One of the most striking things about Schumpeter's political writings from this period is his subordination of all other issues to the health and well-being of the multinational monarchy, and to the formation of a conservative political movement, goals whose value was apparently so obvious to Schumpeter that he took virtually no pains to defend them. It is crucial to realize that Schumpeter first wrote about democracy from the standpoint of a die-hard monarchist whose foremost concern was the "consequences" of a variety of issues and problems for the "innermost essence of the Monarchy" (translated in Stolper 1994, 177).[25] He discussed and acknowledged a variety of problems and policies, to be sure—especially the proposal of a tariff union with Germany—but he insisted on examining each question from the standpoint of the monarchy, an orientation that he emphasized repeatedly throughout the memos and letters of this period (Schumpeter 1985, 251, 252, 253, 271, 272–273, 289; Schumpeter 1992, 361, 364, 366, 368). Equally significant is the fact that all Schumpeter's political memos and letters of this period, no matter the particular topics addressed, were oriented toward the same practical political objective: the formation of a conservative-aristocratic political movement to dominate Austria-Hungary's democratized politics and to defend the position of the monarchy and the conservative elements of Austro-Hungarian society (Schumpeter 1985, 265, 266, 270–271, 279, 283, 302, 303; Schumpeter 1992, 361, 362, 364, 366–367, 368, 370–371, 373, 374).

These characteristic features of the political memos and letters bear emphasis for two reasons. First, political theorists are professionally predisposed, in their interpretation of others' work, to look for and accord weight to substantive philosophical propositions and rigorously logical arguments. But nowhere in the wartime political letters and memos does Schumpeter provide either philosophical premises or intellectually convincing arguments on behalf of monarchy. In these writings, monarchy—or, more specifically, Austria-Hungary's multinational monarchy—simply existed as a *good in itself,* to be defended by practical political actions. Thus there is a danger of granting insufficient weight to Schumpeter's support for monarchy in these writings if we look only for the philosophical grounds of his argument rather than the practical grounds. This danger is compounded by the fact that Schumpeter actually never—here or anywhere else—formulated such coherent and persuasive intellectual defenses for monarchy.[26] In his writings of 1916 to 1918, Schumpeter's desire to defend monarchy apparently preceded any systematic philosophical reflection on the subject. Nevertheless, his intention to defend the monarchy—not a set of philosophical premises—is clearly what "produce[d] the guiding thread" for these early political writings.[27]

A second, related reason to stress these two main features of the letters and memos is that these writings may easily be mistaken for a set of generally conservative policy pronouncements on a somewhat disjointed series of issues. It is not enough to acknowledge that *one* of the things Schumpeter was *saying* in these writings was that a conservative political movement would strengthen the monarchy. It is far more important that the *primary* thing Schumpeter was *doing* in writing these memos and letters was attempting to encourage a specific set of individuals to initiate an aristocratic conservative political movement.[28]

A RESPONSE TO DEMOCRATIZATION.   Schumpeter clearly linked democratization and democratic institutions to the broad set of changes that threatened the monarchy. Writing, as he constantly stressed, with an eye toward the interests of the monarchy, he doubted that it was yet time for a reordering of the relationship between parliament and the kaiser, he regarded the development of democratic debate as unfortunate, and he viewed the establishment of general voting rights regrettable. In sum, Schumpeter contended that for anyone interested in the maintenance of traditional Austro-Hungarian institutions, especially the monarchy, there was much to be regretted in the growth of "modern politics" and political institutions (Schumpeter 1985, 270). In writing to Count Otto Harrach, he expressed a view quite different from that of Social Democrats:

> Your Erlaucht[29] is absolutely right: we do not suffer a lack of democracy, one could rather say that the social structure of Austria cannot stand so *much* democracy—and in particular so much giving in to every slogan of the day—that it does not correspond to its [the social structure's] nature, and that it was imposed artificially . . . And because we have created so democratic institutions which, however, we—unlike English society—are unable to handle, these organs, in particular Parliament and the Press, get so easily out of hand. (Translated in Stolper 1994, 195)[30]

One of Schumpeter's fears was that the war itself would strengthen those in favor of democratic change and weaken conservatives. Past wars, he wrote, might have strengthened existing states and conservative groups, but this war, because it had caused so much bitterness and deprivation, would be bound to weaken them (Schumpeter 1985, 291). Specifically, he wrote, it would almost certainly bring about a "democratization" of voting rights in Prussia, which in turn would weaken conservative circles there; it had already, because of special circumstances, enabled the quick success of the March revolution in Russia and the consequent establishment of a "democratic Russia" (Schumpeter 1985, 290–291).[31]

ELITE DEMOCRACY AS A POLITICAL PROGRAM. It is difficult to isolate distinct passages in which Schumpeter referred to democratization or to democracy as a transformative tendency, because these references are so intricately and completely interwoven with expressions of the practical purpose behind his memos and letters: the fostering of a conservative political movement or party, led by members of the high aristocracy, that would employ the "technique of Tory democracy" to defend the monarchy. It is important to perceive the connection between these two elements of Schumpeter's thought in this period before moving on to the component parts of that proposed action. One way to understand this intermingling of themes is to look again at a passage cited above, this time in its entirety. The passage illustrates the way in which Schumpeter's fear that Austria-Hungary's social structure was imperiled by too much democracy was directly related to his analysis of the range of actions that conservatives should take to counteract this democratic tendency:

> Your Erlaucht is absolutely right: we do not suffer a lack of democracy, one could rather say that the social structure of Austria cannot stand so *much* democracy—and in particular so much giving in to every slogan of the day—that it does not correspond to its [the social structure's] nature, and that it was imposed artificially: *to guide and dominate such a far-reaching democracy with us is a very difficult task for which our government unfortunately is totally incapable.* And because we have created so democratic institutions which, however, we—unlike English society—are unable to handle, these organs, in particular Parliament and the Press, get so easily out of hand. (Translated in Stolper 1994, 195; emphasis added)[32]

The passage continues:

> *Here I arrive at a point that, in my opinion, one cannot emphasize enough: were there leadership on the part of the government, an actual political effort on its part, matters could never have come to the events in parliament.* But without a guiding hand, as it were, letting them to themselves, the parties immediately fell into the old habit of reciting their radical phrases. (Schumpeter 1992, 371; emphasis added, my translation)

Schumpeter commended a set of tactics that he summarized as "that technique of public life which has been perfected in England and which even in periods of sharpest democratic tendencies has preserved the influence of the aristocracy and generally of conservative interests: the technique of Tory democracy" (translated in Stolper 1994, 180).[33]

The goals of the conservative political movement for Tory democracy that Schumpeter was proposing could be described most generally as these: to lead and to dominate [*zu führen und zu beherrschen*] parliament, the press, and the public (Schumpeter 1985, 283). Although Schumpeter discussed a number of policy aims and positions that conservatives should take, he stressed that a Tory democracy program of this kind was a prerequisite for the accomplishment of virtually any of these goals (Schumpeter 1985, 266, 271, 279, 283; Schumpeter 1992, 361, 365, 374).

ELECTORAL AND PARLIAMENTARY ASPECTS OF SCHUMPETER'S PROGRAM. Schumpeter insisted that the movement should be led by aristocrats—and not just ordinary aristocrats, but those high aristocrats whose names had historic importance, those who were most closely associated with the purposes of the Austro-Hungarian monarchy and whose active role would resonate with those who still were loyal to it (Schumpeter 1985, 269, 302–303). It seems likely that this is partly why Schumpeter used the term *Tory democracy* to describe the type of movement and strategy that he meant. He wrote, after all, that the techniques of Tory democracy preserved the influence of aristocrats in England (ibid., 271).

But the movement would have to cultivate an extensive electoral base as well. And thus it was conceived by Schumpeter as not merely a cabal of aristocrats with the kaiser's ear, but as a movement that expressly set out to "deal with the public, to impress it, perhaps to fascinate it" (Schumpeter 1985, 270–271; my translation). For that reason, Schumpeter was highly critical of those government ministers, for example, whose idea of governance was simply to look after policy in the interests of the kaiser within the bureaucracy (Schumpeter 1992, 363, 365–366, 370). That might have been an adequate approach for earlier times, but in a democratizing society a conservative movement had to dominate democratic institutions as well.

The first thing to do, then, was to reconvene parliament. The growth of a "modern" political realm, in which there was a public, public opinion, and public discussion, meant that the monarch did not have a choice between consulting or not consulting parliament; rather, he faced a choice between organizing public opinion through what means were at his disposal, or allowing public opinion to remain disorganized. Schumpeter emphasized repeatedly that one of the worst problems Austria-Hungary faced was that of the "disorganization" of public opinion, or sometimes of "will" (Schumpeter 1985, 269, 301, 303). It was not sufficient to summon parliament; the kaiser and the conservative party needed a plan to use parliament as their instrument, to dominate it, to steer its debates and ensure that it did what the conservatives wished, to make sure that its deliberations included an expression of loyalty to the kaiser (ibid., 266–267). The parliamentary session, in Schumpeter's view, would have to be "boldly executed" (Schumpeter 1992, 362); it would have to convey the impression of a "strong government that knows what it wants" (ibid., 373; my translation). Individual heads of government ministries would have to see it as their job to address and to persuade parliament and, when they encountered opposition, to make their enemies feel their strength (Schumpeter 1985, 268–269, 271; Schumpeter 1992, 363, 365).

The precise meaning that Schumpeter attached to such a parliamentary policy is somewhat difficult to fathom, except that it clearly did not mean an actual delegation of power or prerogative to parliament, since Schumpeter doubted that the time had come for a true parliamentary regime and regretted the actual course of events, once parliament had been convened in 1917, when Social Democrats and Slavs seized the initiative (Schumpeter 1992, 370, 373). In all of this discussion, then, there is no evidence to support the idea that Schumpeter favored a convening of parliament as a democratizing measure, as a way of altering the balance of power in favor of a democratically elected body, let alone establishing full parliamentary sovereignty. And thus there is no reason to see Schumpeter as a proponent of either constitutionalism or parliamentarism, as these doctrines are normally understood.

On the contrary, Schumpeter regretted the suppression of the parliament from the beginning of the war until 1917 because without parliament and a parliamentary policy, the kaiser did not find "that help, which would allow him to stand out, to lead the public, to have an effect from above, to win a basis of support in the mass of voters, in short to create the prerequisites for domestic and foreign success, on which basis a conservative party organization could exist, of which I once dreamed" (Schumpeter 1992, 365, my translation). Indeed, one of the main purposes of Schumpeter's parliamentary proposals was to "strengthen the domestic authority of the Government" and to "give conservative circles a basis [of support] among the mass of voters" (translated in Stolper 1994, 190).[34]

DOMINATING PUBLIC OPINION THROUGH A CONSERVATIVE NEWSPAPER.   The other main strategic element of Schumpeter's Tory democracy proposal—one he discussed with Harrach, who apparently had the means to carry it out—was the establishment of a newspaper to voice the aims of the aristocratic conservative movement. This discussion actually is the most revealing about the means Schumpeter thought could be used to "dominate" the parliament, public opinion, and the press: a combination of an appeal to traditionally conservative voters and an embrace of some of the aims of radical-democrats and socialists. Of course, the general purpose of such a paper would be to spread conservative ideas to as wide an audience as possible—as Schumpeter conceived it, an audience ranging from the "Prince of the Church to the businessman" (translated in Stolper 1994, 193).[35] Schumpeter's description of this proposed newspaper suggests more particularly, however, that he recognized the power of the traditional Austro-Catholic ideas with which the Christian Social Party worked. "The strictly Catholic character and the specifically Catholic point of view would everywhere have to be brought out, which could only help the success of the paper, for this point of view is frequently latent in the consciousness of the Austrian even where it is not apparent" (translated in Stolper 1994, 193).[36]

But Schumpeter was insistent that the deployment of such traditional ideas took on a different meaning in the context of a modern, democratizing society. He argued that the newspaper would have to "clothe this program in modern phraseology" and, somewhat more cynically, that it would have to harness the "modern political technique of dominating public opinion" to serve "old Austrian ideas and interests" (translated in Stolper 1994, 193).[37] In part, this seems to have meant that conservatives would have to accept that Austrian workers had been largely won over to social democracy, and that to slow the working-class climb toward power would necessitate embracing some elements of the SDP's political and social program: including "civil liberties" and a "bouquet of social measures [*ein Bukett sozialpolitischer Maßregeln*]" (Schumpeter 1985, 288).

WHY "TORY" DEMOCRACY?   Schumpeter derived the expression "Tory democracy" from his understanding of the strategies of both Conservative and Liberal Party patrician politicians in mid- to late-Victorian England. Just a few years after writing these letters and memos, Schumpeter categorized the Liberal William E. Gladstone with the Conservative (Tory) Benjamin Disraeli, as politicians who sought sources of power among newly enfranchised voters; this, as we have seen, was one of the key tactics of Tory democracy as Schumpeter described it (Schumpeter 1920–21, 330). Schumpeter's praise for Gladstone—a Liberal, not a Tory—centered on his ability to create the political preconditions of what Schumpeter considered to be sound financial policy, and this was also a recurring theme of his Tory democracy writings (Schumpeter 1985, 271). In general, Schumpeter seems to have believed that Gladstone had successfully co-opted radical political movements into supporting a bourgeois, liberal political-economic program, Gladstonian liberalism. This has in fact been a standard view of mid- and late-Victorian politics (Biagini 1992, 4–6; Biagini and Reid 1991, 3–4; Finn 1993, 1–3).[38]

Schumpeter saw Victorian politics in terms of two sets of phenomena: radical democratic movements, the growing power of previously disenfranchised people, and democratization, on the one hand, and the ways in which those movements merged with or were co-opted by more aristocratic or patrician interests, on the other. Writing about Disraeli and Gladstone in 1920 and 1921, Schumpeter placed their political strategies in the context of a general trend of democratization—the extension of the suffrage and the attending development of new forms of political participation—and contended that they, like socialist intellectuals in other European countries, simply served as the leaders of those classes that were gaining political power before those classes had come fully into their own:

> As the bourgeoisie was at first content that the power of the state should be oriented toward its interests, although the feudal aristocracy or the bureaucracy held the leading positions, so the working class for a long time renounced the fight for voting rights. But in both cases these wishes had finally to surface. In England, the wish was characteristically anticipated by politicians who towered with ambition (Disraeli, Gladstone, Chamberlain), who sought new sources of power in the new layers of voters. Elsewhere it was left to the intellectual leaders of the working class. But the end result was the same. (Schumpeter 1920–21, 330; my translation)

At least from 1916 to 1918, Schumpeter thought that "even in periods of sharpest democratic tendencies" the strategy of Disraeli and Gladstone had "preserved the influence of the aristocracy and generally of conservative interests," and it was for precisely the same purpose that he commended the same Tory-democratic approach in Austria-Hungary (translated in Stolper 1994, 180).[39]

ASSESSING THE EVIDENCE ON SCHUMPETER'S ORIENTATION TOWARD DEMOCRACY. It is crucial to recognize the way in which aristocratic reaction shaped Schumpeter's political thought from 1916 to 1918, because without this recognition, it is possible to seriously misinterpret his practical goals. According to Wolfgang Stolper, Schumpeter's early political writings demonstrate, among other things, that Schumpeter was a proponent of greater adherence to constitutionalism, a stronger parliament, and a vigorous, independent press. In Stolper's estimation, the fact that Schumpeter favored, as a short-term aim, the reconvening of parliament is evidence that he sought to convert the Habsburg monarchy "into a constitutional monarchy" and to "strengthen parliament" (Stolper 1994, 197). Likewise, in Stolper's view, Schumpeter's interest in founding a new conservative newspaper is evidence that he was no friend of censorship and in fact favored a free press modeled along contemporary American lines—"a paper, such as the *Wall Street Journal* or the *New York Times* (or the *Neue Zürcher Zeitung*), conservative in its editorials, but *really* bringing 'all the news that's fit to print,'" (Stolper 1994, 180 n. 23, 193).

By failing adequately to investigate or acknowledge why Schumpeter favored reconvening parliament and establishing a conservative newspaper—failing to give weight to the political impulse behind these practical aims—it is possible to misconstrue these goals as evidence that Schumpeter was fundamentally liberal in outlook, a proponent of "a monarchy restricted by a constitution and restrained by a parliament" along with "maximum personal, civil, and economic liberties for individuals" (Allen 1991, 2: 192, 193; see also Stolper 1994, 200).

But as soon as we read Schumpeter's writings in light of the actual problems of democracy at this time, and compare them with the positions of the SDP, which actively opposed the war dictatorship and worked to restore civil liberties, it is evident that Schumpeter was a critic of the actual, existing democratizing tendencies and democratic institutions in Austria-Hungary and directed his energies toward staving them off. During the war years the Social Democrats were becoming more united around a sharp democratic critique of the dictatorial war measures by which Kaiser Franz Josef and his heir, Karl, ruled. Already long committed to universal suffrage and thus a critique of the electoral system of Austria-Hungary, the Social Democrats advocated strongly during the war for restoring parliament, which had been suspended. When parliament reconvened, bringing back some semblance of constitutional government, Social Democrats joined with Slavic deputies to make use of the political opening to oppose the suspension of trial by jury and the imposition of military justice on civilians, and to continue their campaign against the forced-labor measures taken by the government.

The contrasts with Schumpeter's positions on these matters is quite clear. Nowhere in his wartime writings—or indeed in his later work—did Schumpeter join with the SDP in its principled stand for the expansion of suffrage or the abolition of privileged voting rights. On suffrage, his recorded position was one of resignation; one may regret the establishment of general voting rights, but such rights could not be revoked without unpleasant political repercussions, he argued (Schumpeter 1985, 284). Schumpeter never even hinted at any *principled* objection to the suspension of parliament and the constitution during the war. He was a critic of trying to govern centrally without parliament, but he favored a reconvening of parliament not out of concern for democratic principle but because of his desire to increase the influence of the monarchy in what he perceived to be an already democratizing society. Indeed, in his wartime writings, Schumpeter doubted if the time had yet come for a true parliamentary regime in Austria-Hungary, and he questioned whether such a time would come at all (Schumpeter 1992, 373). As for the success of the Social Democrats in weakening the war dictatorship and restoring some institutional supports of democratic politics during the parliamentary session of 1917, Schumpeter was not gratified by this success but shared in the aristocratic view that the session had been a disaster. He differed with some aristocrats only in that he argued that it was not convening parliament, but failing to dominate it, that had been a mistake (Schumpeter 1992, 370). Finally, in contrast to the SDP, Schumpeter argued during this period that political debate founded on freedom of expression was in many cases not desirable, but that its suppression was too difficult (Schumpeter 1985, 305). Conservatives had to learn to plan and act in a world characterized by open political discussion.

Schumpeter's position, like that of the Christian Socials, was not support for democratization but, at best, acceptance that democratization was the background tendency against which conservatives had to act. In fact, the argument that conservatives had to take concerted action to cope with and counteract the democratization of Austro-Hungarian society and politics combined the two main strands of Schumpeter's view of democracy in this period: first, a conception of democratization as a broad tendency transforming political, social, and economic institutions, and second, an argument for a conservative political program to counteract that democratizing tendency.

SCHUMPETER'S CONSERVATIVE-ARISTOCRATIC PLOT. There exists a strange postscript to Schumpeter's writings on Tory democracy: evidence that in the spring of 1919, after Schumpeter had become finance minister in a Social Democratic–led cabinet in the first Austrian republic, he participated secretly in an aristocratic-monarchist plot concerning the overthrow of the short-lived Hungarian Soviet of Béla Kun. The incident demonstrates Schumpeter's continuing allegiance to aristocratic politics, even after the fall of the Habsburgs—an allegiance apparently stronger than his loyalty either to the democratic republic in which he held appointed office or to the policies of the Austrian Social Democrats, who had emerged the victors of the first elections of the republic and who had given him his appointment.

The Hungarian Soviet, which survived only from March to August 1919, was announced when the previous postwar government abdicated in response to the territorial demands by the allied powers (Bauer [1925] 1970, 102; Gulick 1948, 71). Béla Kun's soviet soon became a thorn in the Austrian Social Democrats' side, calling for the declaration of an Austrian soviet and supporting Austrian communists, who made two coup attempts in April and June 1919 (Bauer [1925] 1970, 105–108; Gulick 1948, 76, 79; Rabinbach 1983, 23). But despite the threat the Hungarian Soviet represented to Austria and the Austrian SDP, the government was in no position to take military action against Hungary and responded mildly to the calls for the establishment of a soviet, even continuing to sell industrial products to Hungary (Gulick 1948, 74). It is in this context that Schumpeter, according to an account by an English journalist-turned-counterrevolutionary, briefly participated in the aristocratic-monarchist plot.[40]

The plot itself, involving first the seizure of the Hungarian embassy in

Vienna and the theft of currency stored there, and later a disastrous invasion of Hungarian territory, appears to have been incompetently planned and executed—is a historical footnote at best (Ashmead-Bartlett 1923, 161–173; Stolper 1994, 18–20). More interesting is the way Schumpeter apparently presented himself to the aristocratic counterrevolutionaries. Not only was he, an official of the Austrian government, willing to take part in an extralegal plot to violate Hungarian sovereignty by seizing the embassy (and help the plotters raise money from private sources by allowing the financier Louis Rothschild to evade currency regulations), but he claimed, perhaps only bragging, that he also would have provided public money for the purpose if he had not had to account for it (Ashmead-Bartlett 1923, 159). Schumpeter, though appointed by the Social Democrats who led a democratically elected government, and though serving in office during the first few months of the first Austrian republic, also allowed that he supported neither socialism nor republican government (Ashmead-Bartlett 1923, 159).[41]

Thus it seems evident that Schumpeter remained practically committed to monarchy even after the kaiser's fall from power and even after taking office in a republic during the height of the Social Democrats' prestige. Although an attempted invasion of Hungary shortly after the immediate scheme in which Schumpeter participated was a failure, aristocratic-monarchist officers eventually did take power in Hungary, after Béla Kun's fall and a period of occupation. And because the new government declared itself committed to a Habsburg restoration, it became just as much a threat to the Austrian republic as the Hungarian soviet had been (Gulick 1948, 101, 115).

Democratic Socialism, the Postwar Council Movement, and Transformative Democracy

The sudden collapse of the German and Austro-Hungarian empires at the end of World War I and the advancement of Social Democrats in Austria and Germany to power shifted the range of practical and theoretical problems to be resolved and discussed in the first postwar years. For the first time, and for only a brief time, the means of bringing about socialism democratically became a pressing practical matter in these countries. Schumpeter's later view of the situation—that socialists had achieved power at a time when conditions were not ripe for socialism—

appears in hindsight to have been correct. Nevertheless, the years 1918 and 1919 saw a particular flourishing of tracts on the "socialization" of industry and the economy—meaning the conversion of capitalist enterprises into socialist ones. And the short-lived socialist-dominated governments in both states established commissions to study the problem.

Socialization, democratization, and their relation to each other also occupied a considerable amount of Schumpeter's own attention in the years following the First World War. His famous 1918 essay, "The Crisis of the Tax State," asked whether the fiscal strains of the war would lead to a collapse of the capitalist economy and the liberal state, and to their replacement by socialism ([1918] 1991). That very essay, and his close ties to some of the commission members, may have helped Schumpeter get his invitation to join the German Socialization Commission in Berlin, which in early 1919 recommended socialization of the coal industry and prominently discussed the question of how democratic the socialized industry should be.[42] His involvement with the commission gave Schumpeter, along with several other members, the idea to write a "Platonic dialogue" on "the principles and problems of socialism" (Vogelstein 1950). From his work with the German commission, Schumpeter was summoned back to Austria to serve for a few months as finance minister, a position that embroiled him in a controversy over the government's long-term plans to both democratize and socialize Austrian industry.[43] By late in 1919 he had fallen out with the Social Democrats and was dismissed.[44] Looking back on these experiences a few years later, Schumpeter wrote an essay in which he discussed—critically, but with some sympathy—the dilemmas of a social democratic government at the head of a parliamentary, democratic state attempting to take decisive steps toward socialism under conditions that, he said, still favored capitalism ([1924] 1952).

But it is above all in an essay entitled "The Socialist Possibilities of Today" (*"Sozialistische Möglichkeiten von heute"*), published in 1920–21, that Schumpeter expounded on the links between democratization and socialization, developing a transformative conception of democracy according to which the contemporary "council" movement entailed a fundamental reorganization of society that, "alone, can force complete socialization" (Schumpeter 1920–21, 338, my translation).

Schumpeter could not have been unaware that in making this argument he was adopting a central premise of prominent social democratic writers and numerous members of the working class in Germany and Austria. In the aftermath of the war, the council movement attempted, among other things, to democratize and socialize plants and industries through the creation of councils *(Räte)* that took over the tasks of management.[45] Radicals in the Berlin labor movement and delegates to the Second Council Congress in April 1919 believed that such representative councils at the plant and industry level could be "the cutting edge of socialism" (Maier 1975, 139). Karl Kautsky, the leading "orthodox" theoretician of the German SDP and the chairman of the Socialization Commission, similarly favored giving workers' plant councils a prominent role in socializing industries (Salvadori 1979, 236; Steenson 1978, 216, 233). And perhaps most important for Schumpeter, his cabinet colleague and longtime acquaintance, Otto Bauer, arguably the most important Austrian writer on socialization and the chairman of Austria's own Socialization Commission, considered the council movement to be the prime means of achieving democratic socialism democratically. These facts make Schumpeter's adoption of a similar view of the council movement all the more significant, for it is nearly impossible to believe he would have incorporated such ideas lightly, or without knowing how and by whom they were being deployed.

Austrian Social Democrats on Democracy and Socialization

The most astonishing feature of Schumpeter's essay "The Socialist Possibilities of Today" is his incorporation of so many of the key elements of the Austrian SDP's position on democracy and socialism—expressed most fully by Bauer—according to which the spread of council democracy would be the most crucial factor transforming liberal capitalist societies into socialist ones. (Of course, since Schumpeter generally deplored democratization of any kind, and since he was, by 1920, no friend of the socialist movement, his writings contain none of Bauer's enthusiasm for democratization, and little of Bauer's confidence that it would entail a flowering of human potential.) Of all those who wrote about socialization and democracy in the immediate postwar years in Austria, those with the most influence were certainly Bauer and other Social Democrats, who temporarily led the postwar government and attempted to put into practice their vision of democratic socialism. For these theorists, a theory of democracy was just one part of a fuller conception of social change—more specifically, one part of their conception of capitalist development and the transition to socialism.

Rudolf Hilferding's *Finance Capital*—one of the works that, like Rosa Luxemburg's *Accumulation of Capital*, contributed to the early twentieth-century flourishing of Marxist theory—formed the basis for many of the Austrian social democratic theories of social development. Beginning his book with an exploration of money and circulation, and emphasizing the reasons for the emergence and proliferation of credit instruments, Hilferding described the capitalist tendency toward the development of "finance capital," meaning an interlocking relation between large banks and manufacturing cartels (Hilferding 1910 [1981]). He drew a number of consequences from the growth of "finance capital." First, and most famously, he argued that cartelized and bank-dominated industries tended to seek an imperialist foreign policy. (Schumpeter disagreed famously with this theory in his essay "The Sociology of Imperialisms" [(1918–19) 1991], where he argued that imperialism had to be understood as an atavistic holdover in capitalist societies; capitalism itself, he claimed, had no propensity toward foreign expansion.) Second, Hilferding argued that the tendency toward finance capital represented a tendency for capitalism to become less anarchic and more a product of conscious organization. This had two implications for the transition to socialism: that it should not be expected as a result of economic crisis, and that the forms of conscious economic organization that would be needed in socialism were developing within capitalism itself.

Austrian Social Democrats like Bauer who relied on Hilferding's theories of capital thus put great emphasis on the need for political action to put those consciously organized sectors of the economy at the disposal of democratic control, and tended to devote considerable attention to the ways in which workers could prepare themselves for the tasks of democratic economic management.

THE INFLUENCE OF G. D. H. COLE.   Otto Bauer was deeply influenced by the English guild socialist G. D. H. Cole (Rabinbach 1985, 138; Bauer [1925] 1970, 146; Rabinbach 1983, 39).[46] Cole has been rightly cited as one of the most important figures in the tradition of participatory theories of democracy: he stressed the importance of meaningful participation, the democratization of nonpolitical institutions, and the educational and developmental significance of democracy (Pateman 1970,

36–38). These positions are usually held to be in stark contrast to Schumpeter's elite conception of democracy, but Cole influenced Bauer quite profoundly, and (as I will show) Schumpeter incorporated in his own 1920–21 essay, "The Socialist Possibilities of Today," many of Bauer's most important assumptions about the council movement. Thus there is actually a surprising lineage from Cole to Schumpeter that deeply underscores the need to reexamine the most widespread understandings of Schumpeter's views of democracy.

Cole's approach to the problem of democracy was to derive theoretical arguments from an analysis of empirical social tendencies and movements, rather than to make arguments based on abstract philosophical premises (Cole 1915; Cole 1920). "This book on Guild Socialism," he explained,

> is an attempt to explain the real character of this demand [for popular control of industry] . . . and at the same time to present the central ideas of Guild Socialism . . . The Guild Socialist theory, while, like all other social theories, it makes certain fundamental assumptions concerning the objects of human association of and men's life in Society, arises essentially out of the actual historical situation in which we are placed at the present time. (Cole 1920, 2–3)

For Cole, then, this form of democracy could be understood as an actually existing social tendency.

Cole argued, moreover, that the principle of democracy demanded not just representation but actual participation in decision making, and he contended that this principle should be applied in every form of association, not merely in politics, narrowly defined (Cole 1920, 4–5, 7, 22–23). Cole based this argument in part on the claim that individuals were not unitary egos but complex beings who pursued a variety of ends in different social contexts. Thus, he claimed, it was insufficient to be represented democratically only as a citizen, and not, for example, as a worker (Cole 1920, 22–23). "All true and democratic representation is therefore *functional*," Cole argued (23–24).

He was also convinced that democracy had developmental importance—that by extending democratic practices to areas where they did not yet predominate, workers and others who played only a small role in representative government would teach themselves to participate fully in the direction of society. Cole linked this educational value of democratic practices to the transformation of capitalist society into socialist society, arguing that the slow democratization of the economy along the lines his work suggested would represent the "consolidation of all forces on the lines of evolutionary development" and would prepare the way for a final, possibly revolutionary, transition to a socialist society that would represent "a culmination of tendencies already in operation" (Cole 1920, 168). Cole argued neither for a state-centered socialism nor a syndicalist model, in which socialism would mean only the democratic participation of workers in the economy, but rather for a socialist society that enfranchised workers in guilds and consumers in cooperatives while democratizing local government, creating participatory cultural and health councils, and leaving the state in something like a brokering role (Cole 1920, 53–143). All these features of Cole's thought were important influences on Bauer's own conception of transformative democracy.

TRANSFORMATIVE DEMOCRACY AND SOCIALIZATION. Like Cole, Bauer viewed democracy as a transformative social tendency. There are a number of perspectives from which to view this feature of his thought. Since Bauer viewed democratic practices as the basis or substance of socialism, he argued that the creation of such forms and the spread such practices would bring about a crucial social transformation. Looking back at the spread of democratic *political* practices, he saw the expansion of democratic *economic* practices as analogous—indeed as a later historical manifestation of the same tendency. In particular, Bauer regarded the spread of the council movement as evidence that members of the working class were seeking the institution of popular self-governance outside the political sphere. And he adopted much of Cole's educational and developmental conception of democracy, arguing for democracy as a form of social learning. Experience with democratic practices and institutions would, over time, prepare society for the popular control of the economy as a whole, and this was the central feature of democratic socialism.

In general, both Austrian and German Social Democrats envisioned some form of democratic socialization. As Wolfgang Stolper puts it, in describing the socialization plans of German Social Democrats, "the social policy involved was democratization" (Stolper 1985, 162; see also März 1981, 166; Stolper 1994, 206). And as Anson Rabinbach points out, the Austrian Social Democrats' whole legislative program of social welfare measures "was the basis for a thorough democratization of society, conceived by the Socialization Commission, set up in the first weeks of April [1919] and headed by Bauer himself" (Rabinbach 1983, 24). Bauer thought only democratization could lead to viable and desirable socialism, because neither determinate economic-historical laws nor a sudden expropriation of the means of production could accomplish it. According to Rabinbach, he was committed to democracy "as the basis for the emergence of socialism" and to "gradual democratization through 'radical reforms' which progressively introduced greater participation by workers and consumers in the decision-making process" (Rabinbach 1983, 121). "Socialism," Bauer contended simply, "is necessarily based upon democracy" (Bauer [1907] 1978, 112).

Bauer was especially clear about tying his conception of democracy to the actual flourishing of the council movement throughout much of Europe and especially in Russia and in German-speaking lands. The sailors whose mutiny in Kiel contributed to the end of hostilities in November 1918 immediately formed a "council" to govern themselves and press their demands (Craig, 1978, 399). The tactic quickly spread throughout Germany and Austria in the postwar months. Delegates from all types of newly formed councils—factory councils, workers' councils, and soldiers' councils—met in Berlin just a month after the collapse of the Central Powers (Kolb 1988, 15). Although they borrowed the idea of councils from revolutionary practice in Russia, the majority of these delegates did not favor replacing parliamentary government by a state consisting only of councils. Rather, they met to advance "a program for which there was a broad consensus in the democratic mass movement of those weeks, amounting to a 'democratization' of the army (especially), the civil service and the economy" (ibid.).[47] Socialist thinkers responded in different ways to this council movement. Lenin, as is well known, insisted both that a system of "soviets," or workers' councils, should replace parliamentary government and that the distinctive feature of the workers' councils was that they would exclude the bourgeoisie from participation (Goode 1991, 113; Lenin 1975, 456).

But from the beginning, Austrian social democratic thinkers focused attention not on workers' councils, groups of workers taking on political functions in the state and society at large, but on factory councils and similar bodies that attempted to democratize decision making within specific social and economic institutions. In his book *The Austrian Revolution*, Bauer chronicled the rise of soldiers' councils, factory ("works") councils, and trade union organizations alongside the newly republican government of Austria in the immediate aftermath of the First World War and showed how they made themselves indispensable for accomplishing the work of demobilization and rebuilding (Bauer [1925] 1970, 162–179). "In this way Social Democracy, the trade unions, the works' committees and the soldiers' councils became partners in administration and organs of governmental power at the same time," Bauer argued ([1925] 1970, 165). Karl Renner insisted that the advent of these organizations forced a rethinking of the whole question of what constituted a democratic constitution. "The conception of a uniform, indivisible, purely political democracy is untenable," he insisted; "on the basis of an advanced bourgeois political system a series of voluntary economic democracies, such as the trade unions and the co-operatives have arisen; and their practical value, their indestructible life force, and their social significance for the masses are simply incontestable. Constitutional law can no longer simply ignore them, as it has done on the continent" (Renner [1921] 1978, 199). In ways that I will examine below, Bauer regarded these spontaneously growing councils as the indispensable means of democratizing society and the economy and achieving socialism.

Leading Austrian social democratic thinkers conceived of democracy as an ideology and a set of practices deeply rooted in liberal societies but capable of being extended until the bounds of liberalism were transcended. Renner referred to "the application of the concept of democracy, previously limited to political life, in the investigation and explanation of economic structures" ([1921] 1978, 189). He related this spread of the idea of democracy, of course, to the council movement, which, as I have said, both he and Bauer thought would fundamentally restructure society and politics. Bauer, likewise, sketched out the historical development of attempts to realize democracy "defined as a system of government conducted with the assent of the governed" (Bauer [1925] 1970, 168).[48] He contended that parliamentary democracy, with elections held every three or four years, could not fulfill even this simple requirement of assent (ibid., 169). The ad hoc system of government during the "first phase" of the Austrian revolution, in which the Social Democrat–led government consulted constantly with newly formed councils of all kinds, realized the democratic ideal "more completely" than any other, precisely because it represented the extension of democratic practices beyond what was normally understood as the political sphere, and because it more fully realized the ideal of popular control and participation.

One of Bauer's discussions of this postwar extension of democracy—this transcendence of parliamentary forms—represents perhaps the high point of Cole's influence, with Bauer expressing himself in Cole's language of "functional" democracy:

> In modern capitalist society by the side of political democracy, embodied in the democratic organization of the State and municipality, an industrial democracy is developing . . . Political democracy only recognizes men as citizens; it takes no account of the economic position, occupation, or social function of the citizen; it summons all citizens without distinction to the ballot box; it groups them according to geographical constituencies. Industrial democracy, on the other hand, groups men according to their vocations, their workplaces, and the functions they exercise in the community . . . In the struggle against formal parliamentary democracy the working class has everywhere espoused the ideas of functional democracy, although in varying forms . . . A combination of political and functional democracy was the essence of the policy imposed on the government of the Republic by the redistribution of power which the revolution effected. (Bauer [1925] 1970, 169–170)

Elsewhere, Bauer described the historical extension of democratic practices from politics into social and economic associations, somewhat more simply, in terms of two revolutions, one political and one social. He wrote in "The Road to Socialism," just months after the fall of the empire, that the events of 1918 had represented a political revolution that had "dethroned the Emperor, done away with the upper chamber, and abolished the privileged voting rights in all the provinces and municipalities" (Bauer [1919] 1978, 146).[49] He added: "The semi-revolution arouses the will to total revolution. The political upheaval awakens the desire for a social reorganization. The victory of democracy inaugurates the struggle for socialism" (ibid.).

Both of these revolutions, political and social, involved democratization as the specific means of abolishing privilege and oppression in different spheres of life. Obviously this was so for the "political revolution," which Bauer also referred to as the "victory of democracy" (Bauer [1919] 1976, 91). But throughout "The Road to Socialism" Bauer also described his vision of socialism in terms of close analogies to the development of political democracy. "Democracy in the state is not yet realized if the highest legislative power is transferred to a parliament chosen by general and equal voting rights," he wrote; "in the same way a democratic economic constitution is not yet realized, if each branch of industry is ruled by an [elected] administrative board . . . Rather, economic democracy requires also that the local administration of each individual industrial plant be democratized" (Bauer [1919] 1976, 104–105, my translation). Bauer argued that while the factory at first is an absolute monarchy of the boss (*"Absolutismus des Unternehmers"*), the establishment of a council converts it first to a "constitutional" monarchy, then to a republic (Bauer [1919] 1976, 108).[50] Most of Bauer's 1919 essay was devoted to working out how this democratization, so recently accomplished in political life, could be spread through the economy.

But democracy was far more than a question of formal institutions for Bauer. This can perhaps be best understood by examining the way in which Bauer, like Cole, had a developmental theory of democracy, one that stressed the way democratic institutions and practices fostered social and moral development. It is a notable feature of Bauer's thought that although he clearly conceived of socialism as involving a change in ownership of the means of production, he devoted little attention to this (see Rabinbach 1985, 137). Bauer downplayed the significance of transferring ownership of the means of production because such a transfer, at least theoretically, could take place suddenly and with little change in deeply rooted social beliefs and practices (Bauer [1919] 1976, 93). More important than ownership for Bauer was control: more precisely, the question of how society could develop the capacity for rational, democratic self-management of the economy. "The example of Russia, where the democratic organization of industry which was attempted immediately after the October Revolution had quickly to give way to bureaucratic State capitalism, demonstrates that only bureaucratic State socialism, which merely replaces the despotism of the employer by the despotism of the bureaucrat, is possible *so long as the workers are without the capacity for self-government in their labour process*" (Bauer [1925] 1970, 144; emphasis added).

Specifically, Bauer regarded the establishment of factory councils as "a necessary condition" for socialism, making a new form of society possible through their "essential educational function" (Rabinbach 1983, 25). In the spring of 1919, when Bauer was the president of the Austrian Socialization Commission, the parliament passed a bill to establish these factory councils throughout the economy in such a way as to allow them to develop their capacities for self-management over time (Bauer [1925] 1970, 137–138). Bauer argued that the "origin and development" of the factory councils was "more important . . . than any forcible act of expropriation," because "it is only this self-education of the workers in and through the practice of works' committees which will create the prerequisites of a socialistic mode of production" (Bauer [1925] 1970, 145, 144).

Bauer saw similar educational and developmental benefits to the consultative and consensual manner of politics, involving both the government, led by Social Democrats, and the spontaneously arising workers' councils, factory councils, and soldiers' councils that appeared in the early period of the first Austrian republic. The system was "a potent agency for the self-education of the masses," he argued, one that served to "widen the intellectual horizon of the workers" and led to an appreciation by the masses of their political potency (Bauer [1925] 1970, 170, 171, 172). Bauer described this in the broadest terms, arguing that "it is not too much to say that this social activity created a new type of manhood and womanhood," explaining a few paragraphs later that "the transformation of political and social institutions is not an end in itself; for the development of peoples it has meaning only so far as it promotes the awakening, the inner change, and the upward movement of mankind" (ibid., 177–178). In an earlier essay on nationalism, Bauer argued that in a socialist society, cultural life would be democratized, too, in the sense that "only socialism will give the whole people a share in the national culture" ([1907] 1978, 110). Socialism, he contended, would give ordinary people the "power to determine their own destiny, to decide by free discussion and resolution their own future, and thus make the development of human culture a deliberate, intentional, conscious human act"—all this because "socialism is necessarily based upon democracy" (ibid., 111, 112). These ideas were quite consistent with the actual practice of the Social Democrats—hemmed in though they were by the growing power of the Austrian right wing—in the cultural, educational, artistic, and social renaissance of working class life that constituted the basis of "municipal socialism" in Vienna from 1919 to 1934.

Needless to say, Bauer had no interest in an autocratic state-managed economy (Bauer [1919] 1976, 96). Already we have seen the importance for Bauer of bottom-up democratization, the need for an economic and social democracy to be constructed out of a network of factory councils and similar participatory institutions. Bauer's conception, however, was not a syndicalist one either; it did not involve handing over the control of the economy simply to the workers in each plant. Bauer's 1919 scheme acknowledged the need for coordination between plants, pointed out that workers were not alone in having material interests in the economy, and likened the task of democratizing plants and whole branches of industry to the task of democratizing local and national levels of government (ibid., 100–104). "My plan of organization introduced the organization of consumers as a third partner, with equal rights, in this co-operative process," Bauer wrote in 1925; "I proposed that every branch of socialized industry be governed by a special administrative body, composed of representatives of the workers and employees who were engaged in the branch of industry; representatives of the consumers for whom the products of the industry were destined; and representatives of the State as arbitrator between the conflicting interests of producers and consumers" (Bauer [1925] 1970, 146). Schumpeter incorporated much of this conception of a democratized socialist society in his "Socialist Possibilities of Today"—not as an ideal, but as the model of society toward which he thought the dominant historical tendencies were leading.

Schumpeter's Transformative Conception of Democracy

Schumpeter had written in 1918 that he thought the First World War, though it might prove disastrous to the losing states, would not immediately usher in an era of socialism, a position he continued to espouse for years after the war was over. The "tax state"—the liberal state that drew its resources from the capitalist economy—would itself reach an irresolvable crisis only when and if it taxed so heavily that private enterprise could no longer function ([1918] 1991), and the war would not bring about such a situation. In fact, he concluded that only a capitalist economy could lead the way to recovery from the war (ibid., 131). "By and by," he argued, "private enterprise will lose its social meaning through the development of the economy and the consequent expansion of the sphere of social sympathy" (ibid., 131). But before socialism could take hold, capitalism would have to create a wealthy, capital-rich economy, a theme he developed even further in his essay "Socialism in England and at Home" *("Der Sozialismus in England und bei uns")* ([1924] 1952, 523). As a result, Schumpeter viewed the social democratic and labor parties that came into power across Europe after the war as being in an odd situation. Committed to socialism, they could nevertheless do almost nothing to bring it about; indeed, they were more or less required to administer capitalism (ibid., 524). But despite this view, Schumpeter thought there were dramatic changes taking place that would usher in socialism. His transformative conception of democracy described some of them.

   That transformative conception of democracy first found full expression in his 1920–21 essay, "The Socialist Possibilities of Today." A close reading of that essay demonstrates that Schumpeter shared with Bauer and like-minded Austro-Marxists at least five major premises for how council democracy would pave the way for socialism. First, Schumpeter argued that the spread of the council system would transform social and economic relations so fundamentally as to make possible a relatively smooth transition to socialism. Second, Schumpeter shared the Austro-Marxists' view that the council movement represented a democratization of industry—a process that was analogous to political democratization. Third, in light of his view of the prerequisites for socialism, Schumpeter, like Bauer, doubted the viability of any attempt to usher in socialism before the spread of the council system had done its work. Fourth, Schumpeter and Bauer both saw the antidemocratic tactics and institutions of Bolshevism as evidence of the futility of trying to achieve democratic socialism before such an underlying social development. And fifth, Schumpeter argued, as against certain syndicalist visions of workplace democracy, that democratic socialism would have to include institutions to coordinate between factories.

A THEORY OF SOCIAL REVOLUTION.   Just as Bauer's theory of democracy was part of a broader theory of social change, there was, underlying Schumpeter's transformative conception of democracy, a general theory of social revolution. The heart of this theory was the argument, almost Marxist in character, that a political act establishing new social order—including a revolutionary or a parliamentary expropriation of the means of production—could take place only as the culmination of a deeper process of economic and social transformation (Schumpeter, 1920–21, 305–306, 333). Such a political revolution would only reflect the emergence of a "new social system," a completed process of building new "life conditions" and the "elevation" of new social classes (ibid., 310, 305). The council movement, in his view, was such a process.

THE COUNCIL MOVEMENT.   Given the great interest in socialization measures in postwar Europe, Schumpeter set for himself the task of determining whether there were in fact any tendencies leading toward the emergence of socialism "independent of wishes" (1920–21, 312). He concluded that there were. He described first the broad tendencies making such a transition possible, or even likely. It is well known that Schumpeter considered entrepreneurs to be crucial to the functioning of capitalism, because he believed that the innovations that entrepreneurs introduced into economic life were responsible for economic growth, and indeed for most of the characteristic features by which capitalism as an economic system could be distinguished. Schumpeter had developed this view in his career-making work, *The Theory of Economic Development* ([1911] 1934). It is clear that, in 1920–21, Schumpeter had already developed an embryonic form of his theory of the demise of individual entrepreneurialism as a component of the decline of capitalism, for in this essay, he argued that the historical process of "rationalization" led to the entrepreneur's tasks becoming mechanized and routine, so that the entrepreneur could be replaced by a bureaucracy (1920–21, 314–318). But in Schumpeter's view these tendencies, which loosened the ties between owners and their productive resources, and undermined support for capitalism, merely tended to make socialism more possible and would not actually bring about a socialist order of society (ibid., 322).

Schumpeter argued in "The Socialist Possibilities of Today" that the tendency that would actually beget the transformation from capitalism to socialism was the same one emphasized by Austrian Social Democrats, the growth of the council system. "The council system and socialization belong together, and tend to realize themselves reciprocally and roughly at the same time," Schumpeter argued (1920–21, 324; my translation). Both "democratic socialism"—which he said was "the socialism of the workers' party"—and "full socialization," by which he meant a thoroughgoing socialism based on a new social system, could take place only on the basis of the spread of the council system, Schumpeter contended (ibid., 310, 338; my translation). The German and Austrian laws establishing mechanisms for creating factory councils were a "practical success" for the council movement, he wrote (ibid., 338; my translation). And a further spread of the movement would eventually make a final act of transformation to socialism possible: "If this movement [the council movement] is sufficiently wide, then it, and it alone, can accomplish full socialization in a single act through general strike" (ibid.).

Like Bauer and other Austrian Social Democrats, Schumpeter saw the spread of the council system as an analogue to and an extension of the process of *political* democratization. Schumpeter described parliamentary democracy in this essay in terms very similar to those of the system's radical critics—as little more than the political reflection of the social and economic power of the bourgeoisie. In Schumpeter's account—not, in this case, a unique one—the bourgeoisie had risen to social and economic power through the industrial revolution and had sought political power and representation in order to protect its economic interests (Schumpeter 1920–21, 324). The prewar parliamentary system of a country such as Austria-Hungary or Germany, in his view, reflected a balancing of the power of the bourgeoisie against the combined power of the aristocracy, the clergy, the peasantry, and the bureaucracy (ibid., 325). From the standpoint of the bourgeoisie, at least, such a system met some of the requirements of democratic theory, as he understood them (ibid.).

In Schumpeter's view, however, parliamentary democracy, as the political expression of liberal capitalist society, could not accommodate the ambitions of the working class to have its interests represented. The working class, in his view, sought representation through extra-parliamentary means and particularly through the democratization of the factory by means of factory councils. He argued that "in the factory a process entirely similar to that in the state has taken place," whereby workers first sought an influence over issues of immediate concern, such as discipline and factory safety, but soon recognized their broader interest in "all the technical and commercial policies of the company management" (1920–21, 337; my translation).[51]

Following Bauer almost precisely, Schumpeter argued that this tendency would lead first to a "constitutional" factory—the analogy seems to have been to a constitutional monarchy—and finally to the sole power of the workers within the plant (1920–21, 337).[52] The very same German and Austrian laws establishing mechanisms for creating factory councils *(Betriebsrätegesetz)*—which Bauer saw as a crucial step in fostering the democratic self-education of the workers—Schumpeter saw as a "practical success" for the council movement, which could lead in the distant future to a situation in which workers themselves would be in a position to take on the tasks of technological and commercial management (Bauer [1925] 1970, 138; Schumpeter 1920–21, 338). In the meantime, the growth of working-class political power and participation was already making merely parliamentary democracy obsolete, he argued (1920–21, 328–330).

For a short time, Schumpeter contended, it was possible for elite politicians—Tory democrats—to harness working-class political power for their own ends within the parliamentary system (1920–21, 330). But "just as the rising of the bourgeois circle forced its participation in politics, so must the rising of the working class have the same result," Schumpeter contended; "just as the bourgeoisie was at first content that the power of the state be oriented toward its interests, although the feudal aristocracy or the bureaucracy held the leading positions, so the working class for a long time renounced the fight for voting rights. But in both cases these wishes had finally to surface" (ibid., my translation).[53]

Of course there is not even a hint that the archconservative Schumpeter approved of this process—on the contrary, he regarded it with unconcealed aversion. Herbert Zassenhaus has rightly argued that in this essay, Schumpeter is "extremely critical" of democracy (Zassenhaus 1981, 198).[54] But this hostility is worth investigating, since it could be mistaken for something that it is not. For Schumpeter's "critical" attitude toward democracy did not prevent him from adopting the social democratic view that democratization was a powerful transformative tendency. Schumpeter, for example, elaborated a deeply cynical picture of the functioning of parliamentary democracies in his own time, according to which voters were manipulated by political parties, individual members of parliament were the tools of party leaders, and parliamentary debate itself was far less relevant than the clash of forces outside the parliament (1920–21, 328–329). But this passage should be interpreted in light of the fact that Schumpeter regarded purely parliamentary democracy as a manifestation of bourgeois power; he argued that the system was decaying precisely because of the democratizing pressures created by mass enfranchisement, which brought with it a need for new institutions for participation and stole the focus from the debate taking place within parliament—an institution whose structure, history, and limits reflected bourgeois power and interests (ibid., 329).

Parliamentary decay took place because the parliamentary system could not accommodate the participation of new voters whose core demands would fundamentally alter the social order on which parliamentary democracy was founded (1920–21, 326, 329). Similarly, because he thought that parliamentary democracy was founded on capitalist production and bourgeois power, Schumpeter was convinced that the measures for the transition to socialism could not be approved by the democratic decision of a parliament; a social reconstruction of the kind created by the council movement would be necessary first. For this reason, he argued that those, like Lenin, who favored an immediate establishment of socialist production naturally abandoned democratic procedures; likewise, he contended that bourgeois politicians could not really afford to favor thoroughgoing democratization (ibid., 327). Thus he cynically commended politicians on each side who repudiated democracy (ibid., 327, 328). But though cynically expressed, this argument is nothing more than the logical extension of his theory of revolutions and his associated claim that real socialism could take place only on the basis of the social reconstruction inherent in the council movement—and not before its completion—a view he shared with Bauer.[55]

Finally, Schumpeter had harsh words in this essay for syndicalism, by which he especially meant an emphasis on the workers in a particular plant taking complete control of it—and scorn as well for the idea that workers in a particular branch of industry should alone make all the decisions regarding the direction of that branch (1920–21, 336–337, 341). Schumpeter argued strenuously that syndicalism of this kind would replace "individual capitalism" with "group capitalism" (ibid., 337). In rejecting the sole sovereignty of workers within a particular plant or branch, Schumpeter directed his hostility toward what he called "the old phraseology of democracy," "the way of thinking of the eighteenth century," "rationalistic philosophy," and the "popular notion" of democracy. But it is crucial to note that all of this argument is intended mainly to establish the forms and extent of worker self-management that would be appropriate in "democratic socialism" (ibid., 341). And it is equally crucial to note that Bauer, too, rejected both syndicalism and the idea of sole sovereignty of the workers in a particular plant or branch of industry. As we have seen, Bauer envisioned a system of democratized plants whose policies would be coordinated by a democratized industry body, including representatives of consumers, workers, and the government (Bauer [1925] 1970, 146).

Thus despite his "critical" positions with respect to democracy, Schumpeter clearly linked democratization to the council movement, as did Bauer, and he clearly saw the council movement as a transformative tendency leading to what he called *real* socialism—socialism as the result of an actual historical tendency, socialism as a "new form of society" (Schumpeter 1920–21, 309, 310). Schumpeter was interested in actual historical tendencies that were transforming society, a category that included "rationalization," as well as "leveling" and "democratization" (ibid., 318). Indeed, Schumpeter's entire essay was framed around his view that the council movement was leading to a new form of society that Schumpeter called "democratic socialism," a form of society in which "each would count for one and no one more than one" (ibid., 310, 326; my translation). He acknowledged that others may have a different type of nondemocratic socialism in mind—indeed, that the central direction of production could be structured aristocratically or hierarchically in "countries where strong aristocratic castes rule," and that the extension of wartime controls on the economy could constitute a kind of nondemocratic socialism (ibid., 308, 309–310; my translation). But, he wrote, "here we want only to speak of democratic socialism, the socialism of the workers' party. Only it means a new form of society" (ibid., 310; my translation).

Correspondingly, Schumpeter argued that the type of socialism that would be the outcome of the council movement would be democratic, and on these grounds he explicitly waived the chance to discuss nondemocratic forms of socialism. Thus in "The Socialist Possibilities of Today" he acknowledged that Social Democrats in Austria distinguished between nondemocratic nationalization *(Verstaatlichung)*—the mere taking over of private enterprises by the state—and socialization *(Sozialisierung)* of industry through the spread of the council system and other representative mechanisms. And he conceded the distinction himself, noting that nationalization, unlike socialization, would "leave the essence and the structure of a capitalist enterprise undisturbed" (1920–21, 334–335; my translation). As for the extension of recent wartime economic controls—which, in Austria, as we have seen, included onerous and undemocratic restrictions on workers—Schumpeter rejected the idea that it might be an actual tendency leading toward socialization. As early as 1918, he wrote that "Marx himself" would "laugh grimly at those of his disciples who welcome the present administrative economy as the dawn of socialism—*that administrative economy which is the most undemocratic thing there is*" (1918 [1991], 130; emphasis added). It is important to recollect, too, that if Schumpeter had wanted to theorize an undemocratic form of socialism, or if he had not believed, with Bauer, that it was the democratizing effects of the council movement that would be crucial in creating the prerequisites for a transition to socialism, he had a conspicuous example at his disposal: that of Bolshevism.

But Schumpeter passed up the chance to argue that the Bolshevist model—particularly dictatorial economic measures and an undemocratic system of *workers'* councils (soviets) meant precisely to exclude the bourgeoisie from political power—was the one that would predominate in socialism (see, for example, Lenin 1975, 456).[56] Schumpeter attributed the development of Bolshevism to the attempt to achieve socialism before the council movement had spread widely enough of its own accord to enable the transition without violent opposition, and before capitalist development had run its full course in other ways, and he considered Bolshevism, as well, a "child of the militarism of the absolute princely state" (1920–21, 326–327, 338, my translation; 1918 [1991] 130). Schumpeter did not think that Bolshevism represented the wave of the future; rather, he embraced, as we have seen, much of Bauer's view of the significance of the council movement as a means of achieving industrial democracy and socialism. Schumpeter even treated the council movement—albeit in terms far less enthusiastic than Bauer's—as a form of the development of the masses, whereby they were growing out of political institutions that implied their subordination and tutelage toward a situation in which workers would be equal to all the tasks of industrial management, a world he described as one of "socialist fulfillment" (1920–21, 330, 338).

SCHUMPETER'S ENGAGEMENT IN POLITICS. Scholarly works on Schumpeter's engagement with the problem of socialization in this period have tended to focus on two main controversies that I consider subsidiary to the problems discussed above: how enthusiastic he was in support of socialization as a member of the German Socialization Commission, and whether he deliberately undermined attempts to socialize Alpine-Montan-Gesellschaft, the largest mining company in Austria.

The German Socialization Commission was founded because of the intense pressure from the council movement and from the rank and file of the German SDP to democratize industry and restructure the economy and society (Craig 1978, 413). But the demands of the council movement never found favor with an influential segment of the German SDP leadership that took power after the war (Craig 1978, 413; Maier 1975, 140). Though it was far from a mouthpiece of the council movement, the commission's work was thus probably doomed from the outset. In fact, even before the commission finished its work on socializing the coal industry, the government proposed its own bill for the "socialization" of the industry that essentially built on the extensive cartelization of the industry and on wartime economic planning—but took no steps toward social control of the industry or industrial democracy (Maier 1975, 140–141).

Since Schumpeter's death, scholars have debated how staunch a supporter of socialization he proved to be while serving on the commission. According to Gottfried Haberler's memorial, written shortly after Schumpeter's death, he was sharply critical of socialization plans during the commission's meetings, and likened his own participation in socialization to that of a doctor at someone's suicide (Haberler 1950, 345). But Theodor Vogelstein, a member of the commission, insisted in a letter he sent to Haberler that Schumpeter "sided mostly with the more extreme propagators of immediate and integral socialization" (Vogelstein 1950). This disagreement has been discussed in most of the recent intellectual biographies (Allen 1991, 1: 163–165; Stolper 1994, 204; Swedberg 1991b, 56–58).

But in Schumpeter's own comments during the commission's confidential sessions, he did not really present himself either as a committed proponent of socialization or as an opponent, determined to prevent it. Rather, he seems to have viewed socialization as given, and to have argued for strong powers for the directors of the socialized coal industry and the managers of the individual coal enterprises—in apparent opposition to the widespread demands for democratization and worker control that the commission had to take into account.[57] Obviously this is of great interest for the current study. Again, some context may be useful. The commission's majority report, although it embraced "democratization" as a principle for socialization, did so lukewarmly, at best. While the commission endorsed the principle of democratic organization of industry, it argued not that democracy required participatory decision making, but rather that "every action of the leading personalities is supported by the trust and will of all concerned"; and even that degree of "democracy" was not to infringe on the "leading personalities" in their "freedom to decide and to move as long as they have this trust" (translated in Stolper 1985, 165).[58] "The leadership of the GCC [German Coal Council] must have adequate power and mobility," the report argued; "the Commission is in complete agreement to stress the importance of leadership in economic life" (translated in Stolper 1985, 165). What the minutes show is that Schumpeter argued for precisely this stress on leadership powers (Sozialisierungskommission 1919a, 38, 49, 50, 55, 87). Stolper and Allen point out that, months later, Schumpeter said in a speech that he had gone as far "as he could" on the German Socialization Commission (Stolper 1985, 162; and see Allen 1: 164). What they do not sufficiently emphasize is that Schumpeter said, more precisely, that the commission's report had gone as far as was possible *in the direction of "democratization of the economy"* (translated in Stolper 1985, 182 n. 2; emphasis added).

In any case, none of this really contradicts one of Schumpeter's major premises throughout the postwar years: that socialism's time had not yet come. Much of the commission regarded the socialization of the German coal industry in part as a response to special circumstances—the industry's cartelization and its already-significant penetration by state ownership—and not necessarily as the first step in a long process of socialization. If the industry was to be socialized, it should be socialized in a way that would not damage the rest of the capitalist economy, Schumpeter argued, and this explains his attachment to doing the job swiftly and integrally. But given that Schumpeter thought the spread of the council movement and economic democratization would be the eventual path to socialism, why did he so strongly support leadership and centralized powers in his work on the commission? One likely answer to the question seems evident: because Schumpeter did not conceive of the socialization of the German coal industry as a real step toward democratic socialization. The time for such steps had not come. In any case, on the commission his dual attitude toward democracy—on the one hand, recognition of democracy's transformative power, and on the other, practical opposition to the spread of democratic practices—again was evident.

Another controversy concerns Schumpeter's conduct a few months later as Austrian finance minister. The dispute concerns allegations that Schumpeter acted underhandedly to prevent the socialization of Alpine-Montan-Gesellschaft, the largest iron-producing concern in Austria, whose socialization Otto Bauer, as president of the Austrian Socialization Commission, regarded as an important part of his plans (Allen 1991, 1: 174–176; Bauer [1925] 1970, 156–157; Gulick 1948, 139–141; März 1981, 173–176; Stolper 1985, 169–180; Stolper 1994, 269–288; Swedberg 1991b, 62–63). Bauer believed that Schumpeter had done so, and Eduard März has made a plausible case for a somewhat modulated form of Bauer's accusation (Bauer [1925] 1970, 156–157; März 1981, 173–176). Meanwhile, Wolfgang Stolper has presented exhaustive arguments to discredit the charge (Stolper 1985, 169–180; Stolper 1994, 269–288).

From the standpoint of Schumpeter's developing conception of socialization and democratization, however, it must be said that the most significant fact about the affair concerns what Schumpeter said about it more than two decades later. In a letter to Charles Gulick, who was at that time preparing his history of Austria, Schumpeter denied taking any such action, but not, he wrote, "because I consider that such an . . . [action] would have been wrong. On the contrary, I consider that, had I prevented a measure that could have only increased the difficulties of a difficult situation, this would have been a service to the country, the government and, above all, to the Social Democratic party" (Gulick 1948, 140 n. 19). Schumpeter believed that the socialization of Alpine-Montan-Gesellschaft would have been premature in 1919, a view perfectly consistent with his underlying conception of the process leading from liberal capitalist society to socialist society, according to which a massive alteration of the social structure would be necessary before a final transition to socialism was feasible.

Nazi Sympathies and Anti-Semitism

In recent years, evidence has emerged showing that Schumpeter was anti-Semitic, and that he had pro-Nazi sympathies. By the time Hitler took power in 1933, Schumpeter had moved to the United States from Germany, where he had lived for about seven years. He never gave speeches or wrote essays with the purpose of defending or promoting Nazism, and, under the circumstances, he never had even the opportunity to participate in the Nazi seizure of power, the creation and consolidation of the Nazi dictatorship, or the enforcement of Nazi racial decrees. For these reasons, his case is different from that of intellectual figures like Martin Heidegger. But this newly emerging evidence is quite sufficient to warrant serious examination and consideration in a work on Schumpeter's political thought.[59]

In general, scholars have adopted two approaches regarding this evidence. The first has been to attempt to show that Schumpeter's social, economic, and political thought and writings were not colored by Nazi sympathy. This first general approach has taken different forms: denying Schumpeter was ever anti-Semitic or pro-Nazi (Stolper 1994, 10–12), or admitting that he was both, but somehow attempting to extenuate his views or separate them from other, better-known aspects of his thinking (Allen 1991, 1: 283–288; 2: 58, 66–68, 90–92, 100–103, 138–139, 166, 191–193). The second general approach has been to use the evidence of his anti-Semitism and pro-Nazi views simply to discredit Schumpeter (Semmel 1992, 3–16). Neither of these general approaches is particularly fruitful.

I would argue against any interpretive strategy, such as these, that cuts off the possibility of making sense of Schumpeter's Nazi sympathies in light of all that we know about his political and social views, including his published scholarly writings. We should even be careful of putting too much weight on observations, such as Richard Swedberg's, that Schumpeter's more extreme pro-Nazi diary notations indicate that he was "quite out of balance" at certain times (Swedberg 1991a, 150). This may be an accurate characterization of his emotional state—and it may also naturally reflect a contemporary scholar's abhorrence for Nazism, which almost by definition appears deranged, to say the least. But Schumpeter's imbalance in these years seems never to have involved any fundamental break with his longstanding political commitments.

From 1916 on, Schumpeter's most important and consistently expressed political commitment was to thwarting the various democratizing tendencies that he thought were visible in Austria-Hungary, Germany, and other liberal capitalist societies, tendencies that were undermining traditional authority in the economy, society, and the state, and that would ultimately bring about a transition to democratic socialism. Late in the First World War, Schumpeter believed that a conservative aristocratic party would serve this purpose—would even save the Habsburg monarchy—but he was proved wrong within months. By the 1930s and early 1940s, when he was writing *Capitalism, Socialism, and Democracy,* Schumpeter was clearly searching for another social group that could tame democracy (see Chapter 4). By this time he had also clearly embraced an authoritarian vision of politics that did not flinch at serious inroads on democratic freedoms. This aversion to a kind of democratizing change, which he feared would lead to democratic socialism, was the core of Schumpeter's deep conservatism. And it was Schumpeter's "conservative convictions," he told a colleague in 1933, that prevented him from condemning the dictatorial measures Hitler had already initiated by that time (Schumpeter 2000, 243). There is good reason to believe that abhorrence for transformative, democratizing change was central to Schumpeter's view of German politics and society during the period of the Nazis' rise to power. Months before Hitler became chancellor of Germany, Schumpeter was convinced that Germany had entered a "laborite" phase—meaning a transitional period on the way to democratic socialism during which labor interests prevailed in a still-capitalist society, a phase that in one place he referred to as "democracy in the sense of trade-union rule" ([1941] 1991, 346).[60] Schumpeter later told a correspondent that it was in part because he did not wish to live under a such a "laborite" regime—"if I could help it"— that he had left Germany in 1932 (2000, 338–339). This admission of the importance of Schumpeter's disgust at what he took to be the currents of change in Germany in the late 1920s and early 1930s lends weight to Allen's view of Schumpeter's Nazi sympathies: "Because Schumpeter interpreted most German political parties as left of center, sympathetic to labor and unsympathetic to his view of capitalism, he had slight sympathy for most of these parties. His sympathy for the Nazis may have boiled down to accepting the lesser of two evils" (Allen 1991, 1: 286).[61]

The evidence, reviewed below, that Schumpeter had Nazi sympathies is, I think, unambiguous and all but conclusive. In assessing what conclusions to draw from the evidence, scholars must make an interpretive choice: either to sever these views from his other social and political ideas and writings, or to try and read them together as one interconnected, if inconsistent, whole. One can either decide, a priori, that his Nazi sympathies and anti-Semitism and his social thought, considered broadly, are separate matters to be dealt with separately, or one can try to understand the interconnections between them. I consider the latter course to be the more justifiable approach. And given this framework for viewing the evidence of his Nazi sympathies, the most obvious conclusion is that Schumpeter was at the very least disturbingly willing to overlook the horrors of Nazi rule because it might serve political and social ends that he favored.

Examination of the evidence adds two more explanatory elements to Schumpeter's sympathy for Nazism. Related to his strong aversion to the social, political, and economic tendencies leading to democratic socialism was a deep abhorrence for a different path to a different type of socialism, that represented by Bolshevism. This aversion became ever more apparent in Schumpeter's private and public writings throughout the 1930s and 1940s.[62] And then there is Schumpeter's anti-Semitism, to which I give separate and thorough consideration below. Though he did so privately and cryptically, Schumpeter usually expressed his sympathy for Nazism along with his anti-Bolshevism and his anti-Semitism. Far from showing that Schumpeter had unique reasons for his Nazi sympathies, or ones that distinguish him from more open Nazi sympathizers and defenders, this is an all-too-typical mix, similar to the constitutive elements of Nazi ideology itself (Friedländer 1997, 73–112).

It is worth remembering, too, that in considering Nazism as a bulwark against the tendencies he deplored—possibly as Germany's "salvation" from them, as he put it (Schumpeter 2000, 241)[63]—Schumpeter was embracing only a particularly hateful and powerful version of the many related reactionary movements that swept Europe in the late nineteenth and early twentieth centuries—movements with which Schumpeter had had personal experience in Austria-Hungary. We have already seen that after his disastrous stint as finance minister of Austria, Schumpeter joined the Christian Social Party, whose fundamental orientation was antidemocratic, antisocialist, and anti-Semitic. Despite its Catholic orientation, and despite its rivalry with the Austrian Nazis, the Christian

Social Party evolved toward fascist-style politics, employing and defending increasingly violent and authoritarian tactics, including cooperation with fascist armed militias to intimidate and attack opponents, and the establishment in 1933–34 of a dictatorship under Engelbert Dollfuss.

Anti-Semitism

That Schumpeter held anti-Semitic views was actually widely known among his colleagues after he began to teach at Harvard in 1932. And Schumpeter admitted as much to himself in his diary, even though he denied accusations of anti-Semitism publicly (Allen 1991, 2: 66; Swedberg 1991a, 150). "I am as antisemitic as Schmidt or some kind of rich German-American," he wrote in the diary in 1939 (Allen 1991, 2: 66). He is not known to have expressed in any extensive form what Saul Friedländer terms "redemptive anti-Semitism," the crucial core of Nazism, a quasi-religious doctrine holding that German social redemption required the expulsion or the annihilation of Jews (Friedländer 1997, 87). But stories about Schumpeter's comments concerning Jews abounded (Swedberg 1991a, 150, 276 n. 79). Schumpeter was known to tell "stale" if not violent anti-Semitic jokes, to use derogatory or dismissive terms for Jews,[64] and to comment on Jews' alleged clannishness and tendency to bloom early (Allen 1991, 2: 66, 67, 191; Stolper 1994, 10; Swedberg 1991a, 150). In two known cases, Schumpeter discussed a job or fellowship applicant's being Jewish in the context of evaluating his credentials. And while it must be said that in both of these cases Schumpeter favored the candidate, the stories do not paint a portrait of tolerance. For example, Schumpeter respected Paul Samuelson, the Keynesian whom he had as a student and junior colleague, and in 1940 he supported his candidacy for a professorship at Harvard. But after the faculty failed to make Samuelson a job offer, Schumpeter is reported to have said: "I could understand it if they had voted against him because he was a Jew. But they voted against him because he was smarter than they are" (Allen 1991, 2: 95; see also Swedberg 1991a, 139).[65]

Schumpeter's involvement with efforts to help German Jewish professors find jobs in the United States after they lost their positions because of Hitler's "cleansing" of the civil service reveals some complexities and contradictions in his attitude toward Jews. In the winter and spring of 1933, just a few months after Schumpeter's arrival at Harvard, Hitler became dictator of Germany and, in one of his first acts, began "cleansing" the civil service, including the German universities, of Jews and other non-Aryans (Carmon 1976, 134; Friedländer 1997, 49–60). Within a few weeks, Schumpeter was corresponding with economists around the country about trying to place some academic refugees in American universities.[66] The effort demonstrates that Schumpeter valued academic freedom enough to override even his worst prejudices. But his embrace of this endeavor was far from wholehearted. He was concerned that no one think he was Jewish, or that he was a critic of Hitler's dictatorship generally. "In order to avoid what would be a very natural misunderstanding," Schumpeter wrote on 19 April 1933 to a minister whose help he hoped to enlist,

> allow me to state that I am a German citizen but not a Jew or of Jewish descent. Nor am I a thorough exponent of the present German government, the actions of which look somewhat differently to one who has had the experience of the regime which preceded it.[67] My conservative convictions make it impossible for me to share in the well-nigh unanimous condemnation the Hitler Ministry meets with in the world at large.[68] It is merely from a sense of duty towards men who have been my colleagues that I am trying to organise some help for them which would enable them to carry on quiet scientific work in this country should necessity arise. (Schumpeter 2000, 243)

And to Alvin Johnson, who was recruiting German Jewish scholars to the New School, Schumpeter wrote on 2 May 1933:

> When we meet again I shall, to your satisfaction I hope, explain why I can not help you in it personally because of the strong emphasis placed on the element of protest; although I do disapprove just as much as you do of any injustice or harshness, I cannot feel about the Hitler government as many people do because I know the one that went before. If I do not approve of the reaction I could not say with truth that I do not understand it. And many public protests even if directed only against one specific point will in the public mind invariably weld into a general protest. But I greatly sympathize and as I should feel it a duty to help my former colleagues in case your plan should not take care of them, I should be much obliged if you told me how things stand and whether I may with safety discontinue my own efforts. (Schumpeter 2000, 253)

Schumpeter also aided Kläre Tisch, a Jewish former student from the University of Bonn, in her attempts to emigrate from Germany. She never succeeded, however, and was murdered by the Nazis (Allen 1991, 2: 108; Stolper 1994, 12).[69] Despite his ongoing support and her dire situation, Schumpeter apparently failed to open the last letter he received from Tisch—one dated, tragically, just a few days before her deportation in November 1941 and subsequent murder (see Schumpeter 2000, 335 nn. 1 and 5).[70]

The efforts to help Jewish colleagues no doubt weigh in Schumpeter's favor. But his insistence in connection with these very grave matters that he himself was not Jewish and that he was not a critic of Hitler just as surely speaks not to the shallowness but to the depth of his anti-Semitic feelings. In 1938, when he was still trying to help Tisch and only a few years after he had aided other German Jewish scholars, he wrote in his diary: "We must have either Hitler or else the Jews" (Allen 1991, 2: 66). Perhaps it is in light of these conflicting impulses—one anti-Semitic, the other provisionally sympathetic to Jewish colleagues and friends—that we should interpret Schumpeter's postwar insistence that not 6 million but 2 million Jews had been murdered in the Holocaust, and the fact that this "seemed to make some kind of difference to him" (Allen 1991, 2: 166).

Nazi Sympathies

The earliest evidence of Schumpeter's Nazi sympathies dates from 1932, the year before Hitler's rise to power and the year in which Schumpeter moved to the United States. Reflecting on his imminent departure, Schumpeter wrote in his diary: "I have to leave. Everyone who is close to me and with whom I could work stand on one side. And what I feel in my innermost self is around Hitler. But is it really so?" (Allen 1991, 1: 288).

In his farewell address to his students on 20 July 1932, he argued that one had to "orient oneself" toward "parties which have non-rational programs" such as that of the Nazis, noting that the Nazi Party was like a "monster of infinite impulse" which needed to be "counselled properly in economics" (translated in Allen 1991, 1: 285).[71] A proficient young economist inclined toward Nazism could advance his career by joining the Nazi Party, he said, advice he also gave in private to some of his students (Schumpeter [1932] 1952, 606; Allen 1991, 1: 284, 285).[72]

The darker significance of some remarks by Schumpeter that have been quoted but not much scrutinized becomes clearer when they are examined chronologically. Hitler became chancellor of Germany in late January 1933, and he used the next few months to consolidate his power and form the basis of the Nazi state (Craig 1978, 570). While Hermann Göring tightened Nazi control over the police, Hitler took by presidential decree the power to ban the meetings and publications of rival parties. After insisting that parliament be dissolved and new elections be held in March, he orchestrated the intimidation of the Social Democratic and Communist parties in their campaign activities. Hours after the infamous fire in the Reichstag, Hitler convinced Paul von Hindenburg, the president, to sign a decree declaring a permanent state of emergency and the suspension of constitutional government and the basic civil rights of citizens; he had already had 4,000 Communist Party members and intellectuals arrested. Days after the 5 March elections, Hitler arrested all of the 81 Communists chosen by voters to serve in the parliament. On 23 March, with menacing pro-Hitler troops surrounding the parliament's temporary meeting place, only the Social Democratic deputies refused to pass the Enabling Act, which gave Hitler absolute power to make laws and change the constitution. It was just a short time before Hitler, on 7 April, issued the decree mentioned above for "cleansing" the civil service.

This, then, is what Nazism meant in April and May of 1933, when Schumpeter said he could not share in the "well-nigh unanimous condemnation" of the Hitler dictatorship, was unwilling to associate himself with any "general protest" against it, and could even "understand" it in light of the alternatives offered by Weimar history (Schumpeter 2000, 243, 253).

Although he never formulated a systematic public defense of Hitler nor acted in such a way as to aid his cause, nothing in the thirteen years of Nazi rule moved Schumpeter to denounce Nazism either. And to friends and colleagues, in his diary, and sometimes in brief references in public speeches, Schumpeter expressed in three ways what he himself called his "astonishing" sympathy for Nazism (Allen 1991, 2: 66). He repeatedly expressed the view that Nazism was an understandable response to Weimar politics and was a bulwark against forces with the potential to destroy Western civilization, especially Bolshevism (Allen 1991, 2: 66, 91, 101, 102–103, 112 n. 4, 113 n. 21; Swedberg 1991b, 28, 86 n. 90). He favored letting the Nazis maintain control over the countries they attacked and subdued, and predicted that a world structured partly by a strong and stable Nazi bloc was possible (Allen 1991, 2: 91, 92, 112 n. 4; Schumpeter 1941 [1991] 388–389; Swedberg 1991a, 276 n. 75; Swedberg 1991b, 86 n. 90). And until quite late in the Second World War, Schumpeter also voiced the hope or belief that Germany could win; when it was clear it had been defeated, his reaction, as recorded in his diary, was furious and anti-Semitic, a bitter protest against what he termed a "Jewish victory" (Allen 1991, 2: 92, 138, 154; Swedberg 1991a, 149–150). In the immediate aftermath of the war, when asked to join German and Austrian refugees, people who considered themselves "enemies and victims of Nazism," in signing a humanitarian petition that called attention to the plight of ordinary Germans, even while acknowledging their responsibility for "crimes that were committed in their name," Schumpeter scrawled an angry note on the document: "I have not signed nor answered this. I feel that to sign one must be able to answer for every phrase. I am no 'victim' of Nazism and don't believe in Germanys [*sic*] guilt. I cannot sign" (Bachhofer, Franck, and Goffron 1945).

Against this sobering picture of Schumpeter's Nazi sympathies, scholars have marshalled several mitigating arguments and pieces of evidence. All of these deserve attention, but none substantially changes the picture presented here. First, there is evidence that Schumpeter scorned Nazism as an irrational "religion," and this is sometimes said to demonstrate Schumpeter's contempt for Hitler (Allen 2: 92; Swedberg 1991a, 148, 275 n. 71). But, as we have seen, viewing Nazism as a religion or an irrational program did not prevent Schumpeter, in virtually the same breath, from advising students that they could advance their career by joining the party and trying to influence its economic program (Schumpeter [1932] 1952, 606; Allen 1991, 1: 285). Second, some scholars have stressed the fact that Schumpeter feared the Soviet Union and believed that Hitler was serving the interests of the West by invading it. But this can hardly be seen as an extenuation of Schumpeter's Nazi sympathies. Hitler himself believed in the need for a dual redemption of Germany and the West from Judaism, on the one hand, and Bolshevism, on the other (Friedländer 1997, 90–104). Third, Allen contends that Schumpeter naively "believed that the Nazis were just another political party with a political program designed to meet public approval, and that Hitler was just another political leader" (Allen 1991, 1: 285). But this argument appears inadequate even in the context in which it is offered—that is, as an explanation of Schumpeter's 1932 views. Allen himself quotes Schumpeter at roughly the same time calling Nazism "a powerful movement which is *singular in our history*" (Allen 1991, 1: 285; emphasis added). Even more important, this argument cannot possibly explain Schumpeter's sympathy for the Nazis in the spring of 1933, let alone in 1945, when no one could have regarded the Nazis as "just another political party" (Allen 1991, 1: 285). Fourth and finally, at least one scholar reports that Schumpeter told acquaintances he would have been considered an enemy of the Nazis and a candidate for a concentration camp had he stayed in Germany (Haberler 1950, 356–357). If so, he cannot have taken the risk very seriously, because he visited Germany from the United States in 1933, 1934, and 1935, after the Nazis had begun arresting thousands of their political enemies and while he was still a German citizen (Allen 1991, 2: 3, 8, 12, 90).

Corporatism

In the last years of his life, just after the defeat of Nazi Germany, Schumpeter expressed sympathy for a kind of corporatist political and economic program that had become a part of Austrian fascism in the 1920s and 1930s (Schumpeter 1946 [1991], 401–405). Schumpeter discussed corporatism so briefly that it is difficult to know how much weight to give his comments. But what little direct attention has been paid to these comments has been marred by an excessively abstract and depoliticized interpretive approach.[73]

The key point is that, in adopting certain corporatist themes from Pope Pius XI's *Quadragesimo Anno,* Schumpeter was adopting the positions that had been incorporated into a political program by the fascist-leaning Austrian Christian Social Party, with which he had ties dating back at least to 1919, and with which he had shared a common interest in opposing the democratizing platforms of the Austrian Social Democrats. The Christian Socials, it should be noted, put into place what they argued was a corporate constitution in 1934—but only after Engelbert Dollfuss took dictatorial powers in 1933, and lured the socialists into a disastrous civil war. In an address to a Catholic employers' association in Montreal in 1946, Schumpeter used language and arguments quite similar to those used by Austrian Christian Socials in suggesting corporatism and "moral reform" as a solution to the crisis of "leadership" in a "society that is disintegrating," the failure of workers to accept their "duties," and the "spirit of social irresponsibility" springing from nineteenth-century movements and philosophy (Schumpeter 1946 [1991], 403, 404, 405). He explicitly offered corporatism to this audience as an alternative to "Bolshevism" and "democratic socialism," both of which he deplored (ibid., 404). Although Schumpeter emphasized the idea that corporatism was not "centralizing," it should be noted that the Christian Socials also made much of this argument, right up until the time of Dollfuss's dictatorship. In any case, Austrian corporatist doctrine was no less authoritarian for being, in principle, anticentralist. Indeed, it was a profoundly antidemocratic and authoritarian doctrine that envisioned a neofeudal society structured by numerous decentralized hierarchies (Schumpeter 1946 [1991] 404; see Diamant 1960).

3

The New Deal and Transformative Democracy

After his political career collapsed in the fall of 1919, Schumpeter turned to an equally ill-fated venture in banking in Vienna that lasted from 1921 to 1924. In time, however, he returned to academia with an appointment to the University of Bonn, in Germany. He stayed there only seven years, accepting a position in the economics department at Harvard in 1932, the year before Hitler's rise to power. And so Schumpeter arrived in the United States not long before Franklin Delano Roosevelt was elected to his first term, and as the U.S. labor movement prepared for some of the most important years of its history. The New Deal period reshaped Schumpeter's thinking about democracy's transformative potential. His writings on the fate of capitalism and the tendencies undermining it were unmistakably colored by vivid American images of depression and conflict, picket lines and sit-down strikes. His transformative conception of democracy was, in an important sense, Americanized.

In Schumpeter's updated version of the transformative conception, the spread of democratic beliefs, practices, and ideologies was still a potent force for transforming liberal capitalist societies into democratic socialist ones. As in wartime and postwar Austria, Schumpeter still placed great emphasis on the deployment of democratic ideas and arguments against workplace hierarchy, and viewed that process as an extension of the process of political democratization. And in the 1930s and 1940s, just as in the previous two decades, Schumpeter set his analysis of democratization within a broad theory of the development of capitalist societies and the onset of socialism. From at least 1918 until his death,

Schumpeter believed that liberal capitalism was fundamentally unstable, that it fostered the expansion of beliefs and practices that were hostile to its continued existence, devitalizing the social forces driving capitalism while empowering its enemies. And he consistently argued that, as a result, capitalism would be supplanted by a form of democratic socialism. In his 1918 essay "The Crisis of the Tax State," Schumpeter argued that "by and by private enterprise will lose its social meaning through the development of the economy and the consequent expansion of the sphere of social sympathy" ([1918] 1991, 130). The basic elements of this argument about the institutional, cultural, and political collapse of capitalism remained the same in "The Socialist Possibilities of Today" (1920–21), which I discussed extensively in Chapter 2. Indeed, Schumpeter continued to elaborate the theory, with more or less the same elements, seven years later in "The Instability of Capitalism" ([1928] 1951), which he wrote while at Bonn; about eight years after that, in the address he gave in 1936, "Can Capitalism Survive?" ([1936] 1991); three years later in *Business Cycles*, which he published in 1939; and in *Capitalism, Socialism, and Democracy* ([1942] 1976), which he worked on throughout the 1930s and published in 1942.

But Schumpeter's theory of capitalist decline also changed during this period. *Capitalism, Socialism, and Democracy* clearly offered the fullest explication of this theory of economic, social, and political transformation. The transformative conception of democracy that was a part of the theory changed, too. In particular, whereas the earlier transformative conception outlined in "The Socialist Possibilities of Today" emphasized the council movement and the establishment of enterprises managed by workers as the specific mechanism of economic democratization that would help lay the foundations for socialism, the later version said less about such specific structural and institutional developments and emphasized simply a widening democratic critique of workplace hierarchy. And while the earlier conception specifically cast the Social Democrats and other proponents of councils as agents of democratic transformation, Schumpeter's later transformative conception cast the American labor movement generally in that key role. Finally, while both the early and late versions discussed "rationalization" as a general historical tendency that would undermine liberal capitalism, only the later theory systematically related every part of the theory to this process. Thus in later years Schumpeter attributed democratizing change less to a concrete social movement with specific plans for industrial democracy, and more to a generalized underlying historical process of rationalization that entailed, among other things, democratization. In the final section of this chapter, I will review some of the weaknesses inherent in this use of rationalization as a way of explaining democratizing change.

The change in emphasis can be explained partly by the fact that the Austrian council movement and the Austrian Social Democratic Party both declined rather steeply in influence after Schumpeter wrote "The Socialist Possibilities of Today." The Austrian SDP nurtured the council movement and passed a socialization law in 1919, but after 1920 the party never had the influence it would have needed to push for council democracy nationally. The party's retreat into its electoral stronghold in "Red Vienna" meant giving up on socialization and prefigured its crushing defeat in the Austrian civil war of 1934.

The change in emphasis can also partly be explained by developments in the United States. With good reason, some have characterized the 1930s as years in which labor democratized America (Freeman et al. 1992, 373). The 1930s were, of course, years of tremendous labor mobilization, the high points of which were the wave of citywide strikes in Toledo, Minneapolis, and San Francisco; the sit-downs that spread across the country from the Fisher Body Plant Number 1 in Flint, Michigan; the rise of activist industrial unionism; and the redirection of state power inherent in the passage of the National Labor Relations Act of 1935. Schumpeter took great interest in such developments and regarded them, in part, as elements of the social and economic democratization that, along with other tendencies, would ultimately bring an end to capitalism. More and more his writings stressed that certain "rationalizing, leveling, mechanizing and democratizing" tendencies inherent to liberal capitalist societies would eventually transform those societies into socialist ones (1939, 697).

Schumpeter never became involved in American politics to the extent that he was involved in Austrian politics. His early political memos, letters, and essays responded to and addressed specific political and social groups and movements in Austria with practical aims fully in view. But while his later writings clearly reflect on New Deal politics, they do so at a distance. Schumpeter's early memos and letters were shaped by his intent to convince a group of conservative aristocrats in Austria-Hungary to push for a reopening of the parliament and to form a political force capable of leading the session in a particular direction—and by the need to provide the theoretical underpinnings for such a proposal. But Schumpeter's writings on New Deal politics were not targeted to any such private audience, and they reveal mainly an intention to persuade a more general readership of his interpretation of social, economic, and political developments in America, and to bolster the case for his theory of capitalist development by referring to ongoing events.

New Deal Politics and the Transformation of Liberal Capitalism

Most accounts of Schumpeter's theory of capitalist transformation, as it appears in *Capitalism, Socialism, and Democracy* and other later works, focus on his argument that the individual entrepreneur was being displaced as a source of crucial economic innovation, and that with the demise of the entrepreneurial function, capitalism would fade too ([1942] 1976, 131–134). Schumpeter had indeed long argued that whole social classes rose and fell according to their ability to fulfill such socially necessary functions ([1927] 1991). The entrepreneur was, in Schumpeter's view, at the nexus of capitalist economic activity; thus the demise of the entrepreneur and his particular social function was a crucial component of Schumpeter's theory of capitalist collapse. But his theory of the transformation of capitalism into socialism involved not just the extinction of the entrepreneurial species but also the collapse of a set of feudal and hierarchical institutions and of a more recently developed capitalist "institutional framework" ([1942] 1976, 134–142). And the passing of all these institutions—including the entrepreneurial function—he attributed to an underlying process: "the rationalizing, leveling, mechanizing, and democratizing effects of capitalist evolution" (1939, 697).

A crucial aspect of this description of the process of "capitalist evolution" generally goes unrecognized: Schumpeter's assignment of democracy or democratization to a critical transformational role. It is, moreover, rarely noted that woven into Schumpeter's later discussions of the transformation from capitalism to socialism is an interpretation of New Deal politics. For in describing these "rationalizing, leveling, mechanizing, and democratizing" tendencies, Schumpeter drew heavily on examples from the New Deal era in the United States.

Schumpeter was not alone in seeing democratic ideas and democratization at the center of New Deal America. Scholars who have regarded the New Deal era as one in which labor democratized America have done so for several reasons (Freeman et al. 1992, 373).[1]

It was only in the 1930s in America that workers secured the legal apparatuses allowing a semblance of democratic participation in the management of businesses. In addition, this democratization of the workplace necessitated a democratizing shift in power from courts to legislative bodies, because it was the courts and their application of common-law doctrines that had traditionally protected the hierarchical nature of the production regime (Orren 1991, 8, 18, 29–40). Schumpeter's dismay at the breakdown of workplace hierarchy, his fierce denunciation of industrial democracy, and his objection to making the production regime subject to the "humors" of democratic political influence indicate that he had a broad awareness of these changes ([1942] 1976, 299–302; [1941] 1991, 359; [1948] 1991, 435).

Since at least the turn of the century, a wide range of Americans had used the term *industrial democracy*—or associated their ideas with it—in ways that were significant for the labor politics of the 1930s. The term was flexible enough to mean different things to its different users, of course, but its frequent use suggests an awareness of the idea of extending the beliefs and practices that underpinned political democracy into the sphere of social and economic relations, as well as of the ideological force of linking proposed social and economic reforms to democracy (Fraser 1989, 58–59; Plotke 1989, 127). Early in the century, the Industrial Workers of the World advocated industrial democracy (Foner 1965, 141–142). And a long line of socialists and radical liberals (to use John Dewey's phrase), associated at one time or another with the League for Industrial Democracy (LID), used the term or proposed the democratization of industry; examples range from Upton Sinclair to Dewey to Norman Thomas, the socialist presidential candidate in the 1930s (Dewey 1935, 34; Sale 1973, 677; Sinclair 1970, 422–429; Thomas 1938, 28). Schumpeter, who had, of course, witnessed the post–World War I flourishing of the council movement and who was also familiar with the use of the term by English, German, and Austrian social democrats, noticed the disparate uses and complained in *Capitalism, Socialism, and Democracy* that "Industrial or Economic Democracy is a phrase that figures in so many quasi-utopias that it has retained very little precise meaning" ([1942] 1976, 300 n. 9). But this complaint did not keep him from offering what he saw as a useful definition of industrial democracy or from continuing to emphasize the sociological significance of the term and the practices related to it (ibid., 300).

Understanding the sociological significance, for Schumpeter, of movements for industrial democracy and similar tendencies requires a review of concepts that formed, in effect, the building blocks for his mature theory of liberal capitalist development: the capitalist system, the capitalist order, tradition, rationality, and rationalization.

The Stability of the Capitalist System

Although he believed that capitalism would be replaced by a form of democratic socialism, Schumpeter did not think an economic crisis would do capitalism in. In particular, he did not regard the Great Depression as a sign of the imminent demise of capitalism. In part this is because Schumpeter distinguished between the *capitalist system* and the *capitalist order.* By the capitalist system, Schumpeter meant only the capitalist economy, conceived as a set of "independent quantities" such as incomes, costs, and prices, all "mutually determining each other" ([1928] 1951, 50). By the capitalist order, which Schumpeter sometimes referred to as the "civilization of capitalism," he meant a whole set of economic, social, and political institutions, beliefs, values, and practices, many of which aided the functioning of the capitalist system (Oakley 1990, 13; Schumpeter [1928] 1951, 49; Schumpeter [1942] 1976, 121–130).

Schumpeter argued that the Depression—like most downturns—could be explained purely in terms of the economic system and was no more than an unusually bad slump caused by the "coincidence of depression phases" of several independent economic cycles; these were themselves normal features of capitalism (1939, 907; see also Brown et al. 1934, 3–21). More broadly, his theory of capitalist motion, first expounded in *The Theory of Economic Development* in 1911, implied that the capitalist system's cycles of booms and busts would never themselves lead to crisis in the Marxist sense. He had long argued, however, that his prediction that the capitalist system had no inherent tendency toward crisis was no more sufficient to predict the future of the whole capitalist order "than a doctor's diagnosis to the effect that a man has no cancer is sufficient basis for the prediction that he will go on living indefinitely" ([1928] 1951, 71). His belief that capitalism would be superseded by socialism did not rest on a prediction about the capitalist system—

which he regarded as stable though cyclical—but rather on his prediction about the capitalist order, which he regarded as fundamentally unstable.

Rationality, Rationalization, and Tradition

According to Schumpeter, a process of rationalization was undermining the capitalist order, a diagnosis closely connected to his views on entrepreneurial agency, tradition, and rationalization (see Chapter 5). It should be said that his use of the terms *rationality* and *rationalization* was somewhat lax, at times even sloppy, but this reflected Schumpeter's agreement with what he viewed as a scholarly consensus holding that social change in modern European societies was linked to rationalization. As early as 1920 he had described rationalization as a "stock theme" in contemporary sociology (1920–21, 318). It is clear that, from early on, Schumpeter drew a very close link between rationalization and democratization, insisting, in the same passage just cited, that the process of rationalization brought with it "democratization," "leveling," and "great instability for all power positions" (ibid.; my translation).

Schumpeter's understanding of rationality shared some common features with the ideas of Max Weber and Karl Mannheim, both of whom had ties to Schumpeter.[2] All three drew a broad distinction between traditional and rational forms of social action; claimed to perceive a long-term historical tendency toward a preponderance of rational social action; described rationality in terms of self-consciously chosen means and ends; and conceived of rationality broadly enough to include social action in pursuit of diverse values, such as democratic ones (Alexander, 1983, 25–29; Mannheim [1936] 1985, 34–36; Schumpeter [1911] 1934, 86–87; 1939, 99–100; [1928] 1951, 65–66; [1942] 1976, 121–130; Weber 1978, 24–26).[3]

The distinction Schumpeter drew between *traditionally* and *rationally* oriented action was already of great importance in his theory of entrepreneurship and innovation (see Chapter 5), which stressed that entrepreneurs were able to break free from the customary social practices that bound most economic actors ([1911] 1934, 86–87; 1939, 99–100; [1928] 1951, 65–66). In his view, most actors relied on traditional, received norms and habitual, ingrained ways of doing things, practices linked to the social institutions that provided order and stability in society. Thus the maintenance of social structures was to be explained not by "rational considerations" but by "traditions, beliefs, religious beliefs, by such things as honor and beauty" ([1941] 1991, 359). Such beliefs and practices were often premised on a commitment to "sacred or semi-sacred tradition" that could not be rationally defended ([1942] 1976, 144). Even liberal capitalism, like other forms of society, rested in part on "super-empirical sanction," an "inherited sense of duty," and an acceptance of "classwise" rights, by which Schumpeter seems to have meant an almost feudal recognition of differential status in the social hierarchy (ibid., 127).

Rational social action—and the related historical process of rationalization—relied, by contrast, on values, norms, and practices that had been scrutinized, interrogated, or questioned. Schumpeter argued that there had been a "slow though incessant widening of the sector of social life within which individuals or groups" relinquished inherited, traditional conduct and guided their actions rationally, "according to their own lights" ([1942] 1976, 122). In contemporary political science usage, accounts of social action that demonstrate its rationality are generally considered to be alternatives to accounts that seek to explain action by reference to values, ideals, shared social practices, and ideologies. It should be evident, however, that Schumpeter's use of the term *rationality* generally did not imply such a distinction. Just as Weber had devised the concept of "value-rational" action (as opposed to simply "instrumentally rational" action) to include action systematically oriented toward "duty, honor, the pursuit of beauty, a religious call, personal loyalty, or the importance of some 'cause' no matter in what it consists," Schumpeter argued that rationalization could explain not only the efficient organization of the modern hospital but also the development of expressionist art, "the genesis of the modern lounge suit," and even democracy and social criticism (Schumpeter [1942] 1976, 125–127; Weber 1978, 25, 26).

For Schumpeter, the rational orientation toward self-chosen or scrutinized beliefs and practices led to a break with traditional, hierarchical beliefs and practices in modern society. "The capitalist process rationalizes behavior and ideas," Schumpeter emphasized,

and by so doing chases from our minds, along with metaphysical belief, mystic and romantic ideas of all sorts. Thus it reshapes not only

our methods of attaining our ends but also these ultimate ends themselves . . . On the one hand, our inherited sense of duty, deprived of its
traditional basis, becomes focused in utilitarian ideas about the betterment of mankind . . . On the other hand, the same rationalization of
the soul rubs off all the glamour of super-empirical sanction from every
species of classwise rights. ([1942] 1976, 127)

And he insisted elsewhere that "when the habit of rational analysis of,
and rational behavior in, the daily tasks of life has gone far enough, it
turns back upon the mass of collective ideas and criticizes and to some
extent 'rationalizes' them by way of such questions as why there should
be kings and popes or subordination or tithes or property" ([1942]
1976, 122). As even these passages demonstrate, Schumpeter tied this
rationalizing tendency very closely to political, social, and economic democratization.

Tradition and Stability

Schumpeter contended that the stability of the capitalist order rested on
the traditional social institutions, classes, beliefs, and practices that he
considered to be its "buttresses": the bourgeois family, a political elite
that could act in the interest of the bourgeoisie, and—a buttress of
crucial interest here—a regime of severe discipline in the factory or
workplace ([1941] 1991, 343, 359–360; [1942] 1976, 127, 135–136,
139–141, 157–161). He complained that nineteenth-century bourgeois
liberals had all too easily forgotten that their society "was the product of
force and of a discipline inculcated into the lower strata by the feudal
predecessors of the business class" ([1941] 1991, 343; [1942] 1976,
214). He argued further that it was not rational agreement but the
worker's traditional acquiescence to the belief that "his true reward was
a satisfaction of employment, loyalty to the firm, and so on" that helped
"keep society together" ([1941] 1991, 359).

Although labor discipline is the capitalist buttress that I will deal with
most here, Schumpeter stressed others as well. He placed particular importance on the reliance of the European capitalist order on the political
leadership of "feudal classes," but he never explained what application
that claim could have in America or for his interpretation of the New

Deal ([1942] 1976, 135–139). He emphasized the importance of a network of small proprietors who remained attached to the institutions of
property and "free contracting," and he discussed the bourgeois family,
whose maintenance and defense, Schumpeter argued, were the focus of
bourgeois economic activity ([1942] 1976, 127, 139–141, 157–161).[4]

Rationality, Democracy, and Social Transformation

Schumpeter regarded liberal capitalism as unstable because, as we have
seen, he thought it unleashed rationalizing social tendencies. He described two types of undermining tendencies: those that refashioned the
motives behind the "entrepreneurial function," which he saw as the
source of capitalist dynamism, and those that tended to create radical
hostility toward capitalism. But behind both of these tendencies he perceived the same process of rationalization (1939, 400).

Schumpeter did not claim that the beliefs and practices that resulted
from or were part of rationalization were logically necessary extensions
of that process ([1942] 1976, 127). Democratic ideology and democratization, in particular, he regarded as contingent forms or results of rationalization—possible but not necessary parts of the rational critique and
dismantling of traditional social institutions and hierarchies. Rationalization could take different forms, in other words, but one of the most
historically significant was the spread of democracy (ibid., 248–249).
There were several strands tying rationalization (as Schumpeter understood this process) to democracy. First, the rationalization of traditional institutions—insofar as it resulted in greater equality and freedom
from old hierarchies—resulted in a more democratic society. Second,
Schumpeter insisted that democratic ideas were, as a historical matter, a
constitutive part of the rationalist civilization of liberal capitalism (ibid.,
126), and that democratic political movements had been a crucial factor
in the creation of that civilization. "Democracy," he argued, "presided
over the process of political and institutional change by which the bourgeoisie reshaped, and from its own point of view *rationalized*, the social
and political structure that preceded its ascendancy" (ibid., 297; emphasis added). Third, Schumpeter contended that the idealization of a human capacity for rational action was itself a part of democratic ideology.
"The ideology of democracy as reflected in the classical doctrine rests

on a rationalist scheme of human action and of the values of life," he claimed (ibid., 296).

Despite these ties, however, Schumpeter did not attempt to reduce democratic ideology to rationality or rationalism. He believed the process of democratic rationalization could never be understood without an immersion in the particular beliefs and ideologies that motivated the bourgeois political program and in the meaning those ideas had in a particular historical context ([1942] 1976, 265–268). Thus he briefly sketched the ideological materials that he thought had been joined together to form what he called the "classical doctrine of democracy" or "the classical doctrine of collective action" (265).[5] And he related those ideas to the particular historical eras in which they took on meaning, acknowledging reluctantly that, "in the first half of the nineteenth century, the oppositions that professed the classical creed of democracy rose and eventually prevailed against governments some of which . . . were obviously in a state of decay and had become bywords of incompetence, brutality and corruption . . . Under these circumstances, democratic revolution meant the advent of freedom and decency, and the democratic creed meant a gospel of reason and betterment" (267).

Although he had nothing but scorn for many facets of this democratic ideology, he recognized its historical significance—recognized that "action continued to be taken on that theory all the time it was being blown to pieces" ([1942] 1976, 249).

The Dangers of Democracy

The rational critique of traditional norms and the democratic reconstruction of traditional institutions could not be limited to the realm of political institutions. And this was linked, Schumpeter claimed, to the downfall of capitalism. He wrote that "the reason, the deepest reason, why I think that capitalism won't survive is the rationalizing effect the system has on our minds, the effect the system has of doing away with everything traditional" ([1936] 1991, 307). Eighteenth- and nineteenth-century radicals had deployed democratic arguments in tearing down the feudal social and political order without grasping their broader implications, he contended. "The English liberal radical who looked upon the House of Lords as an anomaly and upon aristocratic cabinet ministers with distrust, was blissfully confident that the masses, when sufficiently educated and left free to vote, would recognize the excellencies of the capitalist system and keep it up of their own free will" ([1941] 1991, 343). What such bourgeois radicals failed to grasp was the way in which democratic arguments could become everyone's weapon. "Formerly when people were dissatisfied with a pope or a king, they would revolt against the particular pope or king but they took the institution for granted. Now we ask ourselves, 'Why should there be such things as popes or kings?' The bourgeois asked this question. It did not strike him that the same question would be answered unfavorably to the capitalist" (ibid., 360).

And so the rational critique of hierarchy turned eventually to what Schumpeter had identified as a bulwark of capitalism: labor discipline. As I have already noted, Schumpeter argued that the "workman's readiness to obey orders was never due to a rational conviction of the virtues of capitalist society" ([1942] 1976, 214). Labor discipline was thus vulnerable to rationalist attack. He wrote in 1949: "Capitalist activity, being essentially 'rational,' tends to spread habits of mind and to destroy those loyalties and those habits of super- and subordination that are nevertheless essential for the efficient working of the institutionalized leadership of the producing plant" ([1949] 1976, 417). Since the rational critique that bourgeois democrats deployed in their reconstruction of politics could be deployed against capitalist hierarchies as well, he argued that socialism and democracy were linked. "The ideology of classical socialism is the offspring of bourgeois ideology," he argued. "In particular, it fully shares the latter's rationalist and utilitarian background and many of the ideas and ideals that entered the classical doctrine of democracy" ([1942] 1976, 298–299).

Unlike many nineteenth- and twentieth-century liberals who made sharp analytical distinctions between public and private, and in whose work the family dropped out of discussions of social and political change, Schumpeter was closely attuned to the connections he perceived between the structure of the family and social, economic, and political transformation. According to his conservative analysis, one of the key buttresses of capitalist civilization, a "mainspring of the typically bourgeois kind of profit motive" and thus of entrepreneurial activity, had been the bourgeois family ([1942] 1976, 160).[6] But in Schumpeter's view, just as one of the forms of rational critique of inherited institutions and beliefs was democracy, another was the growth of "feminism" and the tendency for "family life and parenthood" to mean "less than they meant before" to both women and men (ibid., 157; see also 127, 157–161). When rationalization reached "private life," he contended, both men and women were less inclined to have children; not having a private family realm to protect and develop, the typical (male) entrepreneur lost the will to accumulate and to fight in both the economic and the political arenas, in Schumpeter's view ([1941] 1991, 374, 378). Thus "the most obvious symptom of the decay" of capitalist civilization, Schumpeter argued regretfully, was "a fall of the birth rate in the upper strata of society" (1939, 401).

The New Deal and the Dangers of Economic Democracy

The spread of democratic ideology into the economic realm was at the center of Schumpeter's understanding of New Deal era politics. Reflecting on the previous decade in a talk he delivered in the early 1940s, he said: "We have complete disorganization in 1933, a complete disbelief in standards, a disbelief both in the old social relationships and in the new ones" ([1941] 1991, 361). Worst of all, according to Schumpeter, that rational rejection of traditional loyalties meant the contemporary unraveling of labor discipline, which he saw as one of the most obvious processes visible in the New Deal era. In a passage that evoked what many American conservatives saw as the deplorable breakdown of social order in the 1930s—the general strikes of 1934 and the sit-downs of 1937—Schumpeter wrote that it had been a great mistake for the bourgeoisie to accept "equality in the political sphere" and to teach "the laborers that they were just as valuable citizens as anyone else," for that had had dire social and economic consequences ([1942] 1976, 214). "Incessant change," he contended,

> was bound to dissolve the discipline in the factory . . . Gone are most of the means of maintaining discipline, and, even more, the power to use them. Gone is the moral support of the community that used to be extended to the employer struggling with infractions of discipline. Gone finally is—largely in consequence of the withdrawal of that support—the old attitude of governmental agencies; step by step we can trace the way that led from backing the master to neutrality, through the various *nuances* of neutrality to backing the workman's right to being considered an equal partner in a bargain, and from this to backing the trade

union against both employers and individual workmen. ([1942] 1976, 214)

He continued in an explanatory footnote:

> Toleration amounting to encouragement of such practices as picket-
> ing may serve as a useful landmark in a process that has not run a
> straight-line course. Legislation, still more administrative practice, in
> this country is particularly interesting because the problems involved
> have been brought out with unequaled emphasis owing to the fact that
> change, after having been long delayed, has been crowded into so short
> a time. ([1942] 1976, 214 n. 10)

In the light of these tendencies and his arguments for the necessity of
strict labor subordination, Schumpeter was sharply critical of what he
termed "industrial democracy." As one might expect from Schumpeter's
understanding of traditional hierarchies, rationalization, and democracy,
he contrasted industrial democracy with a traditional feudal order that
he regarded as crucial to the capitalist workplace, and he drew an analogy between political and economic democratization. Industrial democracy meant "trade-union rule over industrial relations" and "democratization of the monarchic factory by workmen's representation on boards
or other devices calculated to secure them influence on the introduction of technological improvements, business policy in general and, of
course, discipline in the plant in particular, including methods of 'hiring
and firing'" ([1942] 1976, 300 n. 9). I discuss Schumpeter's harsh denunciation of such mechanisms of industrial democracy in the next
chapter.

The process of democratization and the destruction of traditional hierarchies was made much worse, Schumpeter argued, by the fact that the
bourgeoisie possessed little of the political skill needed to resist the tendency. Though he long regarded this lack of broad social and political leadership ability as a general bourgeois trait—he pointed it out in
his essay "Social Classes in an Ethnically Homogenous Environment"
([1927] 1991, 279)—he professed to see much evidence for it in New
Deal America. "Perhaps the most striking feature of the picture is the extent to which the bourgeoisie, besides educating its own enemies, allows
itself in turn to be educated by them," Schumpeter lamented in the early
1940s. "It absorbs the slogans of current radicalism and seems quite
willing to undergo a process of conversion to a creed hostile to its very

existence . . . In this country there was no real resistance anywhere against the imposition of crushing financial burdens during the last decade or against labor legislation incompatible with the effective management of industry" ([1942] 1976, 161). In fact, Schumpeter reserved some of his sharpest words for describing this phenomenon. He told an audience in 1941 that for the "executive of a company . . . it is better to be patted on the back and be told what a progressive individual he is and go off to Nice while there is a sit-down strike at home" ([1941] 1991, 378; see also [1942] 1976, 214). In light of this weakness of the bourgeois spine, Schumpeter could only reassure himself that in the socialist order that he predicted was to come, "there would no longer be . . . any well-meaning bourgeois of both sexes who think it frightfully exciting to applaud strikes and strike leaders" ([1942] 1976, 212).

New Deal Policy and Transitional States of Society

In addition to the direct effect on the workplace of the democratizing tendencies within liberal capitalism, Schumpeter argued that there was an indirect effect, mediated by the state and its economic and social policies. Schumpeter's most general assessments of New Deal programs and policies are best understood in this context. Understanding those assessments requires a brief detour through Schumpeter's notion of the state and its development. Schumpeter wrote, of course, before the renewed debate that has taken place since the 1970s concerning theories of the state, but like many social scientists interested in the questions raised in that debate, he addressed himself to the role of the state in liberal capitalist societies, and did so in response to the way this problem had been established by Marxists. As against a fairly reductive statement of historical materialism—the contention that "social, cultural, and political situations and the spirit in which and the measures by which they are met, derive from the working of the capitalist machine"—Schumpeter countered that "the state does always reflect the social power relations even though it is not merely their reflection," (1939, 695–696; [1918] 1991, 138 n. 20; see also [1948] 1991, 429–430). This argument, in turn, was based on the view that social, cultural, and political institutions, though linked in an overall process to economic ones, could develop relatively independently (1939, 700). There are "intact societies" in which "class structure, beliefs, values, attitudes, and policy are all consistent with each other," but there are "frequently" also situations in which "the class structure of society and its civilization . . . cease to correspond to each other" ([1948] 1991, 429). This was the case for most of the history of liberal capitalism, he argued. In his 1918 essay "The Crisis of the Tax State," Schumpeter argued that the origin of the liberal capitalist state, which he referred to as the "tax state," had to be located in the political and social transformations in the early modern period that began to mark a distinction between civil society as a sphere of economic activity pursued largely out of self-interest, and the state as a sphere in which the prince (and later, citizens) pursued some conception of public interest, funded by taxes levied on private economic activity ([1918] 1991, 110).

Democratization entered crucially into the argument at this point. Schumpeter had described the first historical stages of democratization as a process of "political and institutional change by which the bourgeoisie reshaped, and from its own point of view rationalized, the social and political structure that preceded its ascendancy"—or, more simply, as the bourgeoisie wresting the state "from the hands of the prince" ([1918] 1991, 108, 111; [1942] 1976, 297). But long after the onset of democratization, Schumpeter argued, the European state remained a key component of an "amphibial" or transitional form of society, in which capitalism and the bourgeoisie were the most important forces in civil society, but in which the state retained some of its feudal characteristics, particularly its being staffed by the aristocracy ([1942] 1976, 135, 134–139, 155; [1918] 1991, 108).

Schumpeter argued that America during and after the New Deal was an example of a different sort of "transitional" state of society, reflecting a different phase of democratization and a different constellation of class forces. As I have shown, Schumpeter argued that the United States in the 1930s was undergoing a partial democratic transformation of society—one that some European nations had seen more immediately after the First World War. But that transformation did not completely undo capitalism. In Europe between the wars, Schumpeter argued, the policies of liberal capitalist states "adjusted themselves to a new social situation, which, whatever political party happened to be in power, substantially amounted to democracy in the sense of trade-union rule" ([1941] 1991, 346). In the meantime, however, the economy remained fundamentally capitalist, putting constraints on the range of action open to the state. Thus there was not a perfect fit between the role of the state and the changing relative power of social classes: "The admission of labor to re-sponsible office and the reorientation of legislation in the interest of the working class was in a sense an adjustment to a new state of things. But, with the two exceptions mentioned [Russia and Italy], all nations never-theless attempted to run their economies on capitalist lines, thus contin-uing to put their trust in an engine, the motive power of which was at the same time drained away by crushing taxation" (ibid., 346–347). Schumpeter believed that the United States reached the same position a few years later. "Consider the case of the United States," wrote Schumpeter in the 1940s: "The business class has lost the power it used to have, but not entirely. Organized labor has risen to power, but not completely. Labor and a government allied to the unions can indeed par-alyze the business mechanism. But it cannot replace it by another mech-anism" ([1948] 1991, 430).

It was not just the growth of working-class power that created this sit-uation, Schumpeter argued. In the New Deal era, "intellectuals veered around to what they believed to be the rising sun. Definitely the intellec-tual interest went into the camp of social reconstruction" ([1941] 1991, 354; see also [1942] 1976, 145–155). Intellectuals "invaded labor poli-tics" and "radicalized" it ([1942] 1976, 153–154). Meanwhile, in the absence of a strong preexisting bureaucratic class, intellectuals invaded the state as well during the New Deal era (1939, 1048; [1942] 1976, 155). "In times of rapid expansion of the sphere of public administra-tion, much of the additional personnel required has to be taken directly from the intellectual group," Schumpeter argued, adding: "witness this country" ([1942] 1976, 155). That fact, he contended, "explains why public policy grows more and more hostile to capitalist interests" (ibid., 154).

Under such circumstances, Schumpeter claimed, New Deal programs and policy had become anticapitalist in the sense that they threatened the functioning of the capitalist mechanism even while they could not replace that mechanism with another (1939, 1046–1048; [1942] 1976, 64; [1941] 1991, 362, 395). "Capitalism produces by its mere working a social atmosphere . . . that is hostile to it, and this atmosphere, in turn, produces policies which do not allow it to function," he argued (1939, 1038). Schumpeter argued that New Deal labor policy put the power of the state behind industrial unions, politicized the wage contract, and discouraged investment (1939, 1042–1043; [1942] 1976, 214; [1941]

1991, 359, 435). He claimed, further, that New Deal fiscal policy diminished "'subjective' investment opportunity"—he meant it discouraged people from taking advantage of existing opportunities—and discouraged savings (1939, 1038–1040). And he contended that, beyond a few early attempts to unfreeze markets paralyzed by the crash of 1929, many New Deal regulatory policies constituted a debilitating "indefinite threat" to capitalists (1939, 988, 1043–1044).

These were dire claims. Schumpeter turned out, as we now know, to have been largely wrong in his predictions about capitalism's future—at least as regards the fifty years following his death. New Deal regulation and collective bargaining did not squeeze out investment and make it impossible for capitalism to function. Here a brief comparison with Schumpeter's rival interpreter of the Depression, Keynes, might be illuminating. A key difference between them is that Schumpeter attributed most of the problems that would really endanger capitalism to forces external to the economic system itself. Yes, capitalism was prone to cycles, he argued, but not to dangerous crises. Keynes, on the other hand, famously purported to find an inherent tension within the economic mechanisms of capitalism. Entrepreneurs would in many situations choose not to invest as much as was necessary to maintain current levels of employment; the government, as a result, would have to jolt the economy out of "underemployment equilibrium" by making the investments that the private economy declined to make. Keynes, in the end, seems to have made the more astute analysis. Had Schumpeter accepted Keynes's diagnosis of an inherent weakness in the capitalist system itself, he might have focused his intellectual energies on economic solutions to capitalism's problems, rather than on those social, cultural, and political forces—democratization chief among them—that he thought were destroying capitalism.

As it was, however, he not merely rejected Keynes but wrote him off, and along with him the success of his *General Theory,* as evidence of his view that capitalism produced intellectual forces hostile to its own existence. Keynes's vision, Schumpeter observed in a 1936 review, "may be entitled to the compliment that it expresses forcefully the attitude of a decaying civilization" ([1936] 1951, 153). And writing years after Keynes's death and the end of the Depression, he still claimed it was ideology—"the vision of decaying capitalism"—not analytical strength, that had won adherents to Keynes's *General Theory* ([1949] 1951c, 278).

The Weaknesses of Schumpeter's Transformative Conception

Schumpeter's conviction, outlined above, that a rationalizing, democratizing historical tendency was undermining liberal capitalism in the 1930s was the background to his elite conception of democracy as method. Before turning to the later development of Schumpeter's elite conception of democracy, however, there is an opportunity here for some summary comments about what it means to have a transformative conception of democracy, and about some of the consequences of emphasizing different aspects of such a view. In certain ways, the earlier version of Schumpeter's transformative conception of democracy, though perhaps less elaborate, was more satisfactory and convincing than the later version. Schumpeter made himself more vulnerable to criticism the more his transformative conception of democracy relied on positing a somewhat disembodied general process of rationalization, attributed to the psychic effects of capitalism, instead of focusing on the action of concrete social groups, and the more he relied on a generalized spread of democratic ideas throughout society instead of the specific ideology of a movement, like council democracy. But these weaknesses of Schumpeter's later transformative conception were by no means necessary features of such a view of democracy.

One might raise several related criticisms of Schumpeter's later transformative conception of democracy, as it is described in this chapter. First, despite Schumpeter's own conservative political leanings, viewing democratization as a transformative social tendency was Whiggish insofar as it seemed to make democratization an autonomous, continuously unfolding social force, or treated "history" as the history of societies continuously democratizing. Second, such a conception took on an idealist quality the more it treated democratization as the mere spread of democratic ideas, and not as a comprehensive and concrete political, social, economic, and ideological process. Third, the more Schumpeter's conception moved away from a theory of how council democracy could restructure certain basic social relations and thus transform society, the more it seemed to neglect social structure and power in favor of an examination of mere disembodied intellectual and cultural tendencies. One could sum these criticisms up by saying that the more Schumpeter moved in these directions, the more his transformative conception had a determinist quality to it.

All these objections can be answered within the context of a conception of democracy as *potentially* transformative—potentially, that is, given the existence of groups prepared to make ideological use of democratic ideas, and potentially, given a society in which some institutions and practices are shaped by democratic beliefs and ideals, while other parts of society remain undemocratic. The objections above deserve separate consideration. First, treating democracy as a transformative historical tendency need not involve claiming that democracy is an autonomous, disembodied social force operating through history, so long as that transformation is understood as a potentiality that must be realized by actual political and social groups. Certainly Schumpeter's early transformative conception, with its incorporation of Austrian Social Democratic thought and its reliance on the council movement, was more satisfactory than his later conception, which relied more on the social tendency of rationalization. But Schumpeter never ceased to emphasize the actual historical action of workers, for example, as his deep interest in New Deal labor politics proves. Thus while his discussion of democratization as rationalization raised the specter of a modified Whig history, Schumpeter ultimately avoided Whiggism by emphasizing the significance of democracy as a particular concrete form of rationalization with a life and logic of its own.

Second, a transformative conception of democracy does not have to be idealist if it recognizes that democratization is work that involves more than the spread of values and ideas. Democratic political action does have to be motivated by a comprehensive democratic ideological framework, but the action and that ideological framework involve more than just democratic ideas or values. Schumpeter's early transformative conception of democracy was stronger in this regard, as well, since it attributed transformation not merely to democratic ideas, per se, but to the specific deployment of democratic ideas by the proponents of council democracy. Nevertheless, even in his later conception, Schumpeter tied democratization in some historical phases to the work of the bourgeoisie in seeking political power, and at other times to working-class action.

Third and finally, a transformative conception need not neglect social structure and power. In dropping his explicit reference to the establishment of councils in favor of a more vague notion of democratically inspired hostility to capitalism, Schumpeter certainly became less specific about the relation between democratic ideas and social structures and power relations. But in his later transformative conception, he continued to make clear that the organization of the workplace was what was at issue, and that the maintenance or collapse of strict workplace hierarchy was at the center of his interest. This was clearly the significance of his lengthy polemic against industrial democracy in *Capitalism, Socialism, and Democracy,* which I will discuss in the next chapter.

In these three ways, then, Schumpeter's transformative conception of democracy became less convincing and concrete as it developed. But by tracing the development of Schumpeter's thought over time, and by understanding that the conception became less satisfactory because of particular choices Schumpeter made, it is possible to see that these problems are not inherent to transformative conceptions of democracy.

4
_____

Schumpeter's Elite Conception of Democracy as Method

While his transformative conception developed, so too did Schumpeter's elite conception of democracy, from his early vision of Tory democracy into the later model of democracy as an institutional arrangement or a method, the model that is so well known to Anglo-American political scientists. What most distinguished the model of democracy as method from Tory democracy was Schumpeter's attempt to present the former not as a political program but as a general statement of the nature and limits of democratic government. And yet, while Schumpeter altered the way in which he presented the elite conception, his reactionary and elitist political commitments remained the same: throughout his life he was concerned to thwart or contain what he saw as the dangerous implications and effects of spreading democratic practices and beliefs.

Many people are familiar with how Schumpeter defined democracy as a method in the key chapters in *Capitalism, Socialism, and Democracy*. But the definition of democracy in those chapters is not as crucial as the assumptions behind that definition—assumptions that allowed him to present the model as a full statement of the limits of democracy. Schumpeter grounded his conception of democracy as method mainly by arguing that no other conception could be realized, by arguing that "human nature in politics" was such that democracy could mean nothing more than elite competition for popular votes. He introduced and framed the model of democracy as method in *Capitalism, Socialism, and Democracy* by adopting certain assumptions that limit democratic possibilities, assumptions that Schumpeter derived in part from Gustave Le Bon's crowd psychology and from the elite theories of Vilfredo Pareto and others. It is his resorting to these elite assumptions about human nature that most characterizes Schumpeter's conception of democracy as method and that leads to the most severe problems inherent in that conception, including those often noted by critics.

Schumpeter built on this elite conception of democracy a surprisingly authoritarian vision of "democratic" socialism. Since his early encounters with Austrian Social Democrats, the problem of democratic socialism had loomed large for him. In *Capitalism, Socialism, and Democracy* he contended that state-centered socialism could be "democratic" so long as it coexisted with elite competition for political office. More than this, however, he argued that democratic socialism would not entail democratic economic institutions; on the contrary, he laid out a vision of rigid factory discipline complemented by elite domination of politics. Schumpeter derived this vision in part from his definition of democracy as a method. In a sense, however, it was this whole vision of democratic socialism that Schumpeter had in mind in discussing democracy in *Capitalism, Socialism, and Democracy* in the first place. Having concluded that the dominant social tendencies of the time were leading to socialism, one of his chief purposes in the book was to theorize a form of democratic socialism in which the most dangerous democratic tendencies, from his standpoint, would be quelled.

What Would Democratic Socialism Be?

It is commonly assumed that Schumpeter's intention in setting out a model of democracy in *Capitalism, Socialism, and Democracy* was either to achieve greater conceptual clarity about democracy or to devise a theory of democracy that was more empirically accurate (Allen 1991, 2: 129). Schumpeter's sympathetic interpreters, like many theorists and social scientists, have taken for granted the autonomy, the self-sufficiency, and the self-justifying nature of reflective knowledge. From this standpoint, *to know and to understand* is valuable in itself, and inquiry neither follows directly from nor necessarily leads to practical activity or problems. But on the basis of such assumptions it is impossible adequately to capture Schumpeter's intentions in returning to the subject of democracy in *Capitalism, Socialism, and Democracy*. To grasp the meaning of Schumpeter's democratic thought, in other words, it is crucial that we *not* abstract the model of democracy as method from the practical activities and problems that gave it meaning for Schumpeter. Schumpeter's own conception of science—like Dewey's conception of philosophy and Mannheim's conception of ideology—situated reflective knowledge within its active context.

The most pressing practical question for Schumpeter as he wrote in the late 1930s and early 1940s was the transformation of liberal capitalist societies into democratic socialist ones, an ongoing process Schumpeter attributed to a combination of related tendencies, including democratization. Schumpeter, as we have seen, had regarded the advent of democratic socialism as extremely likely since at least about 1918, and he elaborated a theory of capitalist transformation into socialism during the 1930s and 1940s—a theory whose most comprehensive expression is found in *Capitalism, Socialism, and Democracy* itself. Among other things, he had argued continuously since about 1920 that the spread of democratic practices throughout the economy would contribute significantly to the advent of democratic socialism.

Schumpeter chose to write about democracy because he believed that the advent of democratic socialism was imminent, because he thought many conservatives seriously misunderstood ongoing social transformation and what could be done about it, and because he wished to demonstrate that even if democratic socialism was imminent—perhaps unavoidable—a complete loss of all that conservative elites valued was not. The fact that Schumpeter was chiefly interested in the nature of democratic socialism and not so much in democracy, conceived abstractly or defined as a universal problem, is evident from the fact that his discussion of the democratic "method" in *Capitalism, Socialism, and Democracy* does not stand alone but is an integral part of an outline of his vision of a democratic socialist society. He explained in a preface that appeared in early editions of the book that "the problem of democracy forced its way into the place it now occupies in this volume because it proved impossible to state my views on the relation between the socialist order of society and the democratic method of government without a rather extensive analysis of the latter" ([1942] 1947, xiii).

That the problem of democratic practices spreading into industry, in particular, loomed ominously large for Schumpeter is evident from the fact that when he finally turned to "Democracy in the Socialist Order," the apparent culmination of the chapters on socialism and democracy, he devoted four of about six pages to attacking industrial or economic democracy and arguing that there would be no such thing in the coming socialist society ([1942] 1976, 296–302). This argument relied crucially on his definition of democracy as a method.

Schumpeter wished to explain what a democratic socialist society would look like. And he wished to explore the possibilities of practical action that existed for someone of his reactionary commitments, given the tendencies leading to socialism. In a general way, Schumpeter addressed this second issue in a series of lectures he gave just before publishing *Capitalism, Socialism, and Democracy*. "No more can be achieved by individual or group volitions than to perform transitions with a minimum loss of human values . . . that is how I should define conservatism" (1941 [1991], 399). Schumpeter's laying out of a vision of democratic socialism—and a conception of democracy as an institutional arrangement—in *Capitalism, Socialism, and Democracy* should be understood in light of this view of conservatism. His was a conceptualization of a democratic socialist society in which he saw some chance of preserving his deeply conservative values. As for the first issue, Schumpeter laid out a form of democratic socialism in which the most dangerous *democratizing* tendencies, especially those that might lead to industrial democracy, would be curbed by elite domination of politics and elite control of industry. It is important to note, however, that Schumpeter seems never to have reached a satisfactory answer as to who would constitute the necessary elite. In contrast to Schumpeter's Tory democracy program, which relied on an existing aristocracy to curb democratizing tendencies in Austria-Hungary, his later elite model of democracy as a method argued merely that "human nature in politics" made elite domination inevitable, in democratic socialist society as in others.

Yet his argument might not have taken the precise form that it did had Schumpeter not also set out to respond specifically to "a controversy that has been going on in this country for some time" about democracy and socialism—to refute "the numerous pamphlets that have been published in this country during the last few years [arguing] . . . that a planned economy, let alone full-fledged socialism, is completely incompatible with democracy" ([1942] 1947, xiv; [1942] 1976, 284). Schumpeter was almost certainly referring to works like Friedrich A. von Hayek's 1939 pamphlet, *Freedom and the Economic System*, the germ of his *The Road to Serfdom* (Hayek 1939; Hayek 1944, vii).

Schumpeter disagreed with Hayek in two specific ways. Against

Hayek, he argued that a socialist central planning agency could engage in rational economic calculation, and that democracy could persist in a socialist society. In *Capitalism, Socialism, and Democracy* it is fairly clear that one of Schumpeter's intentions was to make both of these arguments against Hayek's views. Schumpeter also reviewed *The Road to Serfdom* in 1946—naturally so, since the book dealt centrally with the problems of democracy and socialism that were so crucial to *Capitalism, Socialism, and Democracy*. Schumpeter's review testified to his objection to Hayek's whole approach to political theory. His critique indicates the compromise he was trying to achieve in *Capitalism, Socialism, and Democracy* between his own reactionary convictions and his clear-eyed (or so he thought) assessment of the major tendencies at work in society. He wrote:

> Some readers may be disappointed to find that Hayek fails to present an alternative policy of his own . . . More serious is it, however, that no politically effective program *could* be presented from that standpoint in the event that its sponsor moved into power . . . In fact, the book, for a political book, takes surprisingly little account of the political structure of our time. As soon as we do take account of it, we shall feel more kindly toward those English conservatives who incur Hayek's displeasure because of their socialist proclivities. Perhaps they are the only group in the world that, as a group, combines frank recognition of the data of the situation with an adequate appreciation of our responsibility toward mankind's cultural inheritance—in the best Beaconsfield tradition. But the author deals with ideas and principles as if they floated in the air. If he had gone into the historical conditions from which the ideas arose which he dislikes so much, he could not have helped discovering that they are the products of the social system which he does like. The principles of individual initiative and self-reliance are the principles of a very limited class. They mean nothing to the mass of people who—no matter for what reason—are not up to the standard they imply. (Schumpeter 1946, 269–270)

It is not difficult to see from this quotation Schumpeter's desire to respond to Hayek, and to Ludwig von Mises—to refute their belief in the impossibility of socialist calculation and in the incompatibility of democracy and socialism—intertwined with his view of what would constitute a useful conservative response to leading economic and social tendencies. There was no point in simply protesting against such overwhelming social tendencies as those leading to democratic socialism. The point was to understand those tendencies and theorize a form of democratic socialism that would still be consistent with Schumpeter's conservative values. This Schumpeter did, but on the basis of his elite-dominated vision of democracy. Thus one of the great ironies of Schumpeter's vision of democratic socialism was that it largely acquiesced to Hayek's claim that freedom would be sacrificed in socialist society.

Democracy as a Method or Institutional Arrangement

Schumpeter's famous definition in *Capitalism, Socialism, and Democracy* holds that the "democratic method" is "that institutional arrangement for arriving at political decisions in which individuals acquire the power to decide by means of a competitive struggle for the people's vote" ([1942] 1976, 269).[1] This is what is usually meant by Schumpeter's theory or definition of democracy. This definition is simply a condensed version of a more fully elaborated model of democracy as a method that, in its broadest outlines, presents the existence of elections, parties, and a parliament as the definitional prerequisites of democracy, and, contrary to the idea that democracy could mean rule by the people, regards the behavior of political elites as the prime force of democratic politics. Before examining its roots or critiquing it, it is worthwhile to unpack this definition and its implications.

The Crucial Role of Political Elites

Schumpeter's model of democracy as method leaned heavily on the behavior of political elites within democratic polities. "Collectives act almost exclusively by accepting leadership," Schumpeter argued, and democratic collectives were no different from others ([1942] 1976, 270). Indeed, democracy was, Schumpeter asserted, "the rule of the politician" (285). Given this, the "acceptance of leadership is the true function of the electorate's vote," he insisted—or more benignly, "the role of the people is to produce a government" (269, 273). These assumptions naturally put emphasis on the behavior of leaders or political elites. But Schumpeter insisted not only that the emphasis be put on elites but also that the self-interested actions of elites were the "motive power" of democracy; all else, especially the "social meaning" of democracy, was ephemeral. "It does not follow that the social meaning of a type of activity will necessarily provide the motive power, hence the explanation of the latter," Schumpeter insisted (282).

This dismissal of the "social meaning" of democracy reinforced the idea that real democracy had little or nothing to do with the beliefs, ideals, and practices tied to democratic ideologies. At the same time, of course, it signified the idea that elites were the reality behind democracy even if the masses dominated its appearance. Political conduct in democracies might be *clothed* in democratic beliefs and in the supposed pursuit of the public good, but the explanation for the life of democracies was to be found elsewhere, in the pursuit of votes by elite politicians. Schumpeter summed this up in a "saying attributed to one of the most successful politicians that ever lived": "What businessmen do not understand is that exactly as they are dealing in oil so I am dealing in votes" ([1942] 1976, 285). Thus although democratic theory might be concerned with the way that political decisions could be made substantively to reflect popular inclinations, Schumpeter insisted that political decisions—"legislation and administration"—were epiphenomenal, the mere "by-products of the struggle for political office" (286).

The Diminished Role for Popular Participation

Possibly the most significant feature of Schumpeter's elite model of democracy is its diminished role for popular participation (Pateman 1970, 3–5). And this diminution of popular participation is founded on a pessimistic view of what the people are capable of doing. The corollary of Schumpeter's assertion that democracy means "the rule of the politician" is the claim that "the electoral mass is *incapable* of action other than a stampede" (Schumpeter [1942] 1976, 283, 285; emphasis added). This claim, in turn, is a shorthand summary of Schumpeter's three-pronged attack, discussed below, on the common good, the general will, and the individual will, which he apparently regarded as decisive as against any democratic theory of "collective action" (252–264). By defining democracy as a method by which "individuals acquire the power to decide," Schumpeter clearly meant to exclude a definition of democracy according to which *the people* decided or even took part meaningfully in deciding (269).

Despite the fact that Schumpeter's model of democracy is routinely accepted as nonideological and no more than realistic, his arguments for excluding popular participation from the definition of democracy were openly normative. For example, in a curious passage, Schumpeter's line of argument moves from the observation that most societies exclude someone from suffrage, to the tautology or truism that any set of qualifications for citizenship must imply *some* exclusions, to the claim that no society should be denied the label "democratic" because of such exclusions from the body politic, however offensive, and finally to the rhetorical question, "Must we not leave it to every *populus* to define himself?" ([1942] 1976, 244–245).[2] Clearly these last two were normative claims, and peculiar ones at that. Elsewhere Schumpeter argued that voters "must respect the division of labor between themselves and the politicians they elect," meaning they must understand that "political action is his business and not theirs," a principle that ruled out "instructing" representatives or even "bombarding them with letters and telegrams" (295).

The Undermining of Democratic Ideals

Schumpeter's claim that his understanding of democracy was "realistic" has made it easy for interpreters to assume that he meant nothing more than to assert that some political theorists, because of their unwillingness to put aside their "values," were blind to the "facts" of democracy. But Schumpeter's arguments went far beyond this. Not only did he argue that one should not hold democracy *itself* as a thing to be valued—because otherwise one must commit oneself to defending the decisions of "the rabble" instead of "fight[ing] its criminality or stupidity by all the means at one's command" ([1942] 1976, 242)—but he also denigrated the value of such things as participation and liberty, and took a very equivocal stand on free expression and freedom of the press, problems I discuss below (271–272).

Connections to Tory Democracy

The continuities from Schumpeter's Tory democracy memos (reviewed in Chapter 2) to his discussion of democracy as a method or institutional arrangement are striking. His scheme of Tory democracy was democratic only insofar as it included democratic institutions, such as mass parties and a parliament; as we have seen, his model of democracy as a method clearly identified democracy with an institutional arrangement and nothing else. The Tory democracy memos clearly denigrated participation and equality—these were the things to be averted, according to the memos. Likewise, the model of democracy as a method both attacked the values of participation and equality and asserted their disconnection from democratic reality. But perhaps it is the continued commitment to elite domination that marks the clearest continuity. The need for the Austro-Hungarian aristocracy to mobilize politically to dominate parliament and public opinion and to defend the empire and the imperial house against democratic encroachment obviously structured the early memos. The discussion of democracy as a method, too, was structured by openly normative assertions of the need for elite domination ([1942] 1976, 291, 293, 294, 295, 302).

Schumpeter and Elite Theory

Schumpeter's writings on Tory democracy were structured by his deep commitment to monarchy and aristocratic conservatism; this commitment created the guiding thread for his early political memos and letters. In a practical sense, Schumpeter's Tory democratic program was predicated on the existence of the kaiser and of an aristocracy at least potentially capable of political mobilization. It should be fairly obvious, however, that once the Austro-Hungarian monarchy and aristocracy perished, any such political program would need new grounding. Schumpeter's turning to elite theory and his incorporation of its assumptions into his own work is probably best understood in terms of his need to reground his thought in the decades following the collapse of the Austro-Hungarian monarchy. In this sense, the assumption that society was always dominated by elites—a staple of elite theory—could substitute within Schumpeter's social and political thought for his earlier reliance on the existence of a particular elite.[3] But this assumption was the foundation for most of the basic problems that characterize Schumpeter's conception of democracy as method. Schumpeter took on all the key weaknesses and insufficiencies of elite theory generally by adopting its central theoretic core.

THE POLITICAL AND SOCIAL AIMS OF ELITE THEORY. Turning to the basic premises of elite theory was natural for Schumpeter. Like Schumpeter, most of the elite theorists, and their political-intellectual cousins, the theorists of crowd psychology, were motivated by a strong aversion to democracy and a fear that democratization would bring about an egalitarian, socialist social order. The leading proponents of these theories, Gaetano Mosca, Vilfredo Pareto, and Robert Michels, as well as Gustave Le Bon, who is usually classified as a theorist of the "crowd," influenced each others' work and shared a common anti-democratic and antisocialist political creed—in some cases shared even a desire to restore traditional hierarchies in societies where they were threatened or had been destroyed (Bottomore 1964, 9–10; Nye 1977, 10, 13, 23; Struve 1973, 5).[4]

For example, Mosca, one of the earliest elite theorists, regarded the adoption by the European masses of a democratic creed as dangerous, and viewed a scientific attack on democracy and its intellectual under-pinnings as a way of heading off the potential development from demo-cratic sovereignty to socialism. He identified his explorations in elite theory specifically as a way of battling democracy and socialism by "de-molishing" the "optimistic methods" of much social science and "rul-ing out the possibility of a true democratic government" (Bottomore 1964, 12; Meisel 1962, 185; Nye 1977, 17). Pareto considered himself unaffected by such openly political motivations, but even Schumpeter, who admired Pareto, could see how Pareto's "resentments" and political views structured his social theory (Schumpeter 1949, 168–169).

ELITES AND MASSES.   Most elite theorists relied heavily on some ver-sion of a dual assumption: every society was divided into a minority elite and a majority mass, and every society was governed by its elite minor-ity. Pareto provided a seemingly respectable basis for such an assump-tion with the claim—more often asserted than proven—that the most socially significant individual abilities were distributed throughout soci-ety according to a normal distribution (a bell curve), with only a few ex-ceptional individuals possessing extraordinary talents in any given field (Pareto 1966, 113, 130–131, 158–160). On the face of it, it would seem to be a leap from this assertion to the standard elite claim that there were distinct elite and mass categories. But Pareto in fact often argued, with Mosca, that all societies were divided into elites and masses and that all societies had minority governing classes—and he seemed to imply that such a claim could be derived from the less-controversial claim about the distribution of talents (Bottomore 1964, 2–3; Meisel 1962, 33, 37; Pareto 1966, 155, 267–270).

In any case, such elite-mass distinctions were commonplace. Al-though Michels is sometimes treated as standing for a more sophisticated theory of organization, that theory ultimately rested on the presumption of a natural division between elite and mass that reinforced and was reinforced by organizational imperatives (Michels [1915] 1962, 70, 79, 111; Nye 1977, 29–30). And even Max Weber, not customarily classed as an elite theorist, structured his famous lecture "Politics as a Vocation" around a cognate elite assumption that the electorate, at least, must always be divided into active and passive segments (Weber [1919] 1946, 99).

MASSES.   The polemical and intellectual force of elite theory, however, was not in positing an elite-mass split. As descriptive claims, the assertions that, *at any time,* some were politically active and some were not, and that some had high status while some did not, would have packed little explanatory power. What was significant about elite theory was its assertion that elites and masses were fundamentally different, that the social-structural elite-mass division was rooted in deep distinctions in ability and character.

Elite theorists first of all posited that the great mass of people were generally unable to reason, unable to discern logical argument from emotional appeal, were susceptible to manipulation, and thus, overall, were unable to take part in reasoned purposeful social action. The most intense expression of this view was probably in Le Bon's *The Crowd,* for although that book was supposedly about crowds—groups that came together at particular times and places—Le Bon's looseness as to what constituted a crowd and his obvious antidemocratic tendencies led him to treat whole electorates as "crowds" and to treat democratization as the growth in power of crowds (Le Bon [1895] 1981, 175). According to Robert A. Nye:

> It was widely held that collectivities, or what Le Bon called "crowd mentality," underlay the new vigor of mass working-class unions and political parties, democratic electoral procedures, the irresponsibility of "suggestive" popular press, and even juries and parliamentary assemblies . . . Collective psychology thus articulated a liberal critique of democratic tendencies in industrial societies with a facade of "scientific" and clinical terminology that lent a certain respectability to its pronouncements. (1977, 13)

The great mass of people were intellectually impoverished, unable to understand relations of cause and effect, unable to deliberate, and highly suggestible, in the view of elite theorists (Michels [1915] 1962, 64–65, 107–112; Nye 1977, 12; Pareto 1966, 111). Michels, likewise, tended to be unclear as to whether he was characterizing crowds or the masses. In one place, Michels argued that mass sovereignty was impossible because of the attributes of crowds; in another, he asserted that it was "the incompetence of the masses" that "constitutes the most solid foundation of the power of the leaders" (Michels [1915] 1962, 64–65, 111). But it was not just a question of the masses' lack of education or their intellectual incompetence. In Michels's view, for example, the masses were often distracted by lust, exhausted by physical labor, motivated by a love of strong leadership, and easily coopted by irrational slogans, myths, or beliefs (ibid., 85–89, 105).

Elite theorists especially emphasized their claim that the masses existed in an almost dreamlike state of delusion concerning political possibilities and goals. Each theory was slightly different from the others: Pareto's theory of "residues" and "derivations" as the instinctual and ideological springs of action, Mosca's emphasis on the supposed need of collectivities to believe in illusory political formulas, Sorel's theory of the "myth" as the element motivating social action and, for its participants, *assuring its outcome* (Meisel 1962, 16, 55; Nye 1977, 18, 23; Pareto 1966, 215–250; Sorel 1976, 200–212). But all of these theories could be appropriated as part of an antidemocratic portrayal of the irrational, the chimerical, and the plainly false in the political and social lives of the masses. These theories had much in common with Le Bon's crowd theory, and his view that "crowds are to some extent in the position of the sleeper whose reason, suspended for the time being, allows the arousing in his mind of images of extreme intensity which would quickly be dissipated could they be submitted to the action of reflection" (Le Bon [1895] 1981, 67). But they claimed to be more—to be theories of the behavior of the masses generally.

ELITES. Only a few individuals of exceptional ability in any society could really claim to stand above these attributes and behaviors of the mass, according to elite theory. *Just how* some few could rise out of or distinguish themselves from the mass was a matter about which elite theorists disagreed; it is a problem that cannot be adequately treated outside the context of Pareto's and Mosca's broader theories of the circulation of elites (Bottomore 1964, 6). In general, Pareto paid more attention to the maintenance of the elite-mass social structure through circulation of individuals than he did to the rise and fall of whole social classes, but he was not very clear about this distinction (ibid., 42). He viewed the rise of individuals into the elite as a product of their unusual abilities or valuable attitudes—both sharpened by the struggle to survive among the lower classes of any society (Pareto 1966, 112–113, 132–134, 158, 249–250). Meanwhile, he seemed to view the changing positions of *whole classes* as a function of the failure of individual circulation— a result of less capable individuals accumulating in elite classes and more capable individuals accumulating among segments of the masses (Bottomore 1964, 42; Pareto 1966, 249). Mosca's view of elite circulation rested less on the attributes of individuals and more on the ability of particular classes to fulfill socially necessary functions (Meisel 1962, 43–47). Schumpeter's own essay on social classes laid out a theory of the rise and fall of families within and between classes, as well as a theory of how classes themselves rise and fall according to their fulfillment of similarly conceived social functions ([1927] 1991). As for elites' ability to maintain power, Mosca, Pareto, and Michels all placed strong emphasis on the deployment of legitimating ideologies—something we encountered in reviewing the elite theorists' belief that the masses were highly susceptible to ideological manipulation. Again, although there were differences between Mosca's political formulas, Pareto's "derivations," and Michels's emphasis on the "cult of veneration" of the masses, all referred to the deployment of myth, deception, and ideology to sustain and bolster elite rule (Meisel 1962, 16–17, 55–57; Michels [1915] 1962, 93–97; Pareto 1966, 238–240, 270). As is well known, Weber's political thought emphasized a similar explanation for leadership: the theory that domination could be legitimated through appeals to tradition and legal forms, but most especially, in mass societies, to the "charisma" of leaders (Weber [1919] 1946, 78–79).

DEMOCRACY.   All of this had clear implications for the understanding of democracy; indeed it is not too much to say that much of the polemical force of elite theory was directed against democracy. If all societies were dominated by elites, democracy could be understood only as a special case of elite rule. Mosca wrote: "In all societies . . . two classes of people appear—a class that rules and a class that is ruled. The first class, always the less numerous, performs all political functions, monopolizes power and enjoys the advantages that power brings, whereas the second, the more numerous class, is directed and controlled by the first, in a manner that is now more or less legal, now more or less arbitrary and violent" (Mosca 1967, 50). According to Pareto: "Everywhere there exists a governing class, even in a despotism, but the forms in which it appears vary. In absolute government there is only one figure on the stage: the sovereign. In so-called democratic governments it is parliament . . . The worthy Demos thinks he is following his own wishes, whereas in fact he is following the behests of his rulers" (Pareto 1966, 268).

SCHUMPETER'S DEPLOYMENT OF ELITE THEORY. Schumpeter described his task in the later chapters of *Capitalism, Socialism, and Democracy* as one of stating his "views on the relation between the socialist order of society and the democratic method of government," a task involving an "extensive analysis" of the democratic method ([1942] 1947, xiii). But this substantially understated the extent of the polemical difficulties and historical constraints he faced in revising his long-standing elite conception of democracy. Many years after the fall of the Austrian empire, whose aristocracy was the practical basis and the audience for his original arguments on elite democracy, Schumpeter had to place an updated elite conception of democracy on a new footing, appropriate for contemporary problems, especially those in the United States. But Schumpeter lacked the most obvious basis for such a theory or program—the existence of a conservatively oriented elite, ready to take on the task of creating Tory democracy.

Schumpeter believed a form of democratic socialist society was possible in which democratic tendencies would be curbed by elite domination, but he appears never to have reached a satisfactory conclusion as to how that form of society was to be achieved. This is because he was not at all certain where or how the needed elites for that new form of society could be found, or how they could be organized and mobilized. As Schumpeter elaborated his theory of capitalist development and decline, he incorporated his early practical reflections on the role of Tory elites in liberal capitalist societies, arguing that in Europe during the stable era of liberal capitalism, the feudal aristocracy had provided a necessary element of political leadership. But the processes of rationalization, leveling, and democratization had or would destroy that elite, he argued, as they would soon destroy the bourgeois elite. Thus, in a neglected passage of *Capitalism, Socialism, and Democracy,* Schumpeter wrote that "socialism" had "no obvious solution to offer for the problem solved in other forms of society by the presence of a political class of stable traditions" ([1942] 1976, 302). It was "idle to speculate" about the "quality" of the class that might emerge to fulfill this function. Moreover, the existence of economic leadership in the democratic socialism Schumpeter envisioned was equally problematic. Schumpeter contended that, in Europe, existing bureaucracies might be converted to service as the managers of a socialist economy (155). But the United States lacked a preexisting bureaucracy ready to take on this role (ibid.; 1939, 1048).

In the absence of any existing conservative elite ready to serve as the foundation of a plan for Tory democracy, Schumpeter grounded his argument on premises that made an elite-dominated democracy appear to be the *only type really possible, at least in the long run.* That is, he introduced arguments, drawn partly from his reading of elite theorists such as Pareto, according to which democracy as rule by the people was impossible, elite domination of society and politics was inevitable, and thus democracy could at best mean a method that allowed the masses to accept or refuse the particular elite group that ruled them ([1942] 1976, 270, 273, 285).

Schumpeter and Weber

Despite the similarities in Max Weber's thought to aspects of elite theory, Weber is not generally classified as an elite theorist himself. This is nevertheless an appropriate place to focus directly on Weber's influence on Schumpeter's elite conception of democracy as presented in *Capitalism, Socialism, and Democracy,* because the elements of that influence are closely connected to elite assumptions. Weber's influence on Schumpeter is a somewhat difficult topic, because while Schumpeter explicitly referred to elite theory in the course of laying out his conception of democracy as method, he did not refer in these passages to Weber. And yet the apparent influence is striking.

Weber was a critic of democracy, worried, in particular, about the effect that mass politics would have on what he called an ethic of "responsibility," a willingness of political agents to pursue their values and goals self-critically, self-consciously, and with due regard for the consequences of their actions (Weber [1919] 1946). For Weber, as for Schumpeter, leadership was a key category in politics. Politics, he argued, was "any kind of independent leadership in action," a definition that already seems to call into question the idea that democracy, as a particular form of politics, could really entail rule by the people (ibid., 77). Just as Schumpeter, writing in the 1930s, argued that democracy amounted to "the rule of the politician" ([1942] 1976, 285), Weber insisted that democracy had to mean the "rule" (*Herrschaft*) of politicians—either professional politicians with a calling or vocation, a disciplined and responsible devotion to politics, or mere career politicians without a calling (Weber [1919] 1946, 99, 113). Just as Schumpeter argued in the best-known passages of *Capitalism, Socialism, and Democracy* that one could not understand politics from the standpoint of its "social meaning" or the ends it served ([1942] 1976, 282), Weber argued that one could not define a political association in terms of ends or values ([1919] 1946, 78). Just as Schumpeter saw the motive power of democracy in the struggle of parties and politicians for votes ([1942] 1976, 285), Weber saw existing democracies as dominated by parties "changing their material program according to their chances of grabbing votes" ([1919] 1946, 87). And just as Schumpeter thought that the ultimate benefit of elite democratic politics was the competitive struggle that allowed the most-able politicians to rise, Weber judged political systems according to their ability to nurture professional politicians with a calling (Breiner 1996, 19).

A key difference dividing Schumpeter and Weber, however, arises precisely over these related ideas of professionalism and calling. A true professional politician for Weber was one with a calling—and his purpose in writing about democracy was to promote what he called vocational politicians. Schumpeter, by contrast, showed little interest in such an idea. When he spoke of rule by professional politicians, he meant little more than what Weber referred to as ordinary democratic party politics (see Breiner 1996, 159).

The Attack on "Classical" Democratic Theory

Schumpeter's defense of his own elite model of democracy in *Capitalism, Socialism, and Democracy* rested first on a polemic against what he called the "classical" theory of democracy. Schumpeter surely was misguided in classifying Rousseau, Bentham, and the Mills together as proponents of this alleged classical theory. But it is nevertheless important to note that Schumpeter claimed classical democracy rested on improbable metaphysics or on unrealistic articles of faith about "human nature." By demonstrating that classical democracy rested on such premises, and by showing those premises to be untenable, Schumpeter attempted to clear the ground for his own assumptions about human nature.

Before analyzing the argument more closely, it is worth getting a schematic overview. Schumpeter began his attack on the classical doctrine and its conceptions of common good and common will by, first, insisting that the common good had to be metaphysical—something beyond mere empirical, sensible opinions, judgments, and arguments about the social good—or it could have no moral or political weight. Of course, he could count on most contemporary readers think that the classical doctrine was discredited by this metaphysical association alone. Nevertheless, he continued by, second, casting doubt on the common will—that is, by casting doubt on whether such a metaphysical common good could be accessible by democratic political processes. The conclusion was that the classical doctrine had to be rejected and an alternative account adopted.

Now it should be fairly clear that the decisive move in this progression was the claim that the common good must be something metaphysical or it was nothing at all. Or perhaps one should say that the decisive move was the establishment of several supposedly necessary polar alternatives. Either there was a metaphysical common good or nothing but a chaos of independent value judgments and tastes. Either there was a common will drawn inevitably to this metaphysical common good or nothing but meaningless methods of summing up chaotic values and tastes. Once the reader accepted these as the alternatives, it was useless to resist the tide of the argument.

Classical democratic theory first rested, Schumpeter claimed, on a metaphysical conception according to which the common good, almost like Aristotle's eternal mover, constituted a "center . . . toward which all individual wills gravitate" ([1942] 1976, 252). To serve this purpose, the common good had to persist unaffected by human attempts to know it, and thus independent even of "ignorance . . . stupidity and anti-social interest"; as Schumpeter put it, it simply "exists" (250). Because it was to serve as the "beacon light" of democratic deliberation, the common good of classical democratic thought, Schumpeter contended, must be "obvious," "simple to define," and yet, as a first principle, it had also to be "uniquely determined" and capable, presumably by deduction, of producing "definite answers to all questions" (250, 252). In short, although accessible to reason, it had to stand separate from it, unaffected by deliberation, discussion, or means of demonstration (250).

The only alternative to such an account of the common good, Schumpeter insisted, was recognition that the social world was characterized by myriad individuals with "ultimate values" that "cannot be reconciled by rational argument" ([1942] 1976, 251). In many cases, in fact, there were "irreducible differences of ultimate values which compromise could only maim and degrade" (ibid.).

The common will of classical doctrine, Schumpeter argued, was metaphysical by association. The classical doctrine of democracy required a common will that was "exactly coterminous" with the common good; this will had naturally to tend toward the good. In this view, the common will was a "semi-mystic entity," a supraindividual consciousness drawn naturally toward the common good ([1942] 1976, 250, 252).[5] Indeed, individuals, according to this caricature, who "do not see it" were held to be either ignorant or antisocial (250). The alternatives, as Schumpeter tendentiously characterized them, were either that such a metaphysical common will existed or that there was only an "infinitely complex jumble of individual and group-wise situations, volitions, influences, actions and reactions of the 'democratic process'" that lacked "not only rational unity but also rational sanction" (253). And the problem was not merely that these actual individual and group volitions were, considered together, unrelated, discordant, and chaotic. As we will see shortly, individuals, in Schumpeter's view, could be said to have no more than "wishes and daydreams and grumbles" at best—and more likely "dark urges" and "extra-rational or irrational prejudice and impulse" (261, 262). And groups were even worse, displaying "a reduced sense of responsibility, a lower level of energy of thought and greater sensitiveness to non-logical influences" (257).

Thus Schumpeter set up an essentially intractable problem. Clearly, as he described it, there could be no bridging the gap between the base, mundane, chaotic world of individual bias and group irrationality and the eternal, impossible world of the common good. But the need to bridge such a gap, it must be pointed out, was a spurious problem, a product of the way Schumpeter chose set up the argument.

Contrary to Schumpeter's characterization of the classical doctrine of democracy, conceptions of democracy that have stressed the importance of developing individual and group capacities for deliberation and democratic action have not required any such metaphysical conceptions of the common good and common will, and for this reason, Schumpeter destroyed only a straw man. But my point here is to show how Schumpeter's characterization of the logic and structure of the classical doctrine of democracy made his conclusion inevitable, and cleared the way for his own assumptions about human nature.

First, however, Schumpeter turned to an attack on the classical doctrine's supposed view of individual will. This individual will, he contended, had either to be a fixed point, "homogenous" and rationally determined before action, actually the "prime mover" of action, or it had to be regarded as an "indeterminate bundle of vague impulses loosely playing about given slogans and mistaken impressions," given fixity only when some view was imposed from without ([1942] 1976, 253, 254, 256).[6] Individual wills had either to be "ultimate data" in social science—ultimate causes of politics—or they had to be regarded as purely artificial, manufactured by professional politicians, who were the true motive force of politics (253, 254, 259 n. 12). Schumpeter regarded simply the stating of these alternatives in this manner as enough to settle on the latter, pessimistic view of "individual volition." He provided virtually no argument—just the assertion that it would be "unrealistic" to believe that the individual will was "homogenous," rational, and so on (253, 256).

These attacks on common good, common will, and individual will came together in Schumpeter's discrediting of the idea of "rule by the people." Rule, for Schumpeter, meant having a "will" with respect to some person or matter and having the ability to see that will carried out. He thus clearly equated "rule of the people" with the direct carrying out of "the *will* or the action of the community or the people as such" ([1942] 1976, 246; emphasis added).[7] And thus his discussion of rule embodied or implied the above problems concerning both individual and popular will. His dismissal of rule by the people rested on this alternative: either the will of the people (understood, as above, to be an actual entity, fully formulated a priori or at least distinctly prior to action) was carried out, or popular rule was meaningless (243, 245–247). Indeed, unless the popular will was formed a priori, it could be dismissed as subject to "pressure groups and propaganda," and Schumpeter equated this with a will that was staged, managed, created, or manufactured (254, 263). Schumpeter's rather strange dismissal of the idea that parliaments represent people—formulated on the basis of an analysis of "delegation"—makes sense only on this basis. Unless it could be said that parliamentary representatives were given a completely worked out agenda of the popular will with respect to the entire gamut of public issues, the idea that a parliament represented the people was incoherent, and parliament must simply be said to be "an organ of state" (247–248).

One objection to this line of argument is that Schumpeter lumped together conceptions of democracy that should not have been lumped together, in an effort to write off the whole "classical" doctrine of democracy (Pateman, 1970). Among those he erroneously combined as proponents of classical democracy were such theorists as Rousseau and John Stuart Mill, for whom democratic practices and procedures contributed to the growth and nurturing of citizens' capacities for action, deliberation, and self-governance (Held 1987, 72–104; Macpherson 1977, 44–76; Mill [1865] 1991; Pateman 1970, 22–38; Rousseau 1967).[8] Such theories as these did not require the conception of will—individual or group—attacked by Schumpeter. In fact, such "developmental" theories, which focused on the social development of individual and group capacities and volitions as a main problem of democracy, would not even have been coherent if the individual or common will was regarded as something unproblematically preformed. And as we have seen, such a developmental conception was also at the heart of Austrian Social Democratic thought on democracy. Since Schumpeter incorporated some of Otto Bauer's arguments about democratization in his own early transformative conception of democracy (see Chapter 2), it is surprising that he so badly mischaracterized the history of democratic thought in *Capitalism, Socialism, and Democracy*. But Schumpeter's attack was not so much a careful elucidation of the history of democratic thought as it was a preliminary step toward elaborating his own conception of democracy as a method.

The Curious Instability of Schumpeter's Argument

After his tendentious outline of the classical doctrine of democracy, Schumpeter turned to his own set of claims about "human nature in pol-

itics," in a section with that title. This topic, Schumpeter indicated, specifically included issues of "the voter's will, his powers of observation
and interpretation of facts, and his ability to draw . . . rational inferences
from both," as well as questions of group behavior, public opinion, or
"will of the people," and hence, he said, the question of "collective action" ([1942] 1976, 256, 257, 261–262, 263). It was his intention, in
other words, to link his assertions about these matters to a determinate
view of human nature. These assertions about human nature led directly
to Schumpeter's claim that "the electoral mass is incapable of action
other than a stampede," showing how necessary they were to his theory
of democracy as "the rule of the politician" (283, 285). Schumpeter's ultimate conclusions about democracy as method were essentially deduc-
tions from these; the elite conception of democracy as method, in other
words, could essentially be read off these assumptions.

The authorities Schumpeter cited for an alternative account of human
nature were two of the elite and crowd-psychology theorists discussed
above: Pareto and Le Bon (Schumpeter [1942] 1976, 256, 257). Pareto's
emphasis on the irrational provided Schumpeter with the alternative to
the idea of the "definite will that is the prime mover of action" (256).
Meanwhile, Le Bon's work demonstrated what Schumpeter called the
"realities" of "human behavior" in groups (257). Pareto and Le Bon's arguments, in other words, validated the generalizations about human nature in politics Schumpeter articulated in his attack on the individual
will: that the individual will was actually an "indeterminate bundle of
vague impulses loosely playing about given slogans and mistaken impressions" and that groups may arrive at some contingent agreement—
call it "a common will"—but this outcome and the process leading to
it were arbitrary and irrational (252, 253). In political matters,
Schumpeter asserted, the individual was "primitive" and "his" thinking
was "infantile," "associative and affective"; the typical citizen not only
applied weak rational processes but was prey to "extra-rational" and "irrational prejudice and impulse" and "dark urges" (262). This made citizens vulnerable to manipulation, so that whatever consistency and
structure there was to public opinion was actually imposed (263). "The
mass of people never develops definite opinions on its own initiative,"
Schumpeter concluded; "still less is it able to articulate them and to turn
them into consistent attitudes and actions. All it can do is to follow or
refuse to follow such group leadership as may offer itself" (145).

Schumpeter's Strange Concession

Yet no sooner had Schumpeter articulated this conception of human nature in politics than he argued that Le Bon actually "overstress[ed]" the "realities of human behavior," a curiously phrased admission that led to an even stranger and rarely noted passage ([1942] 1976, 257). Since the passage was at odds with his overall argument, one can only speculate that Schumpeter felt the need to acknowledge and perhaps defuse certain everyday political and social observations that could undermine his characterization of human nature. But he did so with a set of concessions that in no way supported his claims about this subject. "In the ordinary run of often repeated decisions the individual is subject to the salutary and rationalizing influence of favorable and unfavorable experience," Schumpeter began. Consumers, he conceded, may actually have "genuine" and fairly definite wants and may even be able to "act upon unbiased expert advice" (258).[9] The "individual citizen's mind," as well, operates with

> a full sense of reality [when it comes to] himself, his family, his business dealings, his hobbies, his friends and enemies, his township and ward, his class, church, trade union or *any other social group of which he is an active member*—the things under his personal observation, the things which are familiar to him independently of what his newspaper tells him, which he can directly influence or manage and for which he develops the kind of full responsibility that is induced by a direct relation to the favorable or unfavorable effects of a course of action. (258–259; emphasis added)[10]

Within this area of interests, Schumpeter admitted, some may even have "relatively definite individual volitions," and this domain even encompassed some "national issues," such as those involving "direct payments, protective duties, silver policies and so on" (259, 260).

In this passage, Schumpeter thus conceded a great deal to the many theorists of democracy who have stressed the importance of developing the capacity for democratic participation and a sense of efficacy within institutions and settings that are familiar and relatively small (Bauer [1925] 1970; Cole 1920; Mill [1865] 1991; Pateman 1970; Rousseau 1967). Schumpeter's language even echoed the theme that such settings and participatory possibilities were educative. "Repeated decisions" and "favorable and unfavorable experience" were both "salutary and rationalizing"; "prolonged experimenting" did away with "irrationalities," he argued; a sense of "responsibility" developed from participation in making decisions in connection with matters where one felt the "favorable or unfavorable effects" of action; the "concerns of daily life" could both "educate and discipline us" ([1942] 1976, 258, 259, 260). All this, it must be said, was directed partly to setting up the argument that, with respect to most national issues, there was "no scope" for will, conceived as "the psychic counterpart of purposeful responsible action," and *"no task at which it could develop"* (261; emphasis added). But such a negative argument was logically dependent on a positive one. If it made sense to argue that people lacked such capacities in national affairs because they had no opportunity to develop capacities in that arena, then this could only be because, by contrast, where such an opportunity existed, people could and did develop these capacities. Of course, Schumpeter simply failed to follow the implications of these crucial admissions.

Schumpeter could not leave matters at this point, and his final few pages on human nature in politics put great emphasis on the influence of the "extrarational, or irrational prejudice and impulse" in areas outside the sector of home, work, local affairs, and national affairs that involve immediate material interests ([1942] 1976, 262). Schumpeter defined this area of irrational impulse as "the political field," so that by definition he could say that in politics a person was necessarily "infantile," "primitive," and prey to the "weakness of the rational processes" (ibid.). The structure of this section of *Capitalism, Socialism, and Democracy* makes it clear that *this* was what he meant by invoking the absolute limits of human nature in politics, for his discussion of the empirical evidence supporting the idea that individuals and groups may, in appropriate institutional and social settings, develop the capacity to make reasonable decisions and act on them, would certainly not support categorical claims about human nature and the roles of elites and masses in democracy. Only the pessimistic assumptions of elite theory can form the basis of the claim that "the electoral mass is incapable of action other than a stampede," that "collectives act almost exclusively by accepting leadership," and that "the acceptance of leadership is the true function of the electorate" (253, 270, 273, 283).

There is something deeply dissatisfying about Schumpeter's ultimate return to human nature. Although he closely scrutinized the supposed assumptions about human nature in classical democracy, Schumpeter showed no equivalent inclination to scrutinize the assumptions he favored with any such care. Indeed, after presenting what can at least be termed mixed evidence about social, political, moral, and deliberative capacities—evidence that strongly supported the idea that context and historically variable institutions and practices made a great difference—Schumpeter provided only the barest justification for resorting to elite assumptions about human nature. He made the transition from his rather optimistic discussion of a "narrower field . . . distinguished by a sense of reality or familiarity or responsibility" back to pessimistic statements about human nature in politics with this claim: "when we move still farther away from the private concerns of the family and the business office into those regions of national and international affairs that lack a direct and unmistakable link with those private concerns, individual volition, command of facts and method of inference soon cease to fulfill the requirements of the classical doctrine" ([1942] 1976, 259, 261). But in general form this stated only what some theorists of democracy would have admitted: that it takes experience, direct participation, and democracy in small settings to foster the capacities needed for democratic decision making. One searches Schumpeter's pages in vain for the argument that would link his pessimistic observations to constant, universal human nature, or that would support any generalizations about human nature in politics at all. Instead one is left with the dissatisfying fact that the coherence of everything else Schumpeter said about democracy rested on elite theory's assumptions about human nature.

Human Nature, Gender, and Democracy

Before leaving the examination of these passages behind, it is important to review their significance for problems of gender and democracy. Although Schumpeter did not make any sustained arguments about gender in *Capitalism, Socialism, and Democracy,* his arguments about democracy and individual and group capacities reflect important assumptions about women's suffrage and political participation, as well as about the family and the realm of the political. Schumpeter's comments on gender are riven by the same tensions that threatened his arguments as a whole. I have argued that Schumpeter failed to trace out the implications of his admission that the "individual" actually did function with "a sense of reality" with respect to the things that concern "*himself*" ([1942] 1976, 258, 259; emphasis added). Embedded in the structure of this curious admission about the "individual" is a problem concerning gender whose implications Schumpeter also failed to pursue.

First it is necessary to locate the issue of gender embedded here. As we have seen, Schumpeter admitted that consumers often learned from experience and developed through exposure to market institutions skills something like the type of deliberative capacities required for democracy. "It is simply not true that *housewives* are easily fooled" when it comes to purchases, Schumpeter remarked ([1942] 1976, 258; emphasis added).[11] A few sentences later, he argued that there was a sphere of rational action and deliberation for the individual consisting "of the things that directly concern *himself, his* family, *his* business dealings, *his* hobbies, *his* friends and enemies, *his* township or ward, *his* class, church, trade union *or any other social group of which he is an active member*" (ibid.; emphasis added). On the one hand, these comments suggest, along with other comments about the educative potential of active participation in arenas such as these, the developmental benefits of participation in decision making, for women as well as men. At the same time, the use of the masculine pronoun—*his* family, *his* business dealings—reflects not just Schumpeter's sexism but also the actual historical ambiguity of these institutions for women, and point to problems theorists of democracy cannot ignore.

The problem for Schumpeter was that he himself made "active" membership in key institutions an important element of his argument. But who exactly *was* an "active member" of a family? If women did not benefit equally from either the structure of the family or the allocation of labor within it, it seems improbable that the family should have provided an appropriate training ground for democratic capacities—Schumpeter's claims notwithstanding. And who exactly benefited from the educational and developmental experience of being an "active member" in such institutions as businesses, ward committees, and trade unions? If a family sent forth only the husband and father as its "public" representative in those institutions, those institutions surely served no educational and developmental purpose for women. If Schumpeter had taken seriously his own argument about active membership and his concessions concerning the significance for democracy of the practices that structure institutions like the family and the workplace, he would have had to deal seriously with such questions. As it was, he did not.

And Schumpeter's definition of the "political field"—as whatever was outside the sphere of those institutions where ordinary individuals could be expected to exercise some capacity for democratic action and deliberation—reinforced his tacit relegation of women to a politically in-active status, even less likely than men to be "carried up the ladder" to-ward participation ([1942] 1976, 262). Thus it should be no surprise that Schumpeter registered no objection to the idea that in "an anti-feminist commonwealth, sex" should have been a measure of fitness for citizenship (244). These problems underscore the strange tensions and contradictions that were at the center of what Schumpeter said about democracy and human nature in politics.

The Deficiencies of Democracy as Method

At least three broad critical attacks have been launched by a variety of theorists against Schumpeter's elite conception of democracy as method. These are widely known. What is not widely recognized is that the central problems such critics have identified in Schumpeter's conception all stem from the process of regrounding his political theory on the categorical assertions about human nature derived from elite theory. These are not problems that can be passed off as idiosyncracies of Schumpeter's. Rather, they are almost unavoidable consequences of adopting elite theory's core assumptions.

Schumpeter's Devaluation of Freedom and Suffrage

In various passages throughout *Capitalism, Socialism, and Democracy,* Schumpeter acknowledged that the several freedoms of expression and a wide, if not universal, suffrage were institutions and practices long valued by proponents of democracy ([1942] 1976, 242, 248–249, 264–268, 295, 297, 411). But his elite conception not only failed to incorporate those valued practices within the meaning of democracy but also undermined the basis for defending them.[12] Critics have focused a great deal of attention on a passage Schumpeter referred to as a "mental experiment," designed in one sense to "prove" that democracy was only a method. There, he used the hypothetical situation of a community that decided democratically to "persecute religious dissent"—a real possibility, Schumpeter argued, because democratic *methods* might lead to such morally "repulsive" outcomes (240–243).[13] The upshot of this experiment was to put forth a theory of democracy according to which democracy was perfectly consistent with the persecution and murder of religious minorities (ibid.). Schumpeter's critics have responded to this in a variety of ways. Some have detected here the disturbing costs of accepting that democracy *is* just a method that includes no protections for minorities (Ashcraft 1995, 21; Bachrach 1967, 19–20).[14] In a similar fashion, Nicholas Xenos, commenting on this passage and others, has argued that democracy is unsustainable when it is treated as only a method, and the "social institutions that promote democratic values and make possible democratic action" are ignored (Xenos 1981, 123).

Schumpeter's willingness to dispense with protections for speech and expression as central to democracy was evident in many passages in the chapters on the elite conception of democracy. Democracy did not necessarily "guarantee a greater amount of individual freedom" than other forms of society, Schumpeter insisted ([1942] 1976, 271). It required enough "freedom of discussion *for all*" to enable elite competition for office, which was the true mechanism or motive force of democracy (272). But Schumpeter pointed out that just as competition in textile manufacturing did not require that every person *actually* be "free to start another textile mill," political competition did not require that the average individual *actually* be free to run for or hold office (272, 272 n). Thus the "relation between democracy and freedom is not absolutely stringent and can be tampered with" (272). In particular, while democracy meant that, during campaigns at least, elite "would-be" leaders had to have their views tolerated, and while actual leaders had to have "freedom of action" while in office, these freedoms seemed not to extend to the masses; in fact, in Schumpeter's view, guaranteeing elite "freedom of action" entailed restrictions on the expression of most individuals, such as banning citizens from engaging in "bombarding [their representatives] with letters and telegrams" (295). In another example of Schumpeter's lack of commitment to free expression as a component of democracy, his vision of the workplace in a "democratic" socialist society included "dictatorship" over workers and the use of factory discipline to curb workers' political expression (302).

This unsteady commitment to freedom as a component of democracy was matched, as discussed above, by a fervent denial that democracy entailed universal suffrage or that it ruled out the conscious exclusion of the propertyless or disfavored groups from voting rights, an argument that Schumpeter conceded would seriously undermine democracy's ties to "liberty" ([1942] 1976, 243–244). This was not at all an abstract matter for Schumpeter, since he listed concrete examples of those who could be excluded from democracy: women, "Orientals," "Jews," and "Negroes" (244, 244 n. 12). It hardly needs to be emphasized that a society that denies some of its members suffrage denies those members a significant measure of freedom to express their beliefs, and Schumpeter even strengthened this link, arguing that exclusions from suffrage *on the basis of beliefs* would be perfectly consistent with the type of elite democracy he envisioned.[15]

Schumpeter recognized in *Capitalism, Socialism, and Democracy* that freedom of expression and wide suffrage had been standard—if not, by any means, noncontroversial—ideals for proponents of democracy. Since he claimed to separate "classical" democratic doctrine from a "realistic" assessment of empirically existing democracies, some interpreters have been inclined to attribute his denigration of these valued practices to his alleged positivistic ambition to separate facts and values (Ashcraft 1995, 21; Bachrach 1967, 19–20). And this interpretation is bolstered by the form of Schumpeter's "mental experiment," purporting to demonstrate that democracy was a method that was perfectly consistent with religious persecution. But the idea of a democracy in which free speech was not necessarily protected for all and in which exclusions from the suffrage based on race, gender, religion, or belief were allowed was founded not on the abstractly conceived distinction between democratic procedures and democratic ideals but on the assumptions about human nature in politics that Schumpeter adopted from elite theory.

The startlingly negative assumptions about human nature in politics Schumpeter adopted called into question the value of freedom, free speech, freedom of the press, and suffrage for most people. Furthermore, these assumptions made it quite difficult to explain what difference there could be between a society that strove to secure freedom of expression for all its members and one that limited freedom of expression to elites competing for office. With regard to the first matter, freedom of expression, it would certainly be difficult to explain what value for society at large there could be in granting most people the "freedom" to express what Schumpeter termed an "indeterminate bundle of vague impulses loosely playing about given slogans and mistaken impressions," or to allow the full expression and development of "public opinion" that lacked "not only rational unity but also rational sanction" ([1942] 1976, 253).

And there would have been little more basis in Schumpeter's assumptions for arguing that such liberty would either allow individuals to make their own ideas heard or help them develop such ideas. Schumpeter's recourse to human nature and not to historically variable institutions in this regard was again unequivocal. "Human Nature in Politics being what it is," he argued, professional politicians were "able to fashion and, within very wide limits, even to create the will of the people," and thus "in reality they [the people] neither raise nor decide issues," but rather "the issues that shape their fate are normally raised and decided for them" ([1942] 1976, 263, 264). Given this analysis of the nature and origin of public discourse, Schumpeter could offer little but empty formalisms to distinguish a politics based on broad freedom of expression and one based on such freedom for political elites only. On Schumpeter's analysis of human nature, both such political systems would involve elite domination of discourse.

And it should be clear that the same was true of suffrage—that given Schumpeter's assumptions about human nature, there could have been little reason to object to restrictions on suffrage, a "right" few individuals would have been able meaningfully to exercise. Within the context of Schumpeter's elite conception, suffrage, like free speech, was meaningful only from the standpoint of the functioning of elite competition. The electorate was merely that group of people whose vote determined (in a nominal sense only) which set of leaders was put in office. It was important insofar as this method, rather than, say, physical battle or a drawing of straws, was used. But since democratic procedures did not guarantee that all, or even any, citizens had meaningful control over political decisions, the *extent* of the suffrage became a fairly arbitrary matter.

The Problem of Distinguishing Democracy

Schumpeter claimed that his elite conception of democracy provided a "reasonably efficient criterion by which to distinguish democratic governments from others," but a variety of critiques of the elite conception, when viewed together, call this claim into question ([1942] 1976,

269).[16] Schumpeter argued that a democracy consisted of an "institutional arrangement for arriving at political decisions in which individuals acquire the power to decide by means of a competitive struggle for the people's vote" (ibid.). But Schumpeter's own arguments destroyed the seeming concreteness of this criterion. Schumpeter was willing to allow that democratic processes were at work in autocracies so long as the autocrat wished "to act according to the will of the people or to give in to it" (241).[17] He envisioned a political system in which elites had the political equivalent of oligopoly power, and considered that there was in fact nothing undemocratic about political "cases that are strikingly analogous to the economic phenomena we label 'unfair' or 'fraudulent' competition or restraint of competition" (271). And he was willing to substitute "the tacit acceptance" of leadership for a real vote—such a procedure "should not be excluded," he wrote—although he argued this would technically violate his criterion of democracy (271 n). In light of these arguments, Schumpeter's seemingly sharply defined criterion of democracy blurred.[18]

C. B. Macpherson has rightly argued that because it envisioned the domination of politics by elites organized as oligopolies, Schumpeter's elite conception of democracy was hardly competitive and thus hardly democratic (Macpherson 1977, 89–91; see also Held 1987, 185). As David Miller quite reasonably points out, "This line of thought cannot be pushed too far without destroying the model's democratic credentials entirely" (Miller 1983, 139). Schumpeter's previously discussed willingness to sacrifice free expression and the like as constitutive of democracy only compounded this problem. Contrary to the idea that Schumpeter's elite democracy was easily distinguished from nondemocratic forms, his democratic criteria were in deep danger of collapsing into those for autocracy or oligarchy.

This deficiency, too, resulted directly from Schumpeter's categorical claims about human nature. He argued that the "competitive struggle for the people's vote" was the key mechanism that distinguished democracy from other forms of society or government ([1942] 1976, 269). This was the crucial difference, he said, between a democratic "parliamentary monarchy" and an undemocratic "constitutional monarchy"; in the first, "the monarch is practically constrained to appoint to cabinet office the same people as parliament would elect," while in the second, electorates and parliaments "lack the power to impose their choice as to the governing committee" (270). But given Schumpeter's assumptions about human nature in politics, this was a distinction without a difference. Schumpeter's own assumptions led to the argument that elections did not represent an articulation and implementation of what voters wanted, that they could not be anything but exercises in elite manipulation, and thus that democracy could not involve the electorate's having "the power to impose [its] choice" about anything. If the underlying mechanism in democratic elections was elite leadership, if "collectivities" of all types acted "almost exclusively by accepting leadership," and if that meant that "acceptance of leadership is the true function of the electorate's vote," then a mere election could hardly make a significant difference as to who controlled a cabinet (270, 273). No wonder, then, that Schumpeter was forced to admit that on his assumptions, the difference between a democratic vote and "the acquisition of political leadership by the people's tacit acceptance" rested on "a technicality" (271). Schumpeter's contention at one point that "the democratic process" did not completely cease "to work in an autocracy" actually reversed the logic of his argument; his argument, like those of the elite theorists, in fact served to prove that *the autocratic process did not cease to work in a democracy* (241). This was no mere slipup to be remedied by a more careful definition of terms. It was the result of Schumpeter's decision to reground his elite conception of democracy on categorical assumptions about human nature.

The Myth of the Classical Doctrine of Democracy

Schumpeter's defense of his own conception of democracy as method rested in large part on an attack on the "classical doctrine of democracy." But as Pateman has remarked, the existence of such a classical theory of democracy is a "myth" (Pateman 1970, 17; see also Held 1987, 178–179; Macpherson 1977, 85; Miller 1983, 137; Santoro 1993, 122–123). The mythological status of the doctrine Schumpeter chose to attack was critical, for the strength of his own model of democracy rested partly on the strength of his attack on this supposed alternative. Or, to put it differently, the strength of his own model rested on the polemical structure he set up, in which his model was made to be the only alternative to certain classical conceptions of the common good, common will, and individual will. Thus Schumpeter's misconstrual of the history of democratic thought cannot be neatly and analytically separated from the weaknesses of his own argument. It is not simply a question of pointing out that there have been many historical conceptions of democracy—although this is true. The chief point is that certain conceptions of democratic thought, especially the ones to which Schumpeter's elite conception was most obviously opposed, were not vulnerable to the critiques Schumpeter made.

A main prong of Schumpeter's attack on the classical doctrine was his claim that it rested on a metaphysical conception of the common will and an unrealistic or rationalistic conception of individual will. But such an attack failed to confront those historical conceptions of democracy that have stressed the development of democratic capacities. Even Rousseau, whose conception of the "general will" has come in for sustained attack on this point, regarded the general will as a social construction, the outcome of a very specific procedure by which individuals were to consult not their own individual interests alone, but their understanding of interests they shared with others (Rousseau 1967, 113). Rousseau took neither the common will nor the individual will as given to politics, but rather assumed that individuals had both individual and shared interests, and that they could be educated to look after those "interests that people really [have] in common" (Wood 1983, 313).[19] In this sense, the concrete existence of individual wills agreeing on some common will depended on education, on proper institutions, and on a form of society in which social and economic inequality was small enough that people would share actual interests (Wood 1983, 314). As both Ellen Meiksins Wood and Nannerl O. Keohane have argued, democratic politics and the procedures Rousseau proposed for them had a concrete, not a metaphysical, meaning, representing for Rousseau ways of breaking down particularist feudal institutions that made political power a personal attribute of nobility, combating commercial moralities that denied the existence of any but individual interests, and supplanting the king's sovereign will as the sole source of social harmony (Keohane 1978, Wood 1983).

John Stuart Mill's qualified commitment to utility as a principle by which to judge policy (Mill [1835] 1973, 114–115) might make him seem vulnerable to the claim that he took for granted the individual's recognition of his or her own utility and the formulation of a common will around some objectively determined maximum. But his actual doctrine of democracy and his interest in creating institutions that could foster stable agreements and cultivate attention to *common* interests were a testament to his appreciation of the difficulties of forming a common will under conditions of class conflict in nineteenth-century England (Ashcraft 1989; Mill [1865] 1991, 120–143).

As for Schumpeter's one-time colleague, the Austrian Social Democrat Otto Bauer, his emphasis on the educative potential of democratic institutions speaks to his rejection of the idea of the individual will as a fixed point, and his understanding of the importance of class conflict in Austria precluded any facile reliance on some readily formed common will as a justification for democracy (Bauer [1925] 1970, 244–250). Although he certainly envisioned democratic socialism as a means of overcoming deep divisions of interest in Austrian society, his commitment to functional democracy, in which individuals would have participatory opportunities not merely as citizens but also as consumers, workers, and so on, and his commitment to democratizing a variety of institutions (both economic and political) at a number of different levels (for example, plant and industry), demonstrated that he anticipated no simple way of ending all divisions of interest, considered as an obstacle to creating a common will (see Chapter 2).

But the heart of the matter, of course, is not that Schumpeter's critique failed to reach these theorists, as historical individuals. What is really at issue is that a commitment to a developmental conception of democracy simply has not entailed the intellectual baggage with which Schumpeter burdened the mythological classical doctrine. The central problem for democratic theorists who have stressed education and development has been the creation of institutions that foster individual and social capacities, and encourage individuals to take account of wider interests. In this sense, most democratic theories have regarded any such thing as a common will—any political agreement among disparate individuals and groups about goals or ways of proceeding—as a necessarily fragile social construction, influenced by historically variable social beliefs and institutional practices. They have regarded individuals and groups with the capacity to conduct their affairs cooperatively, reasonably, and democratically not as an established fact or a given, but rather as a goal of democratization itself.

Here it is worth citing Bauer, whose views on democratization were quite familiar to Schumpeter. Bauer, as I have pointed out, regarded the development of the "capacity for self-government in [the] labour process" as a prime goal of economic democratization and as a prerequisite for democratic socialism ([1925] 1970, 144). He saw council democracy as "a potent agency for the self-education of the masses" and argued that the spread of such democratic institutions "created a new type of manhood and womanhood" (ibid., 178).

Given this, it is not too difficult to see where Schumpeter's argument went wrong with respect to the problem of the common good. For developmental democratic theorists, the common good and the pursuit of it through democratic institutions could not be separated from the educational and developmental benefits of democratization. The common good aimed for was in this sense not distinct from the democratic means of attaining it. Mill's critique of the idea that the "ideally best polity" would be a benevolent despotism epitomizes precisely this idea, which Mill summarized as the argument that "the principal element" of "the idea of good government" is "the improvement of the people themselves" (Mill [1865] 1991, 62). Bauer's argument was just as clear: "the transformation of political and social institutions is not an end in itself; for the development of peoples it has meaning only so far as it promotes the awakening, the inner change, and the upward movement of mankind" ([1925] 1970, 178).

The extent to which a proper understanding of the arguments of these developmental democrats concerning individual and common will and the common good disturbs Schumpeter's argument is difficult to overstate. Schumpeter effectively ceded the polemical territory on which these theorists traditionally made their arguments: the observation that existing political institutions failed to embody full democratic participation and the evidence supporting the idea that properly constructed social, economic, and political institutions could provide opportunities for people to develop their democratic capacities and their control over the decisions that affected them. Schumpeter admitted that when it came to issues tangibly affecting the individual, or matters over which the individual had some actual control, there was evidence that individuals could identify their interests, deliberate, form reasonable conclusions, and act on them.

This left Schumpeter with several options. He could have assumed that the ability to deliberate and a close acquaintance with one's interests were unproblematically given to human beings or were somehow inscribed in human nature. Schumpeter, of course, rejected this option.[20] He could have given up any attempt to link this evidence to fixed, natural, universal human qualities and stood on the terrain of historical contingency and socially developed qualities and capacities. But in standing on this terrain he would have had to justify favoring or opposing the development of the capacities needed for the spread of democracy by pointing to other practical political, social, and economic commitments.[21] In the end, Schumpeter chose not to explain why, given his observations about the ways in which active participation in decision making may foster certain capacities, he still opposed practical, experimental action to widen democratic participation.

As we have seen, he followed a third course and simply reasserted elite theory's assumptions about human nature. But there were severe limits to the usefulness of this polemical strategy. It was simply not clear what compelling reasons could be given for accepting the most negative view of human nature's limits on democracy. To put this differently, given the range of observations Schumpeter cited, the only reason he could have to insist on the elite assumptions about human nature he chose was to preclude the kind of spread of democratic practices proponents of developmental theories of democracy would favor. No one favoring developmental approaches to democracy could have been persuaded on these grounds to adopt Schumpeter's assumptions. And in this sense, Schumpeter's polemical strategy was simply ineffective against developmental conceptions of democracy.

The really serious deficiency here was not simply Schumpeter's misconstrual of the history of democratic thought. It was his failure to recognize that developmental democratic theories were not vulnerable to the types of critiques he offered. And that failure was linked to the requirements of his polemical strategy: attempting to make his categorical assumptions about human nature seem more realistic by mischaracterizing the alternatives as the classical doctrine of democracy.

Schumpeter's Vision of Democratic Socialism

The authoritarian implications of Schumpeter's elite conception of democracy become clear in his vision of democratic socialism. That vision, as elaborated in *Capitalism, Socialism, and Democracy*, rested logically on the elite conception of democracy—not on the transformative one.[22]

The transformative conception, however, was a crucial element of Schumpeter's account of how liberal capitalist societies would become socialist. Recognizing how Schumpeter's authoritarian vision of democratic socialism relied on his elite conception of democracy explains two rather striking discontinuities or contrasts in his thought. The first of these is the contrast between his earlier views of democratic socialism and his later vision in *Capitalism, Socialism, and Democracy.* The second is the disjuncture, within *Capitalism, Socialism, and Democracy,* between his description of the democratizing tendencies leading toward socialism and his authoritarian description of a socialist society.

Schumpeter's own theory of capitalist development toward socialism would lead one to expect that democratic socialism would include democratized workplaces. He had, after all, made the spread of democratic practices and the concomitant collapse of traditional hierarchies in the economy crucial elements in his theory of the decline of capitalism (see Chapters 2 and 3). And earlier in his career he had sided with Austro-Marxists like Otto Bauer in arguing that democratic socialism would include industrial democracy of some kind (Chapter 2), a point to which I will return.

But Schumpeter was deeply opposed to industrial democracy. When he finally turned to the subject of "democracy in the socialist order" in *Capitalism, Socialism, and Democracy,* he devoted four of about six pages to a polemic against industrial or economic democracy ([1942] 1976, 296–302). To construct *his* conception of democratic socialism in *Capitalism, Socialism, and Democracy,* he placed his definition of the democratic method alongside a simple, abstract definition of socialism: centralized state direction of the means of production. The juxtaposition of these definitions allowed him to conclude that "between socialism *as we defined it* and democracy *as we defined it* there is no necessary relation" (284; emphasis added). Given his definitions, democratic socialism could refer only to a society that happened to combine a political system of "competitive leadership" with state control of the economy. Logically this juxtaposition of abstractions meant that there would not *necessarily* be any economic or industrial democracy in a system of democratic socialism. Already it should be clear that this is inconsistent with his account of democratization and the decline of capitalism.

In any case, Schumpeter, led by his own intensely conservative inclinations, went further than this. He declared that "no responsible person

can view with equanimity the consequences of extending the democratic method, that is to say the sphere of 'politics,' to all economic affairs" ([1942] 1976, 299). And he claimed that his view would be shared
by the bureaucratic elites of the future democratic socialist society. As a
result, he argued, "much of this economic democracy will vanish into
thin air in a socialist regime" (300 n). He explained a few pages later:
"effective management of the socialist economy means dictatorship not
of but *over* the proletariat in the factory . . . As a matter of practical necessity, socialist democracy may eventually turn out to be more of a
sham than capitalist democracy ever was" (302).

Schumpeter even noted that bureaucratic elites would be able to
use factory discipline to "restrict" the political expression of workers
([1942] 1976, 302). (His countervailing admission that workers might
be able to use their political rights to soften factory discipline seems
half-hearted, at best, in light of his denial that the masses possessed the
ability to take "purposeful responsible action" [261, 302]). In any case,
it was with obvious relish that he claimed that economic managers in
the socialist society he envisioned would not brook interference from
"fussing citizens' committees or by their workmen" (299). Socialism as
he envisioned it in *Capitalism, Socialism, and Democracy* would break
the workers' resistance, so that "every comrade will realize the true significance of restiveness at work and especially of strikes" as "nothing
else but anti-social attacks upon the nation's welfare" (211–212).

Read in conjunction with Schumpeter's arguments that democracy
did not entail universal or even widespread suffrage, his view that citizens should not be allowed to bombard their representatives with letters, his equivocal stand on freedom of expression, and his belief that
democracies were always elite-dominated, this vision of democratic socialism looks authoritarian indeed.

This elite-dominated, authoritarian description of democratic socialism was clearly a conceptual focus of *Capitalism, Socialism, and Democracy*, yet it was in direct conflict with the way Schumpeter had previously thought and argued about democratic socialism. By 1920,
Schumpeter had incorporated into his own work an astonishing amount
of Otto Bauer's conception of democratic socialism and the way that the
council movement could lead to it (see Chapter 2). Given this vision of
democratic socialism, Schumpeter had rejected at the end of World War
I the idea of building socialism on the structure of the bureaucracies that

had managed the wartime economy. The statist, bureaucratic organization of the economy during the war had also drawn the Austrian Social Democrats' criticism (see Chapter 2). And during the same era Schumpeter, like the Austrian Social Democrats, contrasted "true socialism" with the wartime "administrative economy," precisely on the grounds that the administrative economy was "the most undemocratic thing there is" ([1918] 1991, 130). Similarly, in "The Socialist Possibilities of Today," he was so convinced that socialism, conceived as a wholly new form of society, could take place only after a thorough democratization of the economy carried out by the council movement, that he refused to consider any kind of state-controlled economy to be legitimately socialist (1920–21, 310). He declined even to discuss state socialism grafted onto an aristocratic, elite-ruled country, or socialism achieved through an extension of wartime controls. His reason: "Here we want only to speak of democratic socialism, the socialism of the workers' party" (1920–21, 310; my translation).

The dramatic contrast is due to the fact that he constructed his later vision of democratic socialism around his elite conception of democracy, whereas his earlier vision of democratic socialism had been built on his transformative conception of democracy—and especially his understanding of the council movement and the way in which it would democratize and restructure the economy. Interpreters who abstract Schumpeter's model of democracy as method from his comprehensive focus on the transition from capitalism to socialism fail to see the significance of that model as a foundation for a shockingly authoritarian vision of democratic socialism. They fail to grasp that one consequence of Schumpeter's elevating his elite conception of democracy into a general statement of the nature of democracy was his adoption of such an authoritarian vision of democratic socialism.

A second puzzling discontinuity in *Capitalism, Socialism, and Democracy* exists between what Schumpeter said were the tendencies leading toward democratic socialism and his actual description of a rather authoritarian democratic socialism. If democratization in general, and a turning of democratic ideologies against workplace hierarchy, in particular, were key factors in the overall social, cultural, and political collapse of the capitalist order and the simultaneous rise of socialism, why did Schumpeter describe democratic socialism in such authoritarian terms? If a breakdown of workplace hierarchy was one of the most important tendencies leading to socialism, how could socialism be characterized by such an authoritarian industrial regime?

The discontinuity is perhaps most obvious in Schumpeter's seven-page discussion of "authoritarian discipline in socialism" ([1942] 1976, 212–218). There Schumpeter reviewed the "lesson from Russia" as evidence. He admitted that the actual forces leading to revolution in 1917 precipitated a wave of "'democratic meetingism'—the practice of the workmen's discussing the orders received and executing them only after approval" (216). "The masses got out of hand entirely," he insisted, "and gave effect to their conception of the new order of things by innumerable strikes of the holiday-making type and by taking possession of the factories" (ibid.). He argued further that "management by workmen's councils or by trades unions was the order of the day and was accepted by many leaders as a matter of course" (ibid.). Such conduct by workers was perfectly consistent with the egalitarian tendencies leading to democratic socialism, as Schumpeter had described them in these same pages and elsewhere (214; and see Chapters 2 and 3).

But, he claimed a few pages later, such "wild socializations" or "attempts by the workmen of each plant to supersede management and to take matters into their own hands" were, in his view, naturally to be avoided—they were, in fact, "the nightmare of every *responsible* socialist" ([1942] 1976, 226 n; emphasis added).[23] This was the case, he claimed, in part because of the same elite assumptions Schumpeter articulated elsewhere—here expressed as the problem of the "subnormal performer[s]" who constituted "25 percent of the population" and would need to be reined in (213). And it was true because socialist society would need but would not benefit from the "previous, possibly ancestral, training" in authoritarian discipline that existed in capitalist society, an argument that echoed his account of the breakdown of traditional order in capitalism (212). Now it happened, Schumpeter argued, that a socialist government would have at its disposal exceptional tools for imposing discipline (213–215). But unlike the observations about the spread of democratic ideologies and "democratic meetingism," this claim and subsequent ones about the ease and use of authoritarian discipline in socialism did not follow in any obvious way from Schumpeter's analysis of the transition from capitalism to socialism. Rather, his claim about authoritarian discipline could be deduced only from the particular vision of democratic socialism that Schumpeter based, in turn, on his state-centered definition of socialism and his elite-centered definition of democracy.

Thus Schumpeter's argument in these pages progressed from the claim that a democratic socialist government (after *his* elite definition) would *possess the means* to establish authoritarian discipline, to the argument that a such a socialist government would necessarily exploit those means ([1942] 1976, 215). And the essence of Schumpeter's subsequent portrayal of authoritarian discipline in socialism was well encapsulated in his bitter joke, quoted above: "Socialist democracy may eventually turn out to be more of a sham than capitalist democracy ever was" (302). It is essential to realize that this was true only of democratic socialism as he now chose to define it in *Capitalism, Socialism, and Democracy,* for it certainly would not have been true of democratic socialism as he had understood and discussed it earlier.

All this had repercussions for how Schumpeter treated the historical case of the Soviet Union. Since 1918 Schumpeter had insisted that the Bolshevik revolution had been premature, that it had constituted an attempt to achieve socialism before certain necessary social, cultural, political, and economic changes had occurred. As I pointed out in Chapter 2, Schumpeter argued in "The Socialist Possibilities of Today" that it was, in particular, the fact that the council movement had not spread sufficiently to sustain democratic socialism that accounted for the authoritarian nature of Soviet socialism (1920–21, 326–327, 338). In "The Crisis of the Tax State," Schumpeter linked his argument that "true socialism" could not be achieved on a state-centered model to this view of the Bolshevik revolution as premature ([1918] 1991, 130). Years later, in writing *Capitalism, Socialism, and Democracy,* Schumpeter still insisted that the Bolshevik revolution "was nothing but a fluke," occurring as it did before transformative processes had done their work ([1942] 1976, 359). "The cruelties to individuals and whole groups" in the Bolshevik consolidation of power were "largely attributable to the unripeness of the situation," he insisted (218).

But Schumpeter's discussion of the Soviet model of industrial organization in *Capitalism, Socialism, and Democracy* was pervaded with a euphemism and an evasion strange for someone who was so decidedly a foe of Bolshevism. Schumpeter was in a bind. After all, his own model of democratic socialism now entailed strict authoritarian discipline. And he believed that socialism, as he now envisioned it, "might be the only means of restoring social discipline" ([1942] 1976, 215). Any criticism of the authoritarian discipline of the Soviet model could potentially be deployed against his own vision of democratic socialism. Viewed from another standpoint, it is not clear that any cogent criticism of Soviet authoritarianism could be premised on his own elite-dominated conception of democracy, which made mass submission to authority appear natural. So his argument wavered. On the one hand, Schumpeter argued that authoritarian steps were required to crush worker democracy in revolutionary Russia. He noted that "labor leaders who persisted in recognizing a distinct interest of the workmen have been removed from their positions," and that as a result, the new leaders suppressed "democratic meetingism," helped establish "comrades' courts" and "purge commissions," and made unions "organs of authoritarian discipline" (216–217). He acknowledged that the Soviet state used its position to "enforce . . . conformity with its ends and structural ideas [and] . . . create an atmosphere favorable to factory discipline" (217). "Intellectuals," he observed, were "evidently not at liberty to tamper" with such discipline, and there was "no public opinion" to challenge it (ibid.). But on the other hand, none of this attracted Schumpeter's criticism. He contended strangely (in light of the above) that the "trade unions were not suppressed" (216). Indeed, he argued euphemistically, "self-discipline and group discipline" actually accounted for much of the decline of workplace democracy (217).

In sum, it has proved far too easy for interpreters to avoid looking deeply at Schumpeter's treatment of democracy and democratic socialism, just as Schumpeter avoided looking deeply at the Soviet model of industrial organization. But the full import of his elite conception of democracy is best understood in light of the deeply authoritarian picture he drew of democratic socialism. While this was by no means a picture of Schumpeter's ideal society, it was his vision of a society in which elite rule and conservative values could persist despite the tendencies leading toward socialism.

5

Schumpeter's Vision of Social Science

Schumpeter's transformative conception of democracy is no anomaly in his thought. It is consistent with an approach to social science that he developed over his lifetime, directed toward the study of social transformation. One reason critics and admirers of Schumpeter's political thought have not discerned the transformative conception of democracy in his work is that too many have failed to explore the vision of social science that undergirded it. Most wrongly assume that he shared the basic aims and approaches of either neoclassical economics or contemporary mainstream political science. By imposing on Schumpeter's work the framework of someone else's model of social science, they have obscured crucial features of his work on democracy and the interests motivating it. A more careful interpretation of Schumpeter's vision of social science both clarifies his approach to political and social problems and provides a richer context for some of the issues I have already discussed.

One important mistake made by scholars interested in Schumpeter's political thought has been to isolate features of his political writings that are reminiscent of neoclassical economics and to link them to a view of Schumpeter as an ordinary neoclassical economist. C. B. Macpherson referred to Schumpeter's "equilibrium democracy" and found it "not surprising" that "the man who first proposed this model was an economist who had worked all his professional life with market models" (Macpherson 1977, 79; see also Miller 1983, 135). This approach goes wrong, first, by implying that Schumpeter took an approach to economics that he did not take. Worse, it tends to make the equilibrium-model aspects of Schumpeter's conception of democracy as method appear to be unremarkable, a natural outcome of his methodology. But while Schumpeter started out his career as a proponent of neoclassical economic theory and its equilibrium models, his "methodological" development actually represented a massive shift in the scope and ambition of his project, which transcended equilibrium analysis and moved toward a broader and more ambitious social science capable of comprehending how societies develop from one form to another. His adoption of at least some aspects of equilibrium analysis in his writings on an elite conception of democracy as method actually constitutes a puzzle, and the basis of a critique (see Chapter 6).

A more subtle problem is the frequent failure of Schumpeter's interpreters to put aside certain contemporary assumptions, almost invisible to us today, about the nature, scope, and aims of social science. Although many political scientists and political theorists writing about Schumpeter have actually offered very little explicit analysis of Schumpeter's methodology, in what they have written about Schumpeter's general approach to political science and theory they have surreptitiously introduced crucial assumptions about the nature of social and political science that informed the debate attending the rise of behaviorism in the 1950s and 1960s—assumptions that remain with us in the discipline today. The result of this approach has been the common view of Schumpeter as a disinterested social scientist who merely wanted put to aside ideology and set forth a realistic account of democracy. But not only does this interpretation fail to capture his motives in writing, it also fails to do justice to his complex understanding of the activity of social science.

Recent work by a few sociologists and economists has advanced beyond the usual treatments of Schumpeter's social science methodology. Tom Bottomore (1992), Allen Oakley (1990), Yuichi Shionoya (1990a, 1990b, 1991, 1997), and Richard Swedberg (1989, 1991a, 1991b) have shed new light on Schumpeter's approach to social science and have shown the importance of his explorations in economic sociology. My emphasis in this chapter, though similar, is less on Schumpeter's explorations in economic sociology as a distinct field than on his development of what I term a science of social transformation.

Before writing the book that made his economic career, *A Theory of Economic Development (Theorie der wirtschaftlichen Entwicklung)*, published in 1911, Schumpeter was relatively content with "pure" neoclassical economic theory and its abstract equilibrium models, deduced largely from axioms about consumer behavior. But he soon became dissatisfied with neoclassical methodology as a way of approaching the problems that interested him, and beginning with that 1911 book, it is possible to trace the momentous shift in the ambition of his project toward a social science capable of understanding how societies develop. In fact, Schumpeter came to relate every realm of social science, including the theory of democracy, to this ambitious understanding of social science. This development entailed not only an embracing of dynamic, nonequilibrium models of the economy and the incorporation of economic sociology, but also the development of a theory of innovation as a type of agency, and a reconsideration of the problem of science and ideology. It also entailed a critique of methodological individualism, the explanation of the social world according to the actions, attributes, and motivations of individuals, as if they required no further explanation.

The foregoing chapters should have made it clear that Schumpeter did not offer his elite conception of democracy as method as merely a "realistic" theory of democracy, severed from the distortions of ideology and belief. What might be less clear is that his transformative conception of democracy can be seen as a culmination of his developing approach to social science, while his elite conception can be seen as something of a departure from it.

How the Orthodox View of Political Science Obscures Schumpeter's Approach

During the past forty years, philosophers of science have questioned the logical-empiricist view that mainstream political scientists once set up as a norm. Interpretive social scientists have criticized the naturalistic aspirations of mainstream political scientists. Realist social scientists have attacked the instrumentalist conception of theory. Feminists have attacked the abstract individualism that characterizes some mainstream political science approaches. Postmodernists have attacked the faith in impartial and universal reason that underlies others. Meanwhile, political science itself has presented a moving target, with rational choice theory, for example, growing to prominence, displacing older, explicitly behaviorist paradigms.

But despite these developments it is not too much to say that the implicit philosophy motivating mainstream political science since the behaviorist revolution has remained virtually untouched. Certainly one searches political science journals almost in vain for articles that adopt, for example, interpretivist, feminist, or scientific-realist methodologies—political *theory* articles excepted. Confident of this hegemony within the social sciences, the author of one fairly recent survey argued that virtually all existing social science methodologies can be assimilated to the causal framework of logical empiricism (Little 1991, 3–6). Meanwhile, as both its critics and proponents recognize, rational choice theory, though certainly a departure for political science, still seeks grounding in the same logical empiricism that mainstream political scientists championed in the 1950s (see, for example, Riker 1990, 164–165; Shapiro and Wendt 1992, 197–203). In sum, the practices of mainstream political science have long been constituted by the logical-empiricist "conventional wisdom," despite the fact that, as one critic puts it, "in the last several decades, every key tenet of this 'standard view' has been either abandoned, liberalized to the point of triviality, or thoroughly undermined" (Manicas 1987, 243).

When such assumptions about how to think and structure arguments have been around for so long, they can become invisible to those who hold them. And this may become a problem in its own right. The categories and deep assumptions of the "standard view" of science are still structuring debates in political science in ways we often do not notice. As John Gunnell has pointed out, one of the problems and most curious features of the explicit debate pitting behaviorism against political theory—a debate that unfolded throughout the 1950s and 1960s and died without resolution in the 1970s—was the agreement *by both sides* that a particular logical-positivist or logical-empiricist model could lay exclusive claim to the title "science" (Gunnell 1975, xv–xvi, 12; see also Ashcraft 1984, 516–517; Shapiro and Wendt 1992, 197–201). This acceptance by both sides had the effect of frustrating substantive debate about what methodological approaches were appropriate to the whole range of problems in the social sciences, in favor of polemics that pitted "political science" against "political theory," "facts" against "values," "realistic" against "speculative" approaches, and so on. It is perhaps no surprise, then, given the continuing near-ubiquity of the logical-empiricist assumptions, that Schumpeter's democratic theory has taken on meaning in the context of these same oppositions—no surprise that social scientists have taken up Schumpeter as a cudgel on behalf of their particular conception of social science (Allen 1991, 2: 129–130; Downs 1957; Huntington 1984, 195; Lipset 1959, 71).

Interestingly enough, however, many of Schumpeter's critics have also dealt with his work within this framework. At least implicitly, the claim that Schumpeter's elite conception was meant to provide "an empirically based 'realistic' model of democracy" and to "free thinking about the nature of public life from what he took to be excessive speculation and arbitrary normative preferences" fits Schumpeter's thinking to the terms of logical empiricism (Held 1987, 164). Although this characterization comports with some of Schumpeter's own comments, when combined with a failure to connect his democratic thought to his actual methodological arguments and intellectual development, it distorts his work and makes it appear that he adhered to the methodological orthodoxy of postwar political science, which he did not.

After Schumpeter's death his work itself became a stake in various social-scientific skirmishes. In his foreword to Peter Bachrach's *The Theory of Democratic Elitism*—a work that treated Schumpeter prominently—Sheldon Wolin identified the chief problem in the study of politics as the spread of "the behavioral movement" and "social science," and against this he urged a "moderate reaction" especially to restore the "wonder of politics" (Bachrach 1967, v–vi). That Schumpeter should have come in for such treatment is in many ways understandable, given the way his admirers used his work. Nevertheless, in becoming a banner for one side and a target for the other, his work ceased to be dealt with in its entirety and complexity. His actual vision of social science—which did not fit the view of "science" implicitly accepted by both sides in the debates over behaviorism and logical empiricism—was lost. I aim to recover it here.

Walras and Equilibrium Economics

The work of Léon Walras crowned, for Schumpeter, the accomplishments of neoclassical economics (Schumpeter 1954b, 909, 913).[1] From the late eighteenth century until the 1870s, in Schumpeter's view, mainstream economists worked within a common paradigm, a "classic situation" in economics, well characterized by its best-known early proponent, Adam Smith, and "summed up in the typical classic achievement . . . of J. S. Mill" (ibid., 379–380; see also 51 n. 1). Beginning in the 1870s, however, a new type of economics emerged on the scene, whose purest distillation and highest achievement, in Schumpeter's view, was Walras's *Elements of Pure Economics*. The hallmark of this neoclassical economics was the isolation of "purely" economic relations—most fundamentally, relations between individuals and commodities—from the social relations and social structures within which they were situated, and the description of functional relations between these abstracted elements (ibid., 910, 963, 1038; see also Meek 1967, 206–207).

"Marginalism" refers to the resynthesis of classical economics using the tools of calculus—and especially to the principle of marginal utility, the general idea that consumers, for example, can maximize their utility by distributing their money such that the marginal utility of every commodity they buy is equal to that of every other. The heart of Walras's economics, however, was not so much the principle of utility itself as it was a picture of the economy in general equilibrium—as a system of costs, prices, and incomes all mutually determining each other, such that a change in one of them would ultimately lead to a change in all of them (Schumpeter 1908, 28). His aim, according to Jan van Daal and Albert Jolink, was to show that, given a preexisting distribution of resources, free competition would lead to the greatest possible satisfaction of wants (Daal and Jolink 1993, 3, 39). Walras used a concept of marginal utility to build his economic models toward that end, but whereas Menger and Jevons made marginal utility the center of their work—especially a theory of value premised on marginal utility—for Walras, marginal utility took a backseat to this coordinated view of the economy (Daal and Jolink 1993, 13–19). "So soon as we realize that it is the general-equilibrium system which is the really important thing, we discover that, in itself, the principle of marginal utility is not so important after all," Schumpeter wrote (1954b, 918). Hence even the details of how Walras arrived at a set of equations describing households' willingness or propensity to supply factors of production and to demand goods, as well as functions describing production, aggregate supply, and aggregate demand, were not so important for Schumpeter (Daal and Jolink 1993, 21, 49–50, 56; Schumpeter 1954b, 1011–1013).

What was significant was that, after combining these algebraic equations in a single system, Walras essentially demonstrated that there was a determinate mathematical solution to this set of simultaneous equations; this implied that there existed price levels at which every market in the economy would clear while every person would maximize his or her utility (Daal and Jolink 1993, 40). And this demonstration of a determinate outcome was a brilliant achievement in Schumpeter's view: proof that there was such a thing as an economic system, a complex but self-contained relationship among economic variables.

Walras had abstracted from the social order as a whole a set of variables of interest to the economist. Then, in Schumpeter's view, he had shown something essential about these variables: "whether or not the relations known to subsist between the elements of the system are, together with the data, sufficient to determine these elements, prices and quantities, uniquely" (1939, 41). Walras showed that they were, providing economists with "the magna charta of economic theory as an autonomous science, assuring us that its subject matter is a cosmos and not a chaos" (Schumpeter 1939, 41).

It is worth clarifying the different elements that intertwine in this equilibrium analysis—the key elements of equilibrium analysis generally. Walras's model demonstrated first that there was, at least theoretically, a balance of forces—an equilibrium—attained simply through the conduct of different maximizing agents. He outlined that conduct in terms of fixed behavior rules for those agents, describing how they responded to each other—that is, their mutual interaction and conditioning. Because there was a possible balance of forces, Walras could be said to have demonstrated mathematically the possibility of determinate outcomes. (The one that interested Walras most, of course, was the attainment of the highest possible satisfaction of wants under conditions of free competition.) Finally, by demonstrating that there could be a balance of forces between the variables he isolated for analysis—the particular variables he abstracted from a more complex social world—Walras showed that these variables formed a complete ideal system.

Conceived as a thorough methodological and epistemological review of pure economic theory with this Walrasian vision of the economic system at its center, Schumpeter's first book, *Das Wesen und der Hauptinhalt der theoretischen Nationalökonomie (The Nature and Essence of Theoretical Economics)*, was in many ways a tribute to Walras's accomplishment (1908, xii, xix; Swedberg 1991a, 24–31; Bottomore 1992, 15–20). Everywhere in Schumpeter's economic work there are echoes of this Walrasian model of the economy, viewed sometimes as a technique for understanding economic problems and sometimes as a vision of the economy in itself. His analyses of the "circular flow" (or sometimes "stationary flow") of "economic life," of "static equilibrium" models as a way of understanding the stability in the "economic system," of the history of the conception of a *"tableau économique,"* and of the "businessman's normal" are all examples ([1928] 1951, 51; [1911] 1934, 3–56; 1939, 4, 30–45; 1954a, 43; 1954b, 222–223, 963–971).

But Schumpeter came to have doubts about the completeness of this equilibrium model of the capitalist economy, summarized perhaps most vividly in a preface he wrote to the 1937 Japanese edition of his *Theory of Economic Development,* in which he reconstructed his relationship to Walras and his transcendence of this form of economics early in his career. Schumpeter wrote that he grew dissatisfied with the Walrasian schema not for methodological reasons, per se, but because of his own vision of the capitalist economy.

These first doubts concerned a feature of equilibrium analysis that can be drawn from the discussion above. Since each behavioral rule that made up the ideal equilibrium system described simply how one variable would respond to changes in other variables, nothing in the equilibrium system itself could be said to originate any change. The economist, of course, could model the system's response to change by adjusting the value of one or more of the variables and tracing out the consequences. But such a change—or perhaps, the explanation for it—lay outside the equilibrium system itself. While this was clearly a necessary feature of any such model equilibrium system, Schumpeter thought it was not, in reality, a feature of the capitalist economy.

The capitalist economy was not a "stationary" system, one that simply responded in predictable ways to outside changes. It was itself a dynamic process with its own internal source of change, he contended.

To Walras we owe a concept of the economic system and a theoretical apparatus which for the first time in the history of our science effectively embraced the pure logic of the interdependence between economic quantities. But when in my beginnings I studied the Walrasian conception and the Walrasian technique (I wish to emphasize that as an economist I owe more to it than to any other influence), I discovered not only that it is rigorously static in character (this is self evident and has been again and again stressed by Walras himself) but also that it is applicable only to a stationary process. These two things must not be confused. A static theory is simply a statement of the conditions of equilibrium and of the way in which equilibrium tends to re-establish itself after every small disturbance . . . A stationary process, however, is a process which *actually* does not change of its own initiative . . . If it changes at all, it does so under the influence of events which are external to itself, such as natural catastrophes, wars and so on. Walras would have admitted this. He would have said (and, as a matter of fact, he did say it to me the only time that I had the opportunity to converse with him) that of course economic life is essentially passive and merely adapts itself to the natural and social influences which may be acting on it, so that the theory of a stationary process constitutes really the whole of theoretical economics and that as economic theorists we cannot say much about the factors that account for historical change, but must simply register them . . . I felt very strongly that this was wrong, and that there was a source of energy within the economic system which would of itself disrupt any equilibrium that might be attained. ([1937] 1951, 159–160)

Throughout his career Schumpeter would repeatedly state in different ways the fundamental insight here: that the Walrasian vision, or indeed any economics focused on static theory, could demonstrate only how the economic system responded to external (noneconomic) changes ([1911] 1934, 3; 1954b, 13). Such an economics neither encompassed these *external* sources of change nor theorized any *internal* source of change. What was at stake, then, was not merely a methodological quarrel—especially if methodology is conceived as simply an application of logic to science—but rather a vision of what the economy was.

Schumpeter's entire development of a science of social transformation can be said to derive from two main criticisms of such "pure" equilibrium models. The first was that equilibrium models of capitalism did not illuminate any internal mechanism of change. The second, related, criticism reflected his view that the long-term stability or instability of any social or economic system, such as capitalism, rested not solely on its internal equilibrium processes but also on the stability of the institutions, social practices, and beliefs that supported the system—that is, on questions taken up in "economic sociology." Equilibrium analysis could speak only to the stability of the model system of fixed behavior rules that was abstracted from the social world. It could determine only whether that system would remain stable in the face of changes induced exogenously. But what of the institutions, beliefs, and practices that formed the assumed backdrop for that ideal system? Not only could that backdrop change in the course of history, but also those changes might affect or alter the very behavior rules and categories out of which the equilibrium model was constructed.

   In addition to these central critiques, Schumpeter could be said to have made others. He clearly considered unrealistic Walras's view of equilibrium arising from a sort of auction in which firms and households declared the hypothetical prices and quantities at which they would buy or sell (1954b, 1002). And he had a similar view of making the principle of marginal utility the centerpiece of economics, especially when that meant assuming that consumer demand and decisions, rather than entrepreneurial innovation, drove the economy ([1911] 1934, 65; 1954b, 918). But Schumpeter's judgment on these matters was not harsh. He called the auction assumption "heroic theorizing," and emphasized that "marginal utility was the ladder by which Walras climbed to the level of his general-equilibrium system" and that, having attained this system, principle itself really mattered very little, at least to Walrasian economics (1954b, 918, 1002).

First Steps toward a Science of Social Transformation

It is far easier to grasp the coherence and direction of Schumpeter's development after about 1911 if we recognize that the different methodological issues he considered, the varying topical interests he pursued, and the overall changes in his work all reflected an expanded vision of the subject of economics particularly and social science generally. All these issues were subsumed under the problem of understanding how societies change from one form to another—and more particularly, the problem of understanding the transformation of liberal capitalist societies. Schumpeter's first step toward a science of social transformation was his *Theory of Economic Development,* published in 1911.[2] There he attempted to explicate only those aspects of the complex process of historical change that could be grasped through pure theory as internal, economic sources of change. But it is clear that even at this early stage, he saw this problem as one abstracted from something broader. The opening sentence of *Economic Development* declared the "social process" to be "really one indivisible whole" ([1911] 1934, 3; see also [1937] 1951, 158).[3]

To explain how he would illuminate part of this broad and complex process with the tools of economic theory, Schumpeter made a distinction between static and dynamic theory. In static or equilibrium-based theory, the technique used for analyzing a system's responses to external change Schumpeter called *Variationsmethod,* a term whose meaning is much like the English "comparative statics" (Schumpeter 1908, 443). By dynamic theory, Schumpeter meant an approach that could do more than *Variationsmethod*—an approach that could show how the economy actually generated changes of its own accord. Even in his work prior to the *Theory of Economic Development,* Schumpeter had recognized a special role for dynamic theory, which he said dealt with different problems and had a special set of methods and materials (1908, xix, 182–183; see also Oakley 1990, 1; Swedberg 1991a, 29–30).

Dynamic theory, the pure theory of economic development, however, was not the same thing as a comprehensive description of how a particular economy had actually developed over time. Such a *history* of actual economic development would embrace every factor that figured importantly into that process of economic change, including, for example, wars or the discovery of gold; in a broad sense, the combined result of all these factors could be termed economic development (Schumpeter [1911] 1934, 59–60). But throughout his *Theory of Economic Development,* Schumpeter was careful to distinguish what he called "development in our sense of the term" *("in unserm Sinne")* (see, for example, Schumpeter 1912, 466). What he meant was a type or aspect of development driven not by contingent outside events but by something inherent in the economy.

That something, according to Schumpeter, was innovation by entrepreneurs—an argument generally regarded as his most important contribution to economic theory. Schumpeter contended that in an actually stationary economy—an economy with no internal sources of change—the same commodities would be continually produced in the same way; but in a dynamic, developing economy entrepreneurs found new commodities to produce and new ways of producing them.[4] His entrepreneurial theory of economic development allowed him to provide a unified explanation of capitalist phenomena that in his view were not well explained by traditional theory: credit, capital, profits, interest, and business cycles. In fact, Schumpeter argued that since credit, capital, profits, interest, and business cycles were obviously crucial elements of existing capitalist economies, and since they were (according to his argument) intimately connected to development and change in capitalist economies, the processes and mechanisms of development must be the defining features of capitalism. Since only dynamic theory could get at these processes, dynamic theory obviously was superior to static theory for understanding capitalist economies.

It is necessary to plunge briefly into the substance of his argument for the superiority of dynamic over static theory. According to Schumpeter, credit was at the center of the explanation of capitalist motion. His understanding of the nature of a stationary economy led him to conclude that in a stationary state, there would be (1) no idle productive resources, (2) no profits, (3) no capital (in the sense discussed below), and (4) a zero rate of interest ([1911] 1934, 30–31, 32–37, 44–46). Because of the first of these conditions, an entrepreneur with a plan for a new productive combination—a new commodity or a new way of producing an old one—would need to redirect existing productive resources to the new use (68). Because of the second, the entrepreneur's only source of the means to redirect those productive resources would be *credit*—actually a creation of bankers (ibid., 69, 95–115). (Schumpeter's model of a stationary economy simply assumed away the existence of capital, in the sense of produced means of production that endured for more than one cycle of production [ibid., 44, 45; Oakley 1990, 75].)

Thus it was only in a developing economy that *capital* appeared—in the guise of a fund of purchasing power available to the entrepreneur for the purchase and redirection of existing means of production ([1911] 1934, 122). As the first producer in a new market or as the sole producer with a better method for producing an existing commodity, the entrepreneur would initially earn a premium, which Schumpeter defined as the entrepreneur's *profit* (128–132). Because of the existence of this profit—and only because of it, in Schumpeter's view—the entrepreneur could pay interest on the bank credit, thus establishing a nonzero rate of *interest* (157–158). In this sense, interest was a phenomenon that could be derived wholly from the existence of profits—and thus wholly from the process of economic development.

Only with this schema in mind, Schumpeter argued, could one provide an adequate explanation of economic cycles as a phenomenon driven by the workings of the economy itself.[5] Schumpeter's basic argument was that the initial phases of entrepreneurial activity caused inflation and economic expansion, while later phases caused deflation and contraction ([1911] 1934, 224–236). Schumpeter claimed further that a certain pattern to cycles of booms and busts could be discerned and attributed to the fact that entrepreneurial possibilities arose cyclically and were fairly quickly exhausted, when they arose, by the most able business people (223).[6]

It is important to see how Schumpeter believed a dynamic, developing economy of this description differed from a stationary one. Like the stationary economy, the developing economy *tended* toward equilibrium after being disturbed. But unlike the stationary economy, the developing economy had internal sources of dynamism, and this meant that the economy, *in fact,* would rarely be in equilibrium. While it would tend in that direction, that tendency would constantly be interrupted. The nature of those interruptions was also crucial, for Schumpeter's view was that the interruptions were like periodic restructurings of the institutions and productive capacities of the society. So while he likened the action of the stationary economy to the flowing of blood through the circulatory system, he likened the changes brought about in a developing economy to the physiological growth of the body, taking place while ordinary circulation continued. He wrote: "Development in our sense is a distinct phenomenon, entirely foreign to what may be observed in the circular flow or in the tendency toward equilibrium. It is spontaneous and discontinuous change in the channels of the flow, disturbance of equilibrium, which forever alters and displaces the equilibrium state previously existing" ([1911] 1934, 64). Along these lines, Schumpeter would later in his career refer to the capitalist process of "creative destruction," by which he meant to signify a process that "revolutionizes the economic structure from within, incessantly destroying the old one, incessantly creating a new one" ([1942] 1976, 83).

Schumpeter's Historicism and Economic Sociology

Schumpeter's pursuit of a science of social transformation went further than what has already been sketched here—further, that is, than his theoretical account of the internal causes of economic change and development. To understand his sense of the limits of even his own theory of economic development—and of the need for research in economic sociology—it is important to understand his distinction between what he termed the capitalist "system" and the capitalist "order." By capitalist system, Schumpeter meant to refer to the Walrasian view of an economy as an interconnected, equilibrating system that could provisionally be abstracted from the broader social world and understood on its own. He meant only a set of "interdependent quantities," such as wages and prices, all "mutually determining each other" ([1928] 1951, 50). By capitalist order, which Schumpeter sometimes referred to as the civilization of capitalism, he meant a whole set of economic, social, and political institutions, many of which aided in the functioning of capitalism ([1928] 1951, 49; Oakley 1990, 13). Schumpeter contended that any science of social transformation had to account not only for the economic system but also for the whole economic order.[7] That economic order—its institutions, beliefs, and practices—was subject to historical, transformative processes that could not only impinge on the economic system from without but also fundamentally alter the elements of the system itself.

It is important to stress the continuity between Schumpeter's work on an economic theory of development and his work in economic sociology, because there is a danger of misunderstanding the significance of his case for economic sociology. Schumpeter's methodology was always subordinated to his purpose and ontological vision—his goal of understanding "the social process," which he conceived as "really one indivisible whole" ([1911] 1934, 3). According to this assumption, the designation of some "facts" as "economic" was an artificial one, which had some utility for the analysis of certain problems by use of equilibrium models, but not for understanding social transformation (ibid.). Economic sociology represented a step beyond this analytical distinction between economic and noneconomic toward an understanding of the whole social process.

What, then, was insufficient about economic theory—even his own theory of economic development—as a way of understanding social transformation? Schumpeter answered this question in his 1928 essay "The Instability of Capitalism" ([1928] 1951, 47–72). Much of the essay restated his theory of economic development as it pertained to an explanation of business cycles. He argued that the capitalist system was cyclical, but not unstable or prone to collapse (70). This diagnosis, however, could not serve as a prediction that capitalism would persist indefinitely any more than a clean bill of health regarding cancer could serve as a guarantee of immortality (71). Economic theory (even Schumpeter's own theory of economic development) could explain the formal properties of the capitalist system—and show its tendency toward business cycles—but it could show very little about the fate of capitalism as a whole social order.

With these considerations in mind, Schumpeter by the late 1940s had come to argue that economics comprised four "techniques": not just theory, but also statistics, economic history, and economic sociology (1954b, 12–24).[8] At this point, little more need be said about Schumpeter's view of the importance of pure theory, which he still identified with Walrasian or neoclassical economics. In moving beyond it, Schumpeter was not rejecting pure theory but reconceptualizing its place in the study of the social process as a whole. Indeed, in *History of Economic Analysis* Schumpeter made a very strong case for the importance of theory, not in the sense of "explanatory hypotheses" but in the sense of "creations of the analyst"—concepts like marginal utility, price elasticity, and so on. Likewise, there is not much to say about Schumpeter's discussion of the technique of statistics; its main function, he argued, was to clarify what facts needed explanation (13–15).

What is significant and new about this outline of the four techniques is the fact that it signifies Schumpeter's full embrace of a historical viewpoint. By this I do not mean simply a belief that some comprehension of a set of facts constituting "history" was necessary. I mean by this a historical viewpoint in the strong sense—a commitment to the idea that social structures and institutions are inherently transitory, and that the object of social scientific study is thus a process of change—an approach already suggested by the fact that Schumpeter was seeking a science of social transformation. The mature statement of this historical vision can be found in several places in *History of Economic Analysis*, where Schumpeter commented not only that "the subject matter of economics is essentially a unique process in historic time" but also, far more broadly, that "social phenomena constitute a unique process in historic time, and incessant and irreversible change is their most obvious characteristic" (1954b, 13, 435; see also 814).[9] Although these mature statements were penned in the 1940s, as early as 1918 Schumpeter was attuned to what he called the "laws of social being and becoming" and "the manner in which concrete conditions, and in particular organizational forms, grow and pass away" ([1918] 1991, 101).

A historical perspective of this kind places temporal limits on any lawlike social scientific claim, because such claims typically refer only to an interconnected set of institutions, groups, beliefs, and practices whose characteristic features change over time. Once one embraces this perspective, history becomes a necessary prerequisite for understanding the limits of any approach to social science. Thus Schumpeter began his discussion of the four techniques of economics in his *History of Economic Analysis* with a discussion of economic history that laid the ontological foundation for the discussion of the other techniques. The claim here that "the subject matter of economics" was "a unique process in historic time" implied that the study of history was not merely a self-contained adjunct to economics proper; it was, in a sense, a master subject, because a historical approach revealed the connections between two other fundamental techniques, theory and economic sociology. Insisted Schumpeter,

> Nobody can hope to understand the economic phenomena of any, including the present epoch, who has not an adequate command of historical *facts* and an adequate amount of historical *sense* or of what may be described as *historical experience*. Second, the historical report cannot be purely economic but must inevitably reflect also "institutional" facts that are not purely economic: therefore it affords the best method for understanding how economic and non-economic facts *are* related to one another and how the various social sciences *should* be related to one another. (1954b, 12–13)[10]

Of course it is not far from this argument for the advantages of a historical viewpoint to a defense of "economic sociology," which, in Schumpeter's view, meant the study of "economically relevant" institutions, beliefs, and practices ([1949] 1951a, 286–287). Indeed, Schumpeter distinguished economic history only slightly from economic sociology, writing that the "technique" of economic sociology introduced "social facts that are not simply economic history but are a sort of generalized or typified or stylized economic history" (1954b, 20). Elsewhere he argued that there was scarcely any difference between historians doing "problem" histories—studies concerned with particular, historically bounded sociological problems—and sociologists using historical materials, and least of all sociologists who defined sociology as the historical process (ibid., 786).

Schumpeter's clearest definition of economic sociology distinguished it from "economics proper" in the following manner.

> By "economic sociology," we denote the description and interpreta-tion—or "interpretive description"—of economically relevant institu-tions, including habits and all forms of behavior in general, such as government, property, private enterprise, customary or "rational" be-havior. By "economics"—or, if you prefer, "economics proper"—we denote the interpretive description of the economic mechanisms that play *within* any given state of those institutions, such as market mecha-nisms. ([1949] 1951a, 286–287; emphasis added)

In a similar vein, in his *History,* Schumpeter wrote that whereas eco-nomic theory dealt with "the questions how people behave at any time and what the economic effects are they produce by so behaving," eco-nomic sociology dealt with "the questions how they came to behave as they do," continuing: "If we define human behavior widely enough so that it includes not only actions and motives and propensities but also the social institutions that are relevant to economic behavior such as government, property, inheritance, contract and so on, that phrase really tells us all we need" (Schumpeter 1954b, 21).

Another way to state the point is that economic theory always rested on assumptions about economic sociology—it took for granted the exis-tence of certain institutions and modes of behavior. For example, Schumpeter regarded his own *Business Cycles* as a work of theory—not economic sociology—insofar as it did not directly examine social insti-tutions. The main analytical thesis of that book, concerning innovation, was "a purely economic argument not primarily concerned with the structure of society" (Schumpeter 1939, 96). But he admitted elsewhere in the book:

> It should be emphasized once more that our model and its working is, of course, strongly institutional in character. It presupposes the pres-ence, not only of the general features of capitalist society, but also of several others we, no doubt, hold to be actually verified but which are not logically implied in the concepts either of economic action or of capitalism. Our argument rests on (abstractions from) historical

facts which may turn out to belong to an epoch that is rapidly passing. (144)

There was nothing wrong, per se, about taking such matters for granted, or of not making such matters an object of study. But there were limits to what one could do without direct study of such matters. As Schumpeter put it: "All social sciences run up against certain fundamental problems of society, and none of them can afford to surrender its claims to some competence in matters of motors and mechanisms of social life" (Schumpeter 1954b, 783).

Richard Swedberg rightly emphasizes that Schumpeter thought the "recognition" of economic sociology as a field solves so many "methodological" problems (Schumpeter 1954b, 819; Swedberg 1989, 510). But it is important to recognize, also, why Schumpeter thought this was so. Schumpeter did not regard economic sociology as a *methodological* resolution to a *methodological* debate—a solution that could be arrived at by reflecting on the logic of scientific inference, for example. Economic sociology appealed to Schumpeter's *ontological* vision of the economy as a "unique process in historic time," his vision of the economy and society as a body that grows and undergoes structural change over time even while the circulation of commercial "blood" continues (1954b, 13; [1911] 1934, 64). By reference to this vision, Schumpeter could defend the study of the social body and its development—economic sociology—while still defending the independent legitimacy of studying the circular flow of economics.

With an understanding of this vision, it is possible to take a second look at certain features of Schumpeter's economic thought and see how they interrelate (in a more complex way than we previously grasped) within the whole of his work. For example, Schumpeter's theory of the entrepreneur, which occupies a vital place in his overall theory of economic development, appeared when we first saw it to be simply a feature of his theory—his pure theory—of economic development. But now that we are in a position to survey the whole of the approach to social science that Schumpeter thought was necessary to enable a dynamic theory of capitalism, we can see that the entrepreneur does not fit comfortably into the category of pure theory. After all, Schumpeter defined economic sociology—in contrast to economic analysis—so as to include "habits and all forms of behavior in general," meaning "not only actions and motives and propensities but also the social institutions that are relevant to economic behavior" ([1949] 1951a, 287; 1954b, 21). This definition of economic sociology is certainly wide enough to include the study of the entrepreneur. And indeed Schumpeter admitted this, as we have already seen in passages in which he wrote that his theory of entrepreneurs and economic development was "strongly [institutional] in character" in the sense that "it presupposes the presence, not only of the general features of capitalist society, but also of several others we, no doubt, hold to be verifiable but which are not logically implied" by the mere definition of capitalism nor by the marginalist theory of economic motivation.

Indeed, the entrepreneurial *class* plays a prominent role in Schumpeter's sociological essay "Social Classes in an Ethnically Homogenous Environment," where it is a prime example of a class with a distinct function to fulfill in a capitalist society—innovation—a class whose fate is linked to that function and its ability to fulfill it ([1927] 1991, 244–245). Richard Swedberg even argues that this is Schumpeter's most successful effort to link sociology with economic theory (Swedberg 1991b, 53). It is clear that by the time he wrote *Capitalism, Socialism, and Democracy,* Schumpeter regarded the decline of the entrepreneur—a key part of his theory of the decline of capitalism—as a sociological problem, a problem intimately interconnected with the structural transformation of liberal capitalist societies and clearly not to be explained by economic theory alone.

Implications of Schumpeter's Science of Social Change

Methodological Individualism and Rationality

Schumpeter is frequently credited with coining the phrase "methodological individualism" in his first major work, to signify economic theory that begins with the assumption of the existence of utility-maximizing individuals (Machlup 1951, 100). Schumpeter's point was that methodological individualism—the assumption of this individualistic standpoint for the purposes of economic theorizing—could be distinguished from political individualism, the assumption of an individualistic standpoint for the purpose of arguing for or against political positions (Schumpeter, 1908, 90). In particular, he was keen to emphasize that methodological individualism did not imply political individualism (ibid.).

While it is true that a whole chapter of *Das Wesen und der Hauptinhalt der theoretischen Nationalökonomie* is devoted to an attempt to "justify" the assumption of individualism in economic theory, some interpreters have drawn only one-sidedly on this chapter, failing to perceive the significance of the way that Schumpeter chose to defend methodological individualism. That defense is based on Schumpeter's insistence that the real nature of the economy is *a matter of indifference to economic theorists* (1908, 94).[11] But if methodological individualism was justifiable only for those who were uninterested in the true nature and structure of the economy, it seems clear that it might not be a justifiable starting point for those social scientists interested in that nature and structure.

His youthful defense of methodological individualism prefigured the strict limits that Schumpeter later placed on the usefulness and appropriateness of individualism as a method. These strict limits had reference, again, to Schumpeter's distinction between the economic system and the economic order, and to the methodological practices appropriate to the study of each. And because of this, the limitations had reference, as well, to Schumpeter's distinction between the science of the static economic system and that of the developing social order. The clearest statement of these limitations is to be found in Schumpeter's *History,* where he again argued (as he had in *Das Wesen*) that the marginalist economists who made use of the methodology of individualism were not necessarily political individualists. For the purposes of economic theory, they did make the "self-governing individual" the "ultimate unit" of analysis, resolving economic phenomena "into decisions and actions of individuals" without giving any thought to "superindividual factors" (Schumpeter 1954b, 888). This procedure, he argued, was perfectly adequate for static analysis, or the study of the "logic of economic mechanisms" (889).

But Schumpeter added that "sociological individualism," the extension of this methodology beyond pure economic theory, was, "of course, *untenable so far as it implies a theory of the social process*" (1954b, 888–889; emphasis added). Even though individualism was, "for a limited range of problems," a "sound methodology," it was "poor sociology and even poorer psychology," insofar as it treated "nations . . . [as] amor-

phous agglomerations of individuals" and "social classes . . . not [as] living and fighting entities but . . . [as] mere labels affixed to economic
functions . . . [and] individuals themselves [not as] living and fighting
beings [but as] mere clotheslines on which to hang propositions of economic logic" (886–887). Elsewhere he commented more acidly that a
commercial enterprise had to be understood as a "structure" or a "living
organism" and not just "the congeries of rational billiard balls that theory represents it to be" (Schumpeter 1939, 108).

The point, then, is that those interested in social development—the
transformation of societies from one form to another—had to transcend
the methodology of individualism and take into account group action
and the actual, socially produced ideas and practices that were en-
meshed in it. As we will see, Schumpeter's understanding of the tendencies that he believed were transforming liberal capitalist societies
was premised on an interpretation of the beliefs and practices that motivated particular modes of social action in a given form of society, and the
consequent treatment of classes and individuals as "living and fighting entities." For Schumpeter, social transformation meant the transformation of social structures and institutions, and he connected the maintenance and continuance of social institutions with the maintenance
of certain characteristic social beliefs and practices. We have already
seen how Schumpeter closely tied behavior—which is by assumption,
for economic theorists, only a matter of individual conduct—to institutions and thus to group conduct, arguing that economic sociology itself meant "the description and interpretation—or 'interpretive description'—of economically relevant institutions," a category in which he
included "habits and all forms of behavior in general" ([1949] 1951a,
286–287).

It is important to recognize that Schumpeter's argument implied more
than just the existence of separate methodologies for static economic
theory and dynamic social theory. Methodological individualism, of necessity, had to take the individual for granted, treating the individual as
the unexplained premise of explanation; underlying this was the assumption that one faced a choice between thus reifying the individual or
reifying some social category. Schumpeter's ultimate rejection of individ-
ualist methodology for his broader social scientific project can be explained in terms of his rejection of the analytical opposition between the
individual and the social apparent in this presentation of the choices

open to social scientists.[12] Schumpeter argued in his essay on social classes that the individual, contrary to the assumptions of individualism, is not an ultimate unit of analysis that needs no further explanation; but he did not embrace the contrary view that some social category—the class or the nation—*is* the ultimate unit of analysis. His argument suggested more subtly that the categories interpenetrate and presuppose each other. "We cannot help those who are unable to see that the individual is a *social* fact, the psychological an *objective* fact, who cannot give up toying with the empty contrasts of the individual *vs.* the social, the subjective *vs.* the objective," he wrote ([1927] 1991, 274). It is this argument that surely underlies Schumpeter's use of categories such as class and ideology in his sociological works.

Schumpeter's statement of the limits of methodological individualism was simultaneously a statement of the limits of the neoclassical model of rationality. In economics, methodological individualism meant the assumption that economic phenomena could be explained according to the *rational* utility-maximizing conduct of individuals. It meant, as Schumpeter put it, treating individuals as "clotheslines on which to hang [the rational] propositions of economic logic." Just as Schumpeter argued that methodological individualism was applicable and useful only in limited contexts, when, as he put it, the real nature of the economy was not of interest, so he argued that the neoclassical model of rationality was applicable and useful only in the same contexts.

In notes on rationality Schumpeter made for an informal discussion group at Harvard in about 1940, he insisted very strongly that the social-scientific practice of assuming that economic actors calculate rationally—setting up a "norm" or "logical rule" of rational behavior—was extremely useful in "constructing" models that could demonstrate the logical relation between economic elements ([1940] 1991, 322). Such a rational model, however, was "the product of the analyst's mind" and did not "say anything about reality or about anybody's actual behavior or rationality"; propositions based on such a model were in this sense "independent of the subjective rationality" of the economic agents in question (321). "We are setting up a model that . . . gives the conditions under which a certain given 'goal,' the maximization of profits, would be attained," Schumpeter argued (322).

Such models, propositions, and assumptions expressed, again, what Schumpeter called "the pure logic of the interdependence between economic quantities" ([1937] 1951, 159). As he explained it, the assumption of rationality was necessary to build a model that illuminated this logic. Thus the idea of treating economic agents as rational utility maximizers "was the ladder by which Walras climbed to the level of his general-equilibrium system," but it was "the general equilibrium system which is the really important thing" (1954b, 918). And because it was the final model that was important in such cases, Schumpeter argued, "propositions such as the one about the monopolist's profit maximum are independent of the [actual] subjective rationality of the individual monopolists" ([1940] 1991, 326). That is, the question of the actual motivations and conduct of monopolists—the *"Realgrund,"* or real reason, for their conduct—did not matter at all (ibid., 327).

But justifications of this kind—procedure *x* is justified when goal *a* pertains—necessarily imply a limit to the justification. When *a* does not pertain, *x* is not justified. So Schumpeter immediately added that the actual motivation and conduct of economic agents was irrelevant only when the question at hand was the creation of abstract models of the logic of interdependence between economic quantities—only "so long as we are interested in that proposition as such and in nothing else" ([1940] 1991, 326). It should be clear, then, that everything Schumpeter argued about the limitations of methodological individualism also pertained to a critique of one aspect of methodological individualism, treating individuals as rational utility maximizers. But to transcend these limits, one could not merely "start from the given behavior of the individual" (1954b, 889). One had to go "into the factors that formed" that behavior, treating the "formative influences of environments, group attitudes, group valuations, and so on" (ibid.).

A word of warning is due here. Schumpeter used the terms *rationality* and *rationalization* in several different senses—not just to refer to the assumption of rational utility maximization discussed above. In the following section I will discuss Schumpeter's distinction between traditional custom-bound social action and innovative social action. This distinction is crucial to understanding how Schumpeter deployed the term *rationalization,* meaning the gradual historical process by which he thought traditional modes of action were being replaced by nontraditional "rational" ones. Rationalization in this sense was already an important theme in Chapter 3.

Agency and Rationalization

Schumpeter's broad historical distinction between traditional and rational forms of action—a key part of the later version of his transformative conception of democracy—grew out of his broad development toward a science of social transformation. More specifically, it grew out of an analogous contrast in his economic writings between traditional and entrepreneurial or innovative action. In fact, at the very center of Schumpeter's theory of economic development was the innovating entrepreneur. Thus Allen Oakley quite justifiably argues that Schumpeter's theory of capitalist motion actually requires a creative agent (Oakley 1990, 95).

Why is this? Schumpeter contended that "the problem that is usually being visualized" in neoclassical economic theory "is how capitalism administers existing structures" ([1942] 1976, 84). But he differed significantly from most neoclassical economists even in envisioning the kind of agency that administers but does not alter existing structures in an idealized static model of an economy. While neoclassical economics envisioned this type of agency as individual rational utility maximization, Schumpeter insisted that the actual maintenance or administration of existing structures relied on economic agents' adherence to tradition and custom. "In theory," Schumpeter argued, economic actors are seen as responding to changes and maintaining the structures of capitalism by "acting in accordance with a knowledge of the best combination of present means under the given conditions," but in reality "every individual can act promptly and rationally" only by relying on customs and social practices, "because he is sure of his ground and is supported by the conduct . . . of all other individuals, who in turn expect the accustomed activity from him ([1911] 1934, 42, 79). The tendency toward equilibrium, or the "circular flow of economic life," was thus best explained, Schumpeter thought, by the fact that "everyone will cling as tightly as possible to habitual economic methods and only submit to the pressure of circumstances as it becomes necessary" (ibid., 8–9).

Now Schumpeter very clearly contrasted this type of action or agency—habitual activity within the confines of existing social structures—with the economic agency exhibited under certain conditions by entrepreneurs or other innovators. "Everyone knows," Schumpeter wrote in *Cycles,* "that to do something new is very much more difficult than to do something that belongs to the realm of routine, and that the two tasks differ qualitatively and not only in degree" (1939, 99; see also [1911] 1934, 85).

For economic purposes, the "something new" that Schumpeter had in mind, of course, was economic innovation. We have already seen Schumpeter's argument that whereas in a stationary economy—an economy with no internal sources of change—the same commodities were continually produced in the same way, entrepreneurs in a dynamic, developing economy found new commodities to produce and new ways of producing them; this was innovation. What was significant about innovation, however, was not simply that it involved doing something descriptively new but that it involved stepping outside of existing institutions, established ways of doing and producing things—specifically, for example, making arrangements for the diversion of resources from existing productive enterprises to new ones.

We have already seen that Schumpeter thought that ordinary economic theory focused on how capitalism administers existing structures, but a theory of economics that focused on entrepreneurial agency and innovation, he continued, shifted attention to the problem of how capitalism "creates and destroys" such structures ([1942] 1976, 84). Or, as he put it elsewhere, the focus on innovation put emphasis not on the continuous flow of economic life but on the larger structural and transformational problem of how *economic agents* were implicated in *"discontinuous change* in the channels of the flow" (Schumpeter [1911] 1934, 64; emphasis added).

Given this, Schumpeter was quite clear that one of the differences between his dynamic theory of economic development and ordinary neoclassical equilibrium models concerned agency. He wrote in *Development:*

> Hence, our position may be characterised by three corresponding pairs of opposites. First, by the opposition of two real processes: the circular flow or the tendency towards equilibrium on the one hand, a change in the channels of economic routine or a spontaneous change in the economic data arising from within the system on the other. Secondly, by the opposition of two theoretical apparatuses: statics and dynamics.

> Thirdly, by the opposition of two types of conduct, which, following reality, we can picture as two types of individuals; mere managers and entrepreneurs. ([1911] 1934, 82–83)

It is important to emphasize from the outset that Schumpeter's skepticism toward methodological individualism usually prevented him from reducing entrepreneurial agency to an individual capacity, either one given universally to all individuals as individuals, or one given only to some individuals and not to others. As to the idea that this form of innovative agency could be understood solely as an individual capacity, Schumpeter contended that to bring about "change in the channels of economic routine," entrepreneurial agents had to confront a series of problems whose dimensions he described not psychologically—as a matter of an individual having a new idea—but sociologically. In part this is evident in Schumpeter's understanding of the nature of an innovation, and his contrast of innovation with invention. Schumpeter regarded an invention as merely a technical or "scientific novelty" or breakthrough (1939, 84; see also 8–10, 84–102). An innovation might take the form of "giving effect, by business action, to a particular invention," but in general, "the making of the invention and the carrying out of the corresponding innovation are, economically and sociologically, two entirely different things" (85). To innovate, entrepreneurial agents had to overcome the tendency to act according to socialized routine, and had, moreover, to organize other groups and individuals to do the same (Schumpeter [1911] 1934, 86–87; Schumpeter 1939, 100). "Successful innovation is, as said before, a task sui generis," Schumpeter wrote in "The Instability of Capitalism"; "it is a feat not of intellect, but of will. It is a special case of *the social phenomenon of leadership*" ([1928] 1951, 65; emphasis added).

By referring to this form of agency as a "social phenomenon," Schumpeter was emphasizing that even in those cases where entrepreneurial agency might be tied to individual ability, the *significance* of it could be understood only sociologically. The significance of an innovation and the problem of carrying it out had to do, that is, with the social organization of production at a given time, and with the beliefs and practices that would simultaneously support the existing methods of production and resist changes (1939, 100). This is one reason why Schumpeter referred to innovation as a "social process" (ibid., 86). There is another. In capitalist society, this social process of innovation relied heavily on individual entrepreneurs. But this was a feature only of "the sociology of industrial society" or of capitalism (1939, 96, 144; [1942] 1976, 131). Schumpeter contended that it was equally possible for innovation to be undertaken not by individuals but by bureaucracies ([1942] 1976, 131–133). In fact, Swedberg argues that, over time, Schumpeter put far more emphasis on the concept of "innovations" than on "entrepreneurs," and stressed that teams and other groups could carry out innovations just as well as could individuals (1991a, 171–173).

As for the idea that innovation could be attributed only to certain individuals—the idea that some people were innovators and some were not—Schumpeter usually rejected this, but not always. "Nobody ever is an entrepreneur all the time, and nobody can ever be only an entrepreneur," Schumpeter wrote in one passage; "this follows from the nature of the function, which must always be combined with, and lead to, others" (1939, 103). Innovation, in other words, was most profitably understood as one dimension of agency.

I stress these related points because the value of defining innovation as a form of agency—the value of recognizing forms of social action that upset or challenge existing social beliefs and practices—is lost when innovation is taken to be nothing other than a natural capacity of certain individuals, in contrast with others. It is one thing to hold that social agency in general can be charted on several dimensions, including action in accordance with given beliefs, practices, customs, and so on, and action that defies or upsets such established patterns. But it is another to link these dimensions of action in a determinate way to particular individuals or classes of individuals. First, it is highly implausible that any action could be either wholly tradition-bound or wholly new.[13] And second, it is no more useful to explain that new social practices and structures come into being because some people, who introduce them, are innovators, than it is to explain that "the reason opium puts you to sleep is that it has dormitive powers."[14]

Schumpeter's theory of entrepreneurial agency exposed some of the limits of the typical neoclassical assumption of rational utility maximization. But it was at its weakest when he suggested in scattered passages that this form of entrepreneurial agency could be understood as the possession of an individual—that it was a characteristic marking some people as a class apart from others, and that it could be reduced in some way to individual rather than sociologically developed abilities. Passages such as the one quoted above in which Schumpeter defined "two types of individuals" that he named "managers and entrepreneurs" can be read this way ([1911] 1934, 83). Others reveal a more complex view.

Science and Ideology

So much is made of Schumpeter's disapproving statements about economists who subordinated science to practical aims that to set oneself against the chorus of interpretive unanimity concerning these statements is daunting indeed. In the view of the chorus, Schumpeter plays the role of a crusading behaviorist, out to purge value judgments from science, where they do not belong. Now there is no doubt that Schumpeter heartily disapproved of economists who, as he put it, "indulged their strong propensity to dabble in politics, to peddle political recipes, to offer themselves as philosophers of economic life" (1954b, 19). There is also little doubt that Schumpeter applied this criticism in particular to John Maynard Keynes. (Although it is difficult to read Schumpeter's pronouncements on this subject without a sense of their irony, given his own political interests and his attempt to "peddle" a finance plan during his disastrous stint as finance minister in Austria.) But Schumpeter's prudential warnings about the dangers of practically oriented social science need to be handled carefully, lest they obscure his sophisticated understanding of the inescapable interpenetration of science and ideology. In fact, given the near unanimity of contemporary political scientists, who accept that discussions of such issues must be structured around a distinction between statements of facts and statements of values, there is a serious danger that Schumpeter's disapproval of Keynes and a handful of other economists will be misrepresented or misunderstood as signifying his assent to a doctrine he did not hold.

This danger is quite evident in the secondary literature on Schumpeter. Robert Loring Allen, in his two-volume biography, makes frequent allusions to Schumpeter's disdain for economists with political ambitions, but he fails to put these statements in their proper context—Schumpeter's own theory of science and ideology—and he resorts to contortions to explain away Schumpeter's political commitments and involvements as somehow purely scientific (see, for example, Allen 1991, 1: 86, 144, 150, 154, 163–164; 2: 60, 155, 168–169). Such contortions would be unnecessary with a realistic assessment of Schumpeter's understanding of the problem of science and ideology. In a quotation already cited above, David Held comes close to attributing to Schumpeter the view that the problems of political commitments and social science can be analyzed in terms of the distinction between statements of fact ("an empirically based 'realistic' model of democracy") and expressions of values ("excessive speculation and arbitrary normative preferences") (Held 1987, 164). But Schumpeter's views cannot be adequately explained using this dichotomy.

Schumpeter did not put great weight on a philosophical theory of facts and values when confronting the problem of social scientists and practical politics. His approach to these problems centered not on these categories but on the categories of *science* and *ideology*—and, in any case, he did not depend on a strong ontological or epistemological distinction between any philosophically defined categories. Schumpeter's theory of the process of science and his criticism of politically minded economists can be understood only by reference to his sociological theory of science and ideology. This alone marks him as quite different from mainstream political scientists today. According to his theory of the process of science, a socially constituted, ideological "vision" of the social world and of particular problems within it was a necessary part of every scientific endeavor. Thus for Schumpeter, unlike many later social scientists, science could not be freed of ideology—but at the same time, its ideological component did not thoroughly discredit a science or a scientific argument.

How did Schumpeter come to develop such a theory of the relationship between science and ideology? Why, that is, did he feel the need to develop such a theory? The answers lie in his early economic training, in the general development of his social science beginning in the second decade of the twentieth century, and in the planning of his massive *History of Economic Analysis* in the 1940s. The first two points can be approached from the standpoint of the last.

The planning of the *History* presented Schumpeter with two general problems: to justify the study of the history of economic analysis—to argue that the history of the discipline of economics was relevant to anyone who wanted to understand contemporary economic theory—and to define the subject matter of his book, to define exactly what he meant by economic analysis and its history. Schumpeter's sociological conception of science and his understanding of the interrelation between science and ideology provided him with a justification for studying the history of economics in answer to those who might otherwise have assumed that the history of a social science was merely an inventory of "concepts, methods and results" that were "outmoded" from the modern standpoint (1954b, 4).

Although these justificatory tasks took on some urgency as Schumpeter turned to the *History,* he did not approach the problem for the first time in the 1940s. Not only did he take on the problem in the context of the approach to social science that he had developed over the course of the previous three decades (as we will see below), but he took it on after years of considering the claim that neoclassical economics was in some sense ideologically vitiated. The problems raised by this claim most likely first appeared to him in the course of a seminar he attended in 1905 and 1906 in which he, along with fellow student Ludwig von Mises and the marginalist professor Eugen von Böhm-Bawerk, debated with Marxist students Otto Bauer, Rudolf Hilferding, and Emil Lederer concerning Marx's labor theory of value and theory of exploitation (Allen 1991, 1: 39; Bottomore 1992, 9, 20).

Hilferding's view was not that the marginalists' class position led them to posit a false or distorted theory of value; marginalist economic theory, to his thinking, had some merits. Rather, Hilferding argued that by assuming that the natural starting point of economics was the relation of the individual to commodities rather than the social relations of human beings, and by assuming the goal of a theory of value was to determine the prices of commodities, Böhm-Bawerk ruled out the possibility of understanding social-structural and dynamic dimensions of economic questions.[15] To point out the ideological bias of the marginalists was to show how the partiality of their conception of economics derived from ignoring the social structure and the process of social change of which they were a part, and to demonstrate the broader political implications of this incomplete conception.

Schumpeter must eventually have felt this attack acutely, since, as we have seen, while he developed his approach to social science, he incorporated more and more of this type of critique of neoclassical economics, arguing that the limitations of this approach could be best understood by reference to the fact that marginalism abstracted economic problems from their sociological context. Of course, I do not mean to imply in any way that Schumpeter came to accept the Marxist theory of value; he did not (see Schumpeter [1942] 1976, 23–29). But like Hilferding, he came to see the limitations of marginalist economics in terms of its inadequate conception of social structure (economic sociology) and historical change (economic development).

We can begin to understand how Schumpeter sought to resolve these issues by looking at another methodological issue that Schumpeter resolved analogously: the problem of economic equilibrium and dynamics. With respect to economic equilibrium and dynamics, Schumpeter had argued that certain crucial economic problems simply could not approached from the standpoint of pure marginalist economic theory, because marginalism abstracted the logic of economic relations from the social structure in which those relations took place. For quite similar reasons, Schumpeter argued that an analysis of the pure logic of a science—or the pure logic of the individual scientist's relation to her subject of study—could not get one very far. First, the field of science contained an irreducibly historical and transitive dimension, namely the set of socially constituted concepts and so on available at any time for scientific work. The pedagogical state of a science, Schumpeter argued, "implies its past and cannot be satisfactorily conveyed without making this implicit history explicit" (1954b, 4). He elaborated: "The problems and methods that are in use at any given time embody the achievements and carry the scars of work that has been done in the past under entirely different conditions . . . [A]ny treatise that attempts to render 'the present state of science' really renders methods, problems, and results that are historically conditioned and are meaningful only with reference to the historical background from which they spring" (ibid.).[16] It should be evident that this introduction of the transitive element of science that took on meaning only in historical and social contexts went far beyond the mere idea that it was *a good idea* to state new conceptions and arguments in terms of contrasts and comparisons with old ones.

Schumpeter took a dim view of methodological arguments that attempted to apply styles of argumentation developed in the specialized field of logic directly to particular scientific endeavors.[17] If scientific methodology could be deduced from timeless pure logic, the history of a science might well be irrelevant to its current practitioners. But rather than trying to deduce their methodologies from the abstract principles of logic, prior to engagement with actual scientific problems, Schumpeter argued that scientists should develop methodologies tailored to the explanatory problems faced by each science. Even in his earliest methodological writings, in *Das Wesen,* Schumpeter argued, based on this, that methodology should comprise the last chapter of any work (1908, xiv). And late in his career, Schumpeter contended that one could not judge actual scientific "habits or rules of procedure" simply by "logical standards that exist independently of them," because actual scientific practice contributed to logic (1954b, 5).[18] Thus the distinction between the philosophy of a science and the study of its actual historical development in relation to changing problems blurred considerably for Schumpeter. "The highest claim that can be made for the history of any science or of science in general," Schumpeter wrote, "is that it teaches us much about the ways of the human mind . . . it displays logic in the concrete, logic in action, logic wedded to vision and to purpose" (ibid.). Again, it should be evident that Schumpeter was going considerably beyond the commonsense view that methodological arguments should be illustrated by concrete examples. As he put it: "A sort of pragmatic or descriptive logic may be abstracted from observation and formulation of scientific procedures—which of course *involve,* or merge into, the study of the history of sciences" (ibid.).

Such arguments, which tended to make indispensable both a sociology of science and the understanding of science as a process unfolding over time, had added force for economists, who after all were engaged in the study of "a unique historical process . . . so that, to a large extent, the economics of different epochs deal with different sets of facts and problems," Schumpeter wrote (1954b, 5). Thus it was necessary to situate economic ideas and doctrines within their proper sociological and historical context. This argument went a considerable way toward the position that a *sociology* of science was a necessary condition for truly understanding it, which was, in fact, Schumpeter's view.[19] Schumpeter was quite clear that a sociology of science was an approach that

> treats of science as a social phenomenon . . . [and] analyzes the social factors and processes that produce the specifically scientific type of activity, condition its rate of development, determine its direction toward certain subjects rather than other equally possible ones, foster some

methods of procedure in preference to others, set up the social mechanisms that account for success or failure of lines of research or individual performances, raise or depress the status and influence of scientists
(in our sense) and their work, and so on. (ibid., 33)

Thus in the study of economics as well as in the study of the economy, a
sociological approach—and a corollary emphasis on *how things came to
be* as they were—was crucial.[20]

It would appear from Schumpeter's embracing of a sociology of
science that the door would be open to just the sort of critique of marginalism that Hilferding had launched. Thus it is worth seeing how
Schumpeter's conception of the process of science—the "filiation" of scientific ideas, as he called it—could partially protect economic theory
from such a critique (1954b, 6).

Schumpeter's mature statements on the problem of the relation between theory and practice or between science and practical political
aims are to be found in his posthumously published *History,* which he
worked on throughout the 1940s, and in his address to the American
Economic Association in 1949, "Science and Ideology," published in the
American Economic Review that year. Schumpeter began by asserting, as
he often had, that the attempts by scientists to "serve their country and
their age" had been a source of error ([1949] 1951c, 268). As a preliminary step toward understanding this problem, he turned first to what he
took to be the Marxist theory of ideology, which he described in fairly
broad terms as the theory that thought is determined by the economic
structure of any society (ibid., 271). Schumpeter argued that, according
to his understanding of the Marxist theory of ideology, classical political
economy could be understood as "nothing but the ideology of the industrial and commercial bourgeoisie" and that "statements which display
ideological influence are ipso facto condemned thereby" (1954b, 35–
36).[21]

Against this theory of ideology, Schumpeter argued that the source of
ideological bias was not the fact that social structure—or social class—
determined one's outlook in its entirety and vitiated it completely. The
source of error was that any understanding of the social world—scientific understandings included—began not with the perception of brute
facts but with an ideological and "prescientific" perception defining the
basic social or economic phenomena to be understood and the facts rele-

vant for understanding them. As Schumpeter put it, scientific procedure "starts from the perception of a set of related phenomena which we wish to analyze" ([1949] 1951c, 272). Schumpeter referred to this perception as the scientist's "vision," and he argued, as we have seen above, that it necessarily included results of others' analyses (ibid.). As Schumpeter put it in a passage cited above, the pedagogical state of a science "implies its past" (1954b, 4). What was essential, however, was that beginning with a vision was not something to be deplored; rather, it was a necessary condition, a necessary step, for science (Schumpeter [1949] 1951c, 281).

Having established this set of problems of interest, Schumpeter argued, the economist turned to a scientific analysis that "operates upon the material proffered by the vision" ([1949] 1951c, 272). Schumpeter's general argument was that in some way this scientific process, operating on the original vision, acted to reduce the ideological vitiation. In part, this analysis involved the employment of a body of theory—not "explanatory hypotheses" or the embodiments of "final results of research that are supposed to be interesting for their own sake," but "mere instruments or tools framed for the purpose of establishing interesting results" or "in [Joan] Robinson's unsurpassably felicitous phrase . . . a box of tools" (Schumpeter 1954b, 14–15). These tools, Schumpeter insisted, were ideologically neutral. Such theory consisted of a set of concepts, such as "pricing, income formation, cycles, international transactions, and so on," an "all-purpose apparatus of analysis"; it was a "simple and harmless sort of thing" (ibid., 16, 18). For this reason, Schumpeter argued, it was a mistake for Marxists, for example, to reject terms such as "price or cost or money or value of the services of land" in describing socialist society because they are "tainted with a capitalist meaning" (ibid., 18; see also [1949] 1951c, 274).

> From the outset it is clear that there is a vast expanse of ground on which there should be as little danger of ideological vitiation as there is in physics . . . The Walrasian system *as it stands* may or may not admit of a unique set of solutions but whether it does or not is a matter of exact proof that every qualified person can repeat. Questions like these may not be the most fascinating or practically most urgent ones but they constitute the bulk of what is specifically scientific in our work. And they are in logic although not always in fact neutral to ideology. ([1949] 1951c, 274)

The second insulation of scientific practice from ideological vitiation, Schumpeter contended, came from a concentration on the facts that were defined as relevant according to the economist's vision. It is important to note that Schumpeter did not argue that there was a theory-neutral observational language whose use could allow the facts to be the ultimate arbiter of theories. He had already rejected the idea that there could be any scientifically relevant preanalytic perception of facts ([1949] 1951c, 272). Thus Schumpeter described as follows the process by which science progressed from ideologically conditioned models:

> This work consists in picking out certain facts rather than others, in pinning them down by labeling them, in accumulating further facts in order not only to supplement but in part also to replace those originally fastened upon, in formulating and improving the relations perceived—briefly in "factual" and "theoretical" research that go on in an endless chain of give and take, the facts suggesting new analytic instruments (theories) and these in turn carrying us toward the recognition of new facts. (ibid.)

This process produced "*scientific models,* the provisional joint products of their interaction with the surviving elements of the original vision, to which increasingly more rigorous standards of consistency and adequacy will be applied" (Schumpeter 1954b, 42).[22]

With this conception of the process of science in mind, it is possible to turn to the question of how Schumpeter viewed the distinction between facts and values. As Schumpeter put it, in discussing the battle of methods,

> the epistemological problem in itself is neither very difficult nor very interesting and can be disposed of in a few words . . . An "ought," that is to say, a precept or advice, can for our purpose be reduced to a statement about preference or "desirability." The relevant difference between a statement of this nature . . . and a statement of a relation . . . reveals itself in the fact that acceptance of the latter depends exclusively upon the logical rules of observation and inference, whereas the acceptance of the former (the "value judgements") always requires, in addition, the acceptance of other value judgements. (1954b, 805–806)

Thus Schumpeter agreed that it was not possible to move logically from an "ought" to an "is" and that "judgements about ultimate values" were "beyond the scientist's range except as objects of historical study"

([1949] 1951c, 271; see also Schumpeter 1954b, 336–337). But since Schumpeter considered an ideology to involve far more than simply value judgments, he argued that this distinction held little interest: "The reader will realize that considerations" such as those discussed above "greatly reduce the practical importance of the issue so far as its purely epistemological aspect is concerned . . . [*This*] *explains, in part at least, why the controversy on value judgements did not produce any very important results*" (1954b, 807; emphasis added).

How, then, should interpreters understand Schumpeter's disparagement of economists' quasi-political activities? First, Schumpeter at times criticized economists who dabbled in policy not for having ideologies or even for making value judgments, but for failing to see the way in which economic theory and economic policy took place in a particular historical and sociological context—and for failing to make that historical and sociological context itself an explicit object of study. Their orientation toward *mere* policy, that is, blinded some economists to the broader problems of the state of society in which a policy took on significance. Schumpeter's essay "English Economists and the State-Managed Economy" has been correctly seen as a screed against particular policy-minded economists. But Schumpeter's actual complaint was that "the work of almost all English economists centers in the problems of postwar readjustment under the conditions set by the long-run tendency toward socialism (in our sense) and by the pattern of laborism *rather than in the problems of that tendency and of that pattern themselves*" ([1949] 1951b, 302; emphasis added).

When Schumpeter turned to the actual problems connected with combining value judgments with scientific work, his argument was prudential, not categorical: it was premised on the consequences for science of mixing the two, not on the epistemological distinction (as Schumpeter called it) between an "ought" and an "is." Putting aside "the logical status of value judgements within a science," Schumpeter argued, "the substitution of a creed for analytic ability as a criterion of selection of the personnel of a science will impede advance," and "those who profess to be engaged in the task of widening, deepening, and 'tooling' humanity's stock of knowledge . . . fail to fulfill their contract if, in the sheltering garb of the scientist, they devote themselves to what is really a particular kind of political propaganda" (1954b, 805). Moreover, once scientific battle took on the tones of political battle, it was difficult for opponents to admit any merit in each others' arguments (ibid., 281–282).

But elsewhere Schumpeter argued that this was not the biggest problem scientists faced. On the contrary, "low standards of rigor and sloppiness of thinking have been worse enemies of scientific economics than has been political bias" (1954b, 233). Furthermore, low standards and sloppiness, presumably, included the failure to take a historical viewpoint in understanding economic problems, for Schumpeter also argued that "most of the fundamental errors currently committed in economic analysis are due to lack of historical experience more often than to any other shortcoming of the economist's equipment" (ibid., 13).

6

Democracy and Equilibrium

Thanks to the enormous prestige of neoclassical economics, it has become common to borrow tools and methods of analysis characteristic of that school and apply them to the study of politics. No one familiar with rational choice and game theory can have failed to note this tendency within political science. Much has been written about the validity, scope, and significance of the theory of agency imported into political science via rational choice and game theory—one premised generally on rational, maximizing individuals—and on the characteristic problems to which this theory of agency is applied and the view of politics that emerges from its application.[1] Equilibrium analysis, which constitutes only a part of rational choice approaches, is also frequently applied to political problems. And it can be applied to politics without necessarily involving rational choice theory.[2]

Contrary to the idea that democracy can be best understood as an equilibrium system of mutually conditioning social and political forces, I argue that there are serious limits to *equilibrium* as a conceptual framework for understanding democracy. The two main lines of argument to support this derive from Schumpeter's two main critiques of equilibrium models, elucidated in Chapter 5. First, equilibrium models of democracy are by design incapable of accounting for the potential dynamism spawned by the deployment of innovative new democratic ideologies. Second, they neglect the role of democratic ideologies in the maintenance, creation, and destruction of political institutions. These two problems are inextricably interlinked.

Like his adoption of elite theory's assumptions (see Chapter 4),

177

Schumpeter's use of some equilibrium tools provides the opportunity for the immanent critique of his view of democracy as method. Schumpeter's development of a science of social transformation provided the basis for a sharp critique of equilibrium analysis (see Chapter 5). And yet the elite, method-oriented conception of democracy that Schumpeter produced rather late in his career, in *Capitalism, Socialism, and Democracy,* contained unmistakable elements of an equilibrium theory.

Mine is thus a Schumpeterian critique of a Schumpeterian model of democracy. But I do not claim that Schumpeter "would have" or "meant to" mount the critique I offer of equilibrium models. The critique here uses Schumpeterian tools but goes beyond what Schumpeter himself expressly argued. I make comprehensive use of the concept of ideology and its place in the analysis of social transformation. I do this because the twin deficiencies of equilibrium analysis pointed out by Schumpeter can be seen to prevent equilibrium models from dealing adequately with ideological change, a point that can be made especially clear by drawing on his understanding of innovation. The procedures necessary to construct equilibrium models make it nearly impossible to grasp the ways in which innovative democratic ideologies may be involved in social transformation. But Schumpeter himself did not explicitly link all of these problems in this way.

In addition, the significance of this critique transcends Schumpeter. Similar critiques apply to the work of Anthony Downs, whose *Economic Theory of Democracy* owed a deep intellectual debt to Schumpeter and is regarded as a progenitor of much of the extensive rational choice literature on democracy. In recent years other political scientists, such as Adam Przeworski, Barry Weingast, and Peter Ordeshook, have, in a different sense, examined democracy from the standpoint of an equilibrium framework (Ordeshook 1992; Przeworski 1991; Przeworski 1999; Weingast 1995; Weingast 1997), and the same critiques apply to this contemporary literature, as well.

Equilibrium in Schumpeter's Elite Conception

Just as his theory of economic development focused on economic innovation as the key to development, Schumpeter's transformative conception of democracy made room for an innovating, internal source of dynamism—the deployment of democratic ideologies; the identification of political, economic, and social problems according to those ideologies; the application of the forms of analysis sanctioned by such ideologies to newly identified problems and social structures; and engagement in forms of social action warranted by those ideologies and carried out in their name. This transformative conception thus clearly broke the bounds of equilibrium analysis.

On the other hand, C. B. Macpherson dubbed Schumpeter's elite conception "equilibrium democracy" (Macpherson 1977, 77). Now this characterization, though apt, is only partly so. Schumpeter's elite conception of democracy includes elements of an equilibrium model. But it is also comprised of forces that tend to undermine the attainment of equilibria, but which can still be modeled using equilibrium analysis, and elements that escape equilibrium analysis altogether.

In particular, Schumpeter's elite conception of democracy shares two important attributes of equilibrium models, an emphasis on outcomes that are due to a balance of forces, and fixed "behavioral" rules (see Chapter 5). To say that equilibrium models attribute outcomes to a balance of forces is to say that equilibrium models view outcomes as a by-product of the interaction of the forces themselves. In social science, where the forces in question are often intentional actions, this usually means that outcomes are viewed as an unintended by-product of the relevant actors' actions. This is a basic assumption of neoclassical economics, which views the price and quantity supplied of a good, for example, as the unintentional result of the attempts of consumers to maximize utility and of sellers to maximize profits. Schumpeter was making an analogy between his elite conception of democracy and precisely this feature of neoclassical economics when he argued:

> It does not follow that the social meaning of a type of activity will necessarily provide the motive power, hence the explanation of [the activity of individuals in society] . . . [T]he social meaning or function of parliamentary activity is no doubt to turn out legislation and, in part, administrative measures. But in order to understand how democratic politics serve this social end, we must start from the competitive struggle for power and office and realize that the social function is fulfilled, as it were, incidentally. (Schumpeter [1942] 1976, 282; and see 279)

Schumpeter's emphasis on democracy as an elite "competitive struggle for the people's vote" also stressed the idea of outcomes resulting from the balancing of forces (ibid., 269).

As for Schumpeter's use of "fixed behavior rules," this is clearest in his famous descriptions of the conduct of politicians. He emphasized strongly the idea that professional politicians were power-seekers who dealt in votes in just the same sense that economic theory presumed businessmen and women to be profit-seekers who dealt in commodities. Politicians who form parties, he argued, simply "propose to act in concert in the competitive struggle for political power" (ibid., 283). The more he emphasized this analogy to profit maximization, the more it appears he devised a fixed behavior rule for politicians.

Like the equilibrium models of pure economic theory, Schumpeter's elite conception largely focused on the political "effects" produced by the behavior of political actors—and not "the question how [people] came to behave as they do" (1954b, 21). This, too, was a hallmark of equilibrium models, in his view.

But Schumpeter did not argue that elite-dominated democracies tended very often to be in a state of equilibrium. In fact, he regarded elite coalitions as the political equivalents of economic oligopolies, which undermined the possibility of perfect competition. He even argued that his elite conception could encompass "cases . . . strikingly analogous to the economic phenomena we label 'unfair' or 'fraudulent' competition or restraint of competition" ([1942] 1976, 271).[3] And he thought that oligopolistic and monopolistic competition in economics was inadequately captured by standard equilibrium models, whose focus was price competition and its equilibrating tendencies. Still, it must be said that from Schumpeter's standpoint, this consideration would not have detracted much from the relevance of an equilibrium model. An equilibrium model could be applied to a system that was itself very rarely in equilibrium, he contended (1954b, 964–965).

Finally, there is a key aspect of his elite conception of democracy that, in Schumpeter's own view, could not be portrayed in a true equilibrium model: his view that professional politicians may act like economic entrepreneurs or innovators. In his most famous economic work, he argued that entrepreneurs do not merely make production decisions according to a fixed production function (behavior rule), but rather innovate, creating what he called new combinations. In *Capitalism, Socialism, and Democracy,* he argued analogously that professional politicians at times do not act merely according to a fixed behavior rule but actually create new combinations, innovative party programs and platforms that exploit long-standing political opportunities, and unmet preferences and needs ([1942] 1976, 270–271, 275–276). Schumpeter even argued notoriously that this innovation amounted to creating and manipulating a "Manufactured Will" (270).

Given this combination of equilibrium and nonequilibrium aspects, what should we make of Schumpeter's elite conception of democracy? How vulnerable is it to his critique of equilibrium models? The answer depends on how much weight we put on the different elements of the model. The more our interpretation singles out his definition of politicians as vote seekers and his view that democratic outcomes are due to just the competition between such vote seekers, the more the elite conception of democracy appears vulnerable to his two critiques. (As we will see, Anthony Downs stressed precisely these elements.) Specifically, such a model appears to lack what Schumpeter termed an internal source of change. Politicians would merely maximize votes by responding to exogenously induced changes in the preferences of voters. And such a model would, as he would have put it, focus on the effect of political behavior, while neglecting the historical-sociological question of how such behavior came to be.

The more our interpretation stresses Schumpeter's idea of politicians as entrepreneurial innovators, the less vulnerable to his critiques of equilibrium models his elite conception of democracy appears to be. This process of innovation would certainly constitute an internal source of change. And a strong emphasis on this feature of his conception would require a corollary de-emphasis on the equilibrium aspects of the conception.

But if we weigh this entrepreneurial-innovative aspect of the model heavily, very little would separate the elite conception from Schumpeter's decidedly nonelite transformative conception of democracy. For if we admit that political agents may deploy new ideologies and innovatively create new coalitions, strategies, and forms of action, why should we be constrained to do so solely within the confines of Schumpeter's narrow definition of democracy as a particular minimalist "institutional arrangement"? After all, his critique of equilibrium models involved the argument that economists must think not only about how economic conduct administers capitalism, but also how it creates and destroys the institutional structure of capitalism. This problem, he insisted, could be answered effectively only by a social science that includes the tools of economic sociology. Should one not also ask how political agents may act innovatively to create and destroy—or to challenge and transform—the institutions Schumpeter posited as "democracy"? But this question leads us toward his transformative conception.

Perhaps more disturbingly for Schumpeter's elite conception, we might ask, why should we suppose that only elite professional politicians can engage in this sort of innovation? As we have seen (in Chapter 4), the entire weight of his position rested on elite-theory assumptions, such as the idea that elite politicians may "act in concert in the competitive struggle for political power" but "the electoral mass is incapable of action other than a stampede" ([1942] 1976, 283). Drop this assumption from an approach to democracy stressing political innovation, and one is no longer dealing with an elite conception of democracy at all. One is left with a conception of democracy that focuses on the radicalizing, dynamic effects of movements that attempt to realize democratic values and act on democratic ideologies, as well as on the social and economic implications of spreading democratic practices—something very much like what I have termed a transformative conception of democracy. But this is not the direction in which Schumpeter's heirs took his argument.

Equilibrium and Ideology

Schumpeter never developed a comprehensive theory of ideology. In developing his "economic sociology," however (see Chapter 5), he did seek a social science that would neither take ideas, "motives," and "propensities" at their face value nor treat them as given, in order to study their effects. He sought an approach that would explain how a pattern of ideas came to be, how such patterns were products of a social system, and how they were the possession of distinct groups (1954b, 21; [1942] 1976, 11, 12; [1949] 1951a, 287, 289; [1949] 1951c, 269–271; 1946, 270). He applied a variety of terms to this problem: the analysis of "ideology"; the "sociology of knowledge"; the study of the "civilization," the "cultural complement," or the "socio-psychological superstructure" of capitalism ([1942] 1976, 11, 121; [1949] 1951c, 269–270; 1954b, 33). In discussing it, Schumpeter attempted to avoid several pairs of opposing problems. He tried to explore ideas as products of "historical conditions" and "social system[s]" and as the attempts of "groups or classes [to] explain to themselves their own existence" without falling into the trap of arguing that ideas were determined, in the strong sense, by these things (1946, 270; [1942] 1976, 10–12; [1949] 1951a, 287–289).

He argued that ideology was a ubiquitous feature of thought, while insisting that this did not mean scientific advance was impossible. He denied that ideology could be reduced to false consciousness, and with this he rejected rigid distinctions between ideology and science ([1949] 1951c; [1949] 1951a, 286 n. 8; 1954b, 33–47). Similarly, while arguing that thought was always socially conditioned, he insisted that ideological constructs enabled, as well as constrained, constructive social thought and investigation ([1949] 1951c; 1954b, 33–47; [1942] 1976, 264–268). His discussion of the social tendencies he thought were undermining capitalism—and his related transformative conception of democracy—should be seen as applications of this understanding.

Drawing on Schumpeter and other sources, then, I wish to treat ideology as a structured system of ideas, concepts, cognitive practices, and values shared by a group, and necessary for orienting their thought and action.[4] Several aspects of this definition are worth elaborating.

1. An ideology is a structured system, not just an undifferentiated list of ideas, concepts, and values. It is not just the elements of an ideology that are important but also the specific way those elements relate to each other. Further, the ideology itself conditions and specifies which ideas or values are relevant and important, as well as the aspects of experience that are held to be so self-evident and incontrovertible as to be accorded the status of facts (see below). As structured patterns of thought, ideologies confront each other as wholes, not as single beliefs that have to be abandoned in light of specific evidence, or as individual values that have to be disavowed in light of targeted refutation.[5] Nineteenth-century bourgeois democrats and twentieth-century working-class democrats, as Schumpeter described them, would have disagreed about whether liberal capitalist societies were democratic, but this disagreement could not have been reduced to mere disagreement over the "facts." Nor could it be understood simply as a clash of values, many of which, after all, were shared. In general, Schumpeter treated democratic ideologies as complex systems of theoretical assumptions, transcendent values, warrants for action, common empirical references, and elaborated philosophical claims ([1942] 1976, 250–252, 264–268).

2. No ideology is merely the creation or possession of a single individual. As Karl Mannheim put it:

It is far from correct to assume that an individual of more or less fixed absolute capacities confronts the world and in striving for the truth constructs a world-view out of the data of his experience . . . In contrast to this, it is much more correct to say that knowledge is from the very beginning a co-operative process of group life, in which everyone unfolds his knowledge within the framework of a common fate, a common activity, and the overcoming of common difficulties. ([1936] 1985, 29)

Schumpeter called methodological individualism "poor sociology and even poorer psychology" precisely because it did not treat classes and other groups as "living and fighting entities" (Schumpeter 1954b, 886–887). Schumpeter's transformative conception of democracy viewed democratic ideologies as forms of thought guiding the political action of particular bourgeois and working-class groups.

3. Since ideologies provide the categories and assumptions that structure active thought, it is impossible to imagine thinking without ideologies. Schumpeter argued that even science—the category of knowledge most often contrasted with ideology—was inextricably intertwined with ideology. His argument that one's ideological "vision" made scientific inquiry possible (Chapter 5) is analogous to Clifford Geertz's view that ideology makes "an autonomous politics possible by providing the authoritative concepts that render it meaningful, the suasive images by means of which it can be sensibly grasped" (Geertz 1973, 218).

4. At any given moment in history, different groups are likely to have different ideologies. One must recognize, then, the possibility of ideological conflict between groups and, more specifically, the likelihood that any serious social, economic, or political conflict will likely have an ideological dimension.

5. Given a particular social group, its ideology may be different at different times. Thus one must recognize the possibility of ideological change, due either to the transformation of a single group's ideology or to a historical development bringing a new group with a new ideology into prominence. Any serious social, economic, and political changes will likely have an ideological dimension. In linking his discussion of bourgeois revolution and capitalist transformation to the deployment of democratic ideologies, Schumpeter subscribed to both points 4 and 5.

6. It is now widely accepted in the philosophy of science that facts cannot be regarded as the final arbiters between competing theories, because theories, in part, constitute the facts that are said to be relevant in

any theoretical controversy.[6] The same may be said in the context of ideological conflict. Ideological systems as a whole determine the relevant facts and issues for debate, and the way in which those facts will be viewed. Bourgeois and working-class democrats, as Schumpeter defined them, would have disagreed about which facts were even relevant in assessing how democratic a liberal-capitalist society was—economic facts, or just political ones.

7. If facts are in this sense "theory-laden," so too are "interests." As E. P. Thompson has pointed out in his history of the English working class, interests—even class interests—are not given facts about a group that can be read off its social position (Thompson 1963, 2–3). Schumpeter described the growth of working-class demands for democratic control of industry not as a recognition of objective interests but as an ideological development (Schumpeter, 1920–21, 337). Similarly, social movement theory no longer assumes that group interests are fixed and given but incorporates "the collective processes of interpretation, attribution, and social construction" that make the articulation of interests possible and that therefore "mediate" between a group's social position and the actions it takes (McAdam, McCarthy, and Zald 1996, 2).

8. As both Schumpeter and Geertz point out, ideologies do not merely delude their bearers as many social scientists suggest; in many cases, they enable them to formulate problems and take action. Given this view, and the recognition that ideologies may change, we should recognize that ideologies may be actively reconstructed, reconsidered, and deployed—not just regurgitated. Schumpeter called bourgeois democratic ideology "the classical doctrine of collective action," and underlined its link to the concrete historical struggles in which it was deployed ([1942] 1976, 265, 266–267).

It is the recognition of an ideological dimension to social change—and the recognition that groups may innovatively deploy ideologies—that makes an adequate conception of ideology seem indispensable for understanding social transformation. More particularly, what is crucial is the recognition that in reconstructing ideologies, groups and individuals are reconstructing whole systems of thought—systems that determine how such things as facts, values, and preferences are to be defined, and provide rules for relating these things to social action.

By design, however, equilibrium models rely on what I have termed "fixed behavioral rules" that purport to explain how people in general relate such things as facts, values, and tastes to courses of action, and on exogenously induced change. Since these rules must remain fixed for each model, such models cannot incorporate changes in ideological systems—changes in the patterns of thought that determine how facts and interests are to be related to action—as endogenous sources of political and social change.

The purpose of a sophisticated conception of ideology is to help us investigate how different groups at different times have interpreted the facts of their social situations, defined their interests, and chosen forms of action. Because equilibrium models take such "behavior rules" to be fixed, they must attribute change to exogenous adjustments in the specification of tastes, facts, interests, and so on. But it is not just an exogenous change in tastes (for example) that may lead to new forms of action and interaction; it is also, more generally, a change in the ideology that sets the relationship between tastes, facts, and interests or defines the very concepts themselves. Equilibrium models, then, must assume that which, from the standpoint of the study of ideology, must be investigated.

The point here is analogous to Schumpeter's first critique of equilibrium models in economics (see Chapter 5). In Schumpeter's view, standard economic theory treated production functions (a kind of behavior rule) as fixed, and thus could attribute change and dynamism in capitalism only to exogenously induced changes in the price and quantity produced of the materials employed in production. He introduced the entrepreneur into his model to introduce internally generated spontaneous changes in production functions. But over time he realized that even the introduction of the entrepreneur—even the introduction of internal, spontaneous innovations in production functions—was insufficient for understanding economic development in the broadest sense. This leads to his second critique, for the manner of producing innovation in different forms of society varied, and the investigation of this problem required the tools of history and economic sociology, not equilibrium analysis. The workings of capitalism itself, he argued, tended to undermine the cultural, ideological, social, and political foundations of the kind of entrepreneurship that was capitalism's engine.

Schumpeter's transformative conception of democracy also incorporated the possibility of endogenous, spontaneous change. Not only did the transformative conception account for the existence of political agents—in this case, whole social groups and movements—who redefined the relationship between such things as tastes, facts, and interests, and thereby generated new forms of political action. It also accounted for the possibility of truly thoroughgoing ideological restructurings of these social relations, as when the bourgeoisie used democratic ideologies to challenge aristocratic power, and when the working class used democratic ideologies to challenge the structure of industry.

Ideological innovation, then, cannot be grasped by equilibrium models as a source of social transformation. But what has this to do with democracy? To answer, let us work backward toward the problems of ideology and equilibrium, beginning with a standard, if somewhat fuzzy, definition of democracy as rule by the people. Admittedly, its denotation is unclear, but the moral and political force of the catchphrase is not. It calls on us to create conditions under which the people—including women, the poor, and disfavored minorities—may act so as to exercise meaningful control over the institutions that affect their interests and their lives. Now even this, of course, leaves such terms as *the people, meaningful control,* and *interests,* and such questions as which institutions are relevant, subject to controversy and interpretation. What shall we do about this problem of interpretation?

If we are to think democratically about the interpretation of these terms, we should consider the way in which various groups may themselves come to define them—or, more specifically, how such groups may come to define themselves, their interests, and the extent of meaningful control that they seek—as well as the facts, problems, issues, and institutions they consider relevant to the articulation and realization of their own democratic vision. Democratic theorists, then, have to be interested in the ideological process by which such groups define democracy.

Naturally there is an analytical distinction between the theoretically best definition of democracy (if there is one), and the definition any particular group may develop at any given time. But it is a mistake for democratic theorists, of all people, to put too much weight on this distinction. The development of political capacities, the recognition of public interests, and the development of a sense of efficacy are classic themes in democratic theory. Since Jean-Jacques Rousseau, participatory and developmental theorists of democracy have insisted that democracy is not just a defined set of institutions but is also a process of development or growth. Rousseau, John Stuart Mill, John Dewey, G. D. H. Cole, and

Carole Pateman have all, in different ways, focused on the problem of developing people's capacities to act democratically (Rousseau 1967; Mill [1865] 1991; Cole 1920; Dewey 1935; Pateman 1970). Indeed they have insisted, in different ways, that the development of these capacities is a significant part of what makes democratic participation itself valuable. These classic issues cannot be separated from the ideological process by which people come to decide on the meaning and application of democratic ideals for themselves and their own situations. Democratic theorists, then, must take a crucial interest in the ideological process by which groups define themselves, their interests, and the meaning of democratic control, as well as the facts, problems, issues, and institutions that they consider relevant to their own democratic vision. But equilibrium models deal inadequately with this process. Democratic theorists must not be indifferent to this weakness.

A Schumpeterian Critique of Equilibrium Democracy

Schumpeter's First Critique Applied

There are at least three related reasons for regarding Anthony Downs's *An Economic Theory of Democracy* as an equilibrium model. First, this characterization comports with Downs's own understanding of his project, as an attempt to devise a theory of democracy that could be integrated into a "general equilibrium" theory of the economy (Downs 1957, 3). Second, the two main features of Schumpeter's elite conception of democracy that had the most influence on Downs were precisely the equilibrium-model features identified above. Downs gratefully acknowledged Schumpeter's intertwined claims that legislative and policy outcomes in democracies were merely the by-products of competing forces, and that what motivated parties to participate in this competition was not principle but the desire for power or votes. "Parties formulate policies in order to win elections, rather than win elections in order to formulate policies," he wrote, attributing his arrival at this axiom to his reading of Schumpeter's "profound analysis of democracy" (Downs 1957, 28, 29 n. 11, 284).[7]

Third, Downs developed these equilibrium model features even further, with the result that his *Economic Theory* displays every one of the aspects of equilibrium models discussed in Chapter 5. His overall goal, he said, was to formulate a set of predictions, a "behavior rule for democratic government" that would indicate what kinds of goods and services it would provide (Downs 1957, 3, 164–204). And virtually all of the twenty-five "testable propositions" with which he closed his book were lawlike claims premised on equilibrium analysis. Further, throughout the book, Downs devised his behavior rules as descriptions of how strategic political actors could be expected to respond to each others' choices. And Downs clearly abstracted his political actors and behavior rules from a social reality he admitted was more complex, and consistently defended his choices in terms of model construction, not plausibility or realism.

Schumpeter's key criticism of equilibrium models was that they could include no endogenous sources of change. Because such models consist of an interrelated system of fixed behavior rules, each of which describes specified responses to specified environmental changes, change must ultimately be attributed to something outside the model itself. Downs's was certainly just such a model. No actor in his model did more than respond to the behavior of others; change had to originate outside the model or not at all. Downs argued, for example, that strategic, election-oriented parties chose their policies and ideological positions based on the ideological distribution of voters. But the reasons for the ideological distribution of voters, Downs argued, were outside the scope of his model (Downs 1957, 140). I argue, however, that ideological innovation can be seen as an endogenous source of change in politics, much as product innovation may be seen as a source of endogenous change in economics.

Let us look at this more closely. Downs argued that voters decide which party to vote for based on a comparison of the utility stream received from the present government with the expected utility stream from the opposition party, were it in power (Downs 1957, 49). But orientations toward such things as utility and information and the way in which they are to be related to a course of action are quintessentially ideological matters, ideologies being structured systems of thought that determine a group's orientation toward the empirical world of facts and information, and its perception of its interests, or its "tastes," or of what is useful. Changes in ideological systems, then, may surely lead to important changes in political action—and as I have already pointed out, such changes cannot be reduced to mere exogenous respecifications of tastes or information.

By choosing equilibrium analysis, Downs chose to forgo an exploration of such endogenous ideological change. Hence the kind of ideological innovation—the kind of spontaneous change in the nature and distribution of ideologies—that Schumpeter envisioned in his *transiformative* conception of democracy was simply not a part of Downs's model.

Serious as they are, such considerations are not reason enough to reject Downs's model for all purposes, however. Schumpeter was right to contend that equilibrium analysis can demonstrate "the logic of the situation" (1954b, 17), or what Satz and Ferejohn term "the structure of certain environments" (Satz and Ferejohn 1994, 74, 87). Downs's model certainly could illuminate the structure of choices faced by parties and voters—*given* certain environmental conditions, and *given* certain fixed assumptions about the actors. But democratic theorists, and those more broadly interested in democratic change, cannot be satisfied with such limitations.

Further, Downs attempted to do more than provide a description of the "logic of the situation" for parties and voters. In his ambition to construct a thoroughgoing theory of democracy, Downs extended his analysis to attempt to explain ideologies themselves and their meaning and significance for political actors. He attempted, further, to explain why citizens would come to agree on particular standards and prerequisites of democracy, satisfied by the existence of a set of political institutions, providing little opportunity for popular participation. His attempt to deal with these matters with definitions and behavior rules devised for use in an equilibrium model led to a series of serious weaknesses.

One sign of such problems can be found in his chapter "How Uncertainty Affects Government Decision-Making," meant to explain why democracy became what he termed *representative democracy*—why, in his terms, there were people who led, persuaded, or purported to represent others (Downs 1957, 82–95).

An economist might say that Downs simply began the chapter with an assumption of "perfect information"—the assumption that voters know exactly which parties and policies will most promote their interests—and that he then relaxed this assumption and traced out the consequences. But Downs assumed more than perfect information. From the outset, he asserted that under conditions of perfect information "no citizen can possibly influence another's vote" (Downs 1957, 83). This assertion equated political certainty or imperviousness to persuasion solely with the possession of facts.[8] Given voters' "taste structure[s]" or definite knowledge of what is "beneficial to them," nothing but facts could influence their votes, Downs argued (ibid.). This entailed assuming that there existed a set of "facts" that were unaffected by any theoretical conception of the world, and that individual voters had tastes that they themselves could regard as fixed and not subject to persuasive reconsideration.[9] These are important claims, and claims virtually forced on Downs by the need to build an equilibrium model out of fixed behavior rules relating given information and tastes to behavior.

But these assumptions are not sensible ones from the standpoint of any reasonably sophisticated conception of ideology. For surely adopting a different theory, a different conception of the world, a different ideology, could change not just a person's tastes but also her sense of the appropriate way of relating her tastes to action, her sense of what her interests were, and her sense of what aspects of the empirical world were relevant to making decisions about a given problem and which purported facts she deemed reliable. The idea that only facts could change a person's voting decisions seems absurd from this standpoint.

Already we can see that Downs's choice of equilibrium analysis made it nearly impossible for him to discuss such ideological change as a source of democratic dynamism. As Downs's argument proceeded, this problem blossomed into a serious internal contradiction, as becomes clear when we turn to the next chapter, "The Development of Political Ideologies as Means of Getting Votes." Downs again assumed that facts (and knowledge of what was personally beneficial) were directly available to voters without the mediation of what he termed "philosophies"; on this basis he argued that *if* voters could "expertly judge every detail of every stand taken," then political parties would not even need to present ideologies (1957, 98). Peculiarly, however, Downs expressed the problem in this way: if voters *could* possess such detailed information, they would relate it to "their own views of the good society" or *"their own ideologies"* (ibid.; emphasis added). The gist of Downs's argument from this point on was that voters *could not make this comparison,* because they lacked sufficient information about parties and their policies. Parties formulated ideologies to make voter decision making possible.

The key for us is the reference to voters' ideologies. If Downs meant that voters' ideologies were their "views of the good society," views that would at the very least determine or condition preferences, then his earlier discussion of persuasion as *fact giving* would have to be regarded as incomplete. Persuasion would have to entail more than giving facts. But this is not necessarily what Downs meant by ideologies in this chapter. Here Downs defined *party* ideologies as nothing but shorthand versions of complete sets of policy stands. He might also have meant that *voters'* ideologies were just shorthand versions of their fully elaborated preferences concerning every issue, but if so, it is difficult to understand why voters would have a difficult time relating parties' positions to their own. According to this definition—ideology-as-shorthand—it should have been no more difficult to assess a party's positions than to formulate one's own ideology.

Downs's failure to resolve this contradiction was again clear when he turned to the subject of "How Rational Citizens Reduce Information Costs" (1957, 220–237). Here Downs argued that voters cared only about streams of utility income, not philosophies or ideologies per se, but that they lacked information about how the various policies undertaken by governments might affect those streams. Therefore, they relied on others—"specialists"—to make those judgments. They chose these specialists, Downs argued, by assessing their criteria for making decisions about policies—that is, *by assessing what he elsewhere termed ideologies.* Thus Downs reproduced the same contradiction in discussing specialists that he had created in discussing party ideologies.

If Downs had held on to his view of persuasion-as-fact-giving and to his conception of facts and tastes as given things—both necessary for the creation of a tractable equilibrium model—then his view of voter decision making would have to be seen as either severely limited or fraught with contradiction. But had he embraced a more complex view of ideology, then his view of persuasion-as-fact-giving would have to be rejected, along with equilibrium analysis. It is impossible to imagine a tractable behavior rule that would incorporate the possibility of open-ended change in styles of argument, suppositions about the nature of the social world, or broadly epistemological presuppositions about what counts as good evidence in political argument. Yet these are precisely the sorts of things that may be understood as sources of endogenous, spontaneous ideological change.

Schumpeter's Second Critique Applied

Schumpeter's second critique of equilibrium models held that in abstracting an equilibrium system from a complex social world, social scientists could highlight the "effects" produced by the given behavior of actors, but could not address "the question how [people] came to behave as they do" (Schumpeter 1954b, 21). Such matters fell victim to a sharp distinction, imposed by the requirements of equilibrium analysis, between what was studied—the effects of the mutual interaction of defined behavior rules—and what was left out. This criticism applies to Schumpeter's elite conception of democracy in two ways. First, the elite conception did address certain beliefs, practices, and motivations that Schumpeter argued were significant in democracy—especially those of vote-seeking professional politicians. But it focused on the effects of those behaviors and did not explain how they came to be—or, more particularly, how they came to be accepted as democratic. Indeed, he could say little about the historical origin of these behaviors, since he regarded them as universal and nearly transhistorical. Virtually all the behaviors, beliefs, and practices that he attributed to elite democracy resulted from supposedly constant, universal features of social interaction. Elite politicians, he said, have the ability to "act in concert in the competitive struggle for political power," but "the electoral mass is incapable of action other than a stampede"; as a result, he claimed, "collectivities act almost exclusively by accepting leadership" (Schumpeter [1942] 1976, 283, 270). Schumpeter's elite conception of democracy rested so heavily on such universal claims that it is difficult to know what is specifically democratic about it.

Now this can be answered by turning to what Schumpeter said was the institutional arrangement of democracy: competing parties, a parliamentary system of government, and limited political freedoms (Schumpeter [1942] 1976, 269–283). But this only leads to the second problem, for these institutional arrangements clearly were what made leadership *generally* into specifically *democratic* leadership. But, how, as Schumpeter put the question, did these arrangements come to be? On this, the elite conception of democracy was virtually silent.

Schumpeter was aware of this problem. His elite conception is famous for its stark dismissal of the so-called classical theory of democracy—of the view of democracy propounded by its supporters. Yet the more he emphasized his elite conception of democracy as *just* a method, the harder it was for him to explain how democracy "came to be" and what beliefs sustained it—a problem he discussed under the heading, "the survival of the classical doctrine" (Schumpeter [1942] 1976, 264–268). When he turned to this problem he admitted that one had to understand that democracy was *not* just a method, not just a mechanism for accepting elite leadership—that is, not just what the elite conception said it was—but that "it actually becomes what from another standpoint *I have held it incapable of becoming,* viz., an ideal or rather a part of an ideal schema of things," a set of beliefs and practices motivating political action (ibid., 266; emphasis added). However, unlike his transformative conception, his own elite conception of democracy had virtually nothing to say about this.

In accentuating the equilibrium aspects of Schumpeter's conception, Downs re-created similar problems within his own conception of democracy. As we have already seen, equilibrium models necessarily rest on a sharp distinction between the fixed behavioral rules whose interaction and effects are the center of attention, and a set of exogenous factors that are not directly studied. Like Schumpeter, Downs abstracted universal behavior rules from the historical complexity of beliefs, practices, and motivations. Similarly, this tended to make Downs's theory one of rational behavior *within* the exogenous constraints of democratic institutions, rather than one explaining the growth, sustenance, and death of democratic institutions. Hence there is something arbitrary about his suddenly proffered list of institutional conditions defining democracy in the second chapter of *An Economic Theory of Democracy:* a single party chosen to govern; periodic elections; universal suffrage; one person/one vote; majority rule; acceptance of nonviolent, democratic procedures by both winners and losers; electoral competition (Downs 1957, 23–24). These democratic institutions and standards appear arbitrary because equilibrium analysis imposes so sharp a distinction between the behavior rules that actually constitute the model and the external circumstances from which those behavior rules are abstracted. They appear arbitrary because they bear no necessary relation to the fundamentals of Downs's model—essentially all based on rational utility maximization.

As with Schumpeter, Downs's willingness to take such institutions for granted hid from view not only their maintenance but also the ideological struggle over their creation, the problem, as Schumpeter put it, of how they came to be. And since his model generally did not or could not account for such matters, Downs's line of argument could collapse into contradiction when he suddenly had to include them in his analysis.

For example, although Downs contended that universal suffrage was a definitional prerequisite for democracy, he added in a footnote that "in some democracies, women or permanent resident aliens or both are not allowed to vote" (Downs 1957, 23 n. 5).[10] Downs's failure to recognize the contradiction here was emblematic of his failure to recognize that the struggle to create the conditions of democracy could not without considerable cost be left out of a theory of democracy. The publication of Downs's book in 1957, a crucial early year of the civil rights movement in the United States, made this failure even more poignant.

Contemporary Treatments of Democracy and Equilibrium

The place of equilibrium models in social science has only grown in the forty years since Downs wrote *An Economic Theory of Democracy*. In fact, a spate of recent work testifies to the fact that equilibrium theories of democracy are alive and well (Ordeshook 1992; Przeworski 1991; Przeworski 1999; Weingast 1995; Weingast 1997).

The spirit of Schumpeter's elite conception of democracy as method lives on in this work, in various ways. Adam Przeworski opened a recent article with the declared purpose of defending "a 'minimalist,' Schumpeterian, conception of democracy" (Przeworski 1999, 23). His reasons for defending such a conception, it must be said, are different from Schumpeter's. But the use of the tools of equilibrium analysis to defend a defanged version of democracy is unmistakably similar. And while Schumpeter advanced an elite conception of democracy in part as an alternative to his transformative conception, which envisioned economic democratization, Barry R. Weingast seems to take it for granted in his articles that a minimally regulated capitalist economy simply *is* a key feature of democracy.[11]

Nevertheless, these are equilibrium theories of democracy in a somewhat different sense. While Schumpeter's and Downs's conceptions were of equilibria *within democratic institutional structures,* much of the recent literature addresses the problem of how democracy can be achieved and stabilized, and thus is concerned with democratic institutions *as equilibrium outcomes of political competition.* Likewise, since these theories are expressly concerned with the transition from authoritarian to democratic systems, it is clearly not true that they simply neglect the problem of transformation. But they do share problems that, in Downs's and in Schumpeter's case, I show to be tied to the neglect of internal sources of change in democracies. The fact that recent equilibrium theories try to incorporate "institutions" and account for dynamism—but still display characteristic problems similar to those in earlier work—actually strengthens the case for the limits of equilibrium analysis. (I have already argued that Schumpeter's two critiques of equilibrium models, though they can be analytically distinguished, tend to merge in practice. The two critiques, that is, refer to different faces of the same general problem. In this section, then, I will not take pains to distinguish the two critiques.)

The recent equilibrium treatments of democracy attempt to demonstrate how it would be rational for various groups in a conflictual, authoritarian society to agree to democratic procedures. From a rational choice perspective, this is a difficult problem, since it may mean some parties forgo their ability to get what they want by undemocratic means. Such a process may involve citizens or political organizations acting together to enforce democratic procedures even though the benefits from this would appear to be collective.

Przeworski posits this as a problem of parties weighing the potential benefits of acting undemocratically (plus the costs of sanctions imposed by others) against the potential benefits of acting democratically. As he puts it, the question is: "How does it happen that political forces that lose in contestation comply with the outcomes and continue to participate rather than subvert democratic institutions?" (Przeworski 1991, 15).[12] Weingast similarly proposes viewing this problem as one of various parties deciding whether to punish a government for transgressions against democratic procedures (Weingast 1997). Since what they are attempting to explain is the adoption and maintenance of such procedures, their focus is overtly institutional.[13] Nevertheless, these political scientists do not assume that adherence to procedural norms is automatic. On the contrary, they show how such norms could be self-enforcing—that is, how agreement on democratic procedures could constitute an equilibrium condition, such that no one would want to violate the agreement, given what others would do (Przeworski 1991, 22; Weingast 1997, 245).

Weingast argues, for example, that the establishment of democratic rules in a nondemocratic society requires a social agreement on policing violations of such rules. Indeed, he assumes that "all citizens have preferences and values about the appropriate limits on government" and that "each citizen, based on his or her preferences and values, is able to classify state actions into two mutually exclusive categories: legitimate actions and fundamental transgressions" (Weingast 1997, 245–246). But surely both the achievement of social agreement about democratic rules and the development of group and individual capacities to "classify state actions" involve ideological change and work. By this I mean that they involve changing or reconstituting values, moving people to reconsider the aspects of social life they consider significant, and validating new forms of political action and expression. After all, it was not until the twentieth century that large numbers of people in this country considered women's lack of suffrage or the systematic oppression of African Americans to be violations of democratic procedures. Weingast's assumption that people can recognize violations of democratic principle effectively treats preferences for democracy or democratic values and the ability to classify state actions according to whether they violate democratic norms as unproblematic attainments and characteristics of individuals, prior to social interaction. But precisely insofar as these are not really individual attainments but are politically and socially developed—precisely insofar as these are inherently ideological—leaving them outside the scope of one's model excludes important problems from consideration. The ability to recognize that Jim Crow laws and discriminatory poll taxes were "transgressions" of democracy was not simply a given in American social and political interaction. Despite two hundred years of American liberal discourse, the growth of anything like a consensus around the idea that these constituted antidemocratic practices was a difficult and precarious achievement. In particular, it required ideological work—performed by the civil rights movement—to demonstrate to most Americans that there was a transgression inherent in practices most people today would admit were racist.[14] Again we are confronted with evidence for Schumpeter's argument that equilibrium models may show the "effects" of "how people behave at any time" but not "how they came to behave as they do" (Schumpeter 1954b, 21). And this is no small problem for models that purport to explain the origin of democratic institutions.[15]

Weingast further argues that "citizens in stable democracies not only must value democracy but also must be willing to take costly action to defend democratic institutions" (Weingast 1997, 261). In a sense, the argument is natural enough; it solves a puzzle that arises in his analysis. But viewed from the standpoint of the historical development of democratic ideologies, this postulate is rather arbitrary. Weingast posits citizen commitment only to the stability and persistence of democratic institutions and to his narrow interpretation of the meaning of democracy, and ignores the fact that democrats, historically, have valued wider participation; social, economic, and political equality; and freedom of expression, association, and dissent, not just the stability of the institutions he identifies as democratic.

Przeworski's model shares many of the same problems. He explicitly sets out his intention to have no recourse to "norms" in explaining the adoption of democratic procedures (1991, 23–26).[16] His conclusion is that "political forces comply with present defeats because they believe that the institutional framework that organizes the democratic competition will permit them to advance their interests in the future" (ibid., 19, 29–31). Here Weingast scores effectively against Przeworski, noting that for Przeworski's "institutional framework" to be meaningful, there must be a "citizen consensus" to enforce the rules (Weingast 1997, 255). But the effect of Weingast's argument is to show that Przeworski can no more do without "citizen consensus" than can Weingast. And thus Przeworski must address the same question Weingast neglects: by what process do people come to believe that certain types of actions violate democratic procedures? How, more broadly, do they come to define democracy?

Democracy's demands are in principle open-ended. The problems and institutions to which democratic ideologies, beliefs, and practices may be applied are diverse and extensive, and the changes that may be brought about by the expansion of democracy are potentially great. It seems unlikely that any attempt to analyze democracy from the standpoint of equilibrium analysis could ever grasp these features. Perhaps the strongest and deepest possible commitment to democracy is a commitment not merely to democratic procedures or democratic institutions, but a commitment to let the spread of democracy reconfigure social relations and structures in ways both foreseen and unforeseen. People who have that sort of commitment to democracy need a clear-eyed assessment of how democratic institutions really work and an honest approach to experimenting with democratization. They cannot be much interested in approaches to studying democracy that by their very nature cannot say much about democratic change or about the beliefs and practices that maintain and reproduce democratic institutions.

It would be a mistake, however, to assume that only those who favor the thorough democratization of societies need to acknowledge the limits of equilibrium analysis, or that its flaws are flaws only from the standpoint of such values. Although those limitations are particularly profound for people who favor more democracy in social and economic institutions and who would like to see ordinary people given more chances to expand their social capacity for democratic action, they are also limitations for anyone who wants to have a thorough and complex understanding of democracy. They impose restrictions as to how much can be seen and understood about democratic institutions, democratic beliefs, democratic history, and democratic change. That is why it is very significant that the limitations of equilibrium analysis can be seen from the standpoint of Schumpeter's own approach to social science.

7

Conclusion

By the time Schumpeter died, in 1950, Soviet-style communism, not democratic socialism, had begun consolidating its hold on Eastern and Central Europe. A half century later, those communist regimes themselves are already fading in memory, replaced by liberal democratic polities whose outlines seem closer in spirit to Schumpeter's democracy as method than to his transformative democracy. Of course liberal democracy, though it centers on a similarly procedural and insubstantial set of requirements, is not synonymous with Schumpeter's elite conception of democracy, which rested on elite theory's low estimate of ordinary people's competence. But the obvious practical success of liberal democracy nevertheless presents a sharp challenge to any attempt to revive the lesser-known aspects of Schumpeter's political thought. Did 1989 refute the conception of democracy as a transformative social tendency?

From some quarters, the answer would appear to be a resounding yes. As communism began to fall in 1989, Francis Fukuyama famously declared an end to history, brought about by "the total exhaustion of viable systematic alternatives to Western liberalism" (Fukuyama 1989, 3). And as Jeffrey C. Isaac points out, many other observers readily infer from the establishment of liberal democratic regimes in former communist countries that liberal democracy is an "ethical-political imperative," and that it represents a fulfillment of all the aspirations of Eastern European dissident movements (Isaac 1998, 155–160).

Against this view, I want to defend the continuing relevance of a transformative conception of democracy. Perhaps it would be best to begin by recalling the chief features of such a view of democracy, as they

contrast with Schumpeter's elite conception. A transformative conception stresses the significance of democratic beliefs, values, and ideologies, in contrast to Schumpeter's elite conception, which treats democracy as just a method, and which insists that the values and
commitments traditionally associated with democracy obscure democracy's real workings. A transformative conception further emphasizes
the importance of social movements and groups who articulate their
interests and formulate their programs of action in democratic terms.
Schumpeter's elite conception stresses only the role of elites motivated
by electoral interests. Finally, a transformative conception emphasizes
that democratic beliefs and practices could be applied to social and economic structures as well as political ones, opening up the possibility of
broad social transformation by way of democratization. Schumpeter's
elite conception, of course, emphasizes that democracy is just a matter
of politics—of basic electoral and parliamentary institutions, and nothing more. How well does such a transformative conception hold up in
light of the Eastern European democratic transitions from Soviet communism?

First, new and innovative democratic ideologies do indeed seem to
have been crucial to the collapse of communism in Eastern and Central
Europe. The interconnected democratic ideologies of "antipolitics" and
"civil society" gave the velvet revolutions of 1989 not just their symbols
and goals but also their distinctive nonviolent strategic vision. In the
language of the dissidents, "civil society," of course, referred to a sphere
of association somewhere between private life and the state, motivated
by public, not private, interests, and not dominated by the party or any
political authority. "Antipolitics" meant both a strategic disavowal of
any desire to challenge state power directly—such a challenge was regarded as futile—and an ethical posture of avoiding the corrupting influence of any such quest for power. Both terms referred primarily to a
vision of a democratized society, to the practices of free expression, and
to the type of self-organizing, participatory democracy that could be
linked to an eclectic set of tactics including petitions, the circulation of
underground literature, prayer meetings, and protest concerts. They expressed, in short, both the ideals and practical necessities facing dissidents in the 1970s and 1980s. They also expressed, of course, a reaction
to the reality of communist parties that as nearly as possible controlled
every institution and every aspect of life—not just through direct coer-

cion but also with the help of ordinary people who perpetuated dishonesty and evasion in their everyday lives, a situation famously explored by Václav Havel (1991).

On one level, "civil society" and "antipolitics" expressed ethical ideals. A frequent theme was the worthiness of a life lived in accordance with the ideal of civil society, even when such a thing did not exist. Leszek Kołakowski, the exiled Polish philosopher, wrote of acting *as if* democratic opposition was possible in Eastern Europe (Ost 1990, 60). Though civil society was "only an idea," George Konrád, the Hungarian dissident writer, contended, "the greatest act on behalf of freedom is to behave toward everyone as though we were free men—even toward those we fear" (1984, 82). But it would not be fair to say that the theorists of civil society and antipolitics were content to propagate only ethical ideals of individual conduct in hard times. Konrád insisted that actual "permanently open democracy" was the "greatest good," and said, with only mild irony, that it was "up to us" to declare "democracy within and among all social units" to be the "goal of history" (35, 191). Jacek Kuroń, a mentor to many Polish Solidarity activists, reconceptualized democracy itself as "the continual expansion of the scope for autonomous, non-coerced social activity," according to David Ost (1990, 65). And the ethical ideal and the social goal were linked by a clear sense of social practice, as the onetime student leader Adam Michnik made clear by arguing: "We need politics of activism" (Michnik 1985, 326). For many dissidents, that meant improvising expressive movements, groups, and activities that furthered or demanded democracy without directly attempting to seize power. But the active ideal of antipolitics was always tinctured with an element of critical self-doubt and awareness of the danger of pursuing absolutes and utopias.

In all this, then, there was a distinctive democratic theory informing the nonviolent movements that were instrumental in bringing down communism. The mass movements that arose in 1989 did not attempt ordinary revolution; they acted as if they already had democratic rights to protest, to demand changes, to give testament. Furthermore, as Isaac has pointed out, although much of antipolitical theory is recognizably liberal—for example, the emphases on voluntarism and self-limiting projects—much of it was also critical of liberal democracy (1998, 165–166). The theories of civil society and antipolitics led naturally to critiques of liberal democracy's "impersonality," its failure to stem "bureaucratization," the "debasement of communication" it fostered, and the disengagement and "domination" by the powerful that it encouraged (ibid., 166).

Along with the significance of democratic ideologies, the transformative conception of democracy also insisted on the instrumentality of political and social movements acting to realize such democratic beliefs. Of course, the transitions to democracy in Eastern Europe involved a variety of elite actors and high-level negotiations. Yet it would be hard to understand these without giving due emphasis to the mass movements and protests that framed and enabled elite actions. The Polish Solidarity movement, the best known of these, was powerful enough in 1980 and 1981 to cause serious speculation about the possibility of a Soviet invasion, and to trigger, in reality, a domestic martial-law crackdown. That crackdown badly undermined the legitimacy of communist rule, since it underscored the lesson that such rule had to be backed up by military power. Eight years later, it was Solidarity's ability to win relegalization and roundtable talks with the government in power, the Jaruzelski regime, that inaugurated the revolution of 1989, setting the pattern for similar negotiations in other countries.

Following the classic pattern of many powerful social movements, Solidarity burgeoned suddenly from a local struggle with fairly limited demands into something much larger and more challenging. Solidarity was born, as is well known, in a strike at the Lenin Shipyards in Gdansk in 1980 (Ost 1990, 75). The workers' key original demand in the early weeks was the legalization of free trade unions, a goal that possessed its own inherently democratizing logic.[1] After the strike spread, Solidarity, the name of the Gdansk union, was adopted as the name of the broader movement at a meeting of many independent trade unions. By the end of the year, Solidarity claimed some 10 million members (Przeworski 1991, 58), including even a "rural" wing of some 3.2 million members (Crampton 1994, 371), and early in 1981 it was able to hold a congress in which it issued an elaborate platform for social and economic change (Raina 1985, 169–197). This organization was decimated by the declaration of martial law later that year. But Solidarity retained some leadership and a network of underground newspapers throughout the 1980s. A wave of strikes in 1988, not planned by the leadership, allowed a new mass base of members to rebuild and retake Solidarity, and to demand that it be again recognized by the state (Ost 1990, 207–228). These strikes led to the roundtable talks relegalizing Solidarity and calling for the June 1989 elections in which it won essentially all the seats available to opposition candidates.

Because events in Poland were so crucial to what happened through-out the rest of Eastern and Central Europe in 1989, it is difficult to ar-gue that any other democratically inspired social movements were as important as Solidarity. But mass demonstrations drawing on dissident traditions of the previous forty years and employing anticommunist and democratic symbolism proved to be crucial factors in Hungary, East Germany, and Czechoslovakia. These took many forms, including pro-tests focused on environmental issues, gatherings at foreign embassies to request visas, and vigils. The cumulative effect of these peaceful dem-onstrations—which embodied the antipolitical idea of behaving as if democratization had already occurred—was immeasurable. Just a few examples should suffice. In Hungary in June 1989, 250,000 people turned out for the reburial of Imre Nagy, a key anti-Soviet figure of the 1956 revolution, in Heroes' Square, an official rehabilitation that had in turn been forced by earlier demonstrations in 1988 (Oberschall 1996, 107–108). And as the Hungarian regime began to weaken and collapse, East Germans headed there in droves seeking a route to the West. Their mass invasions of embassies eventually sparked a collapse of the com-munist countries' visa and emigration policies. This breakthrough, in turn, caused a mushrooming of regular prayer meetings and protests at the Nikolai Church in Leipzig. The prayer meetings had been an oppor-tunity for veiled protest for years. At the beginning of 1989 the regular protests had drawn a few hundred participants at most, but after the "exit crisis" the numbers of demonstrators grew, from 1,000 in early September to 3,000 in late September until, from mid-October until Christmas, 110,000 to 450,000 demonstrators marched from the Nikolai Church to the center of the city each Monday (ibid., 112–113). The marchers chanted, "We are the people," and appropriated other revolu-tionary and mass movement symbols such as the "Internationale," "We Shall Overcome," and "Liberty, Equality, Fraternity!" (111–113).

However crucial innovative democratic ideologies and movements may have been to the transitions of 1989, this still may not lay to rest the most nagging doubts about a transformative conception of democracy. These doubts concern the scope and ambitions of democracy. From Gdansk to Budapest, parliamentary politics and capitalist economies of one kind or another predominate in the former communist states. Ten years after the fall, the former communist states embody the democracy of competitive parties and parliaments, but not of direct participation, councils, or a democratized society and economy. Given the chance to invent democracy for themselves, why did Eastern and Central Europeans show so little interest in these ideas?

Any answer must begin by recognizing that the movements that overturned communism were not nearly so univocal in their interpretations and expectations of democracy as the current situation might suggest. The typical level of participation in liberal democracy looks rather meager in comparison to the stronger democracy envisioned by antipolitics and civil society. And dissidents targeted many more institutions than just those of the state for democratization during the years leading up to 1989. Radical and participatory democracy had a place in their visions. For example, the Solidarity movement outlined its chief aims in an early 1981 article that appeared in its official newspaper, *Tygodnik Solidarność*. Its basic values, according to the article, included "social justice" and "total democracy"—as well as "genuine participation by the working people in the country's social and public life" (Raina 1985, 173–174). In fact, the article blamed many of Poland's economic problems on "the lack of democratic mechanisms for decision-making" in economic matters, and found the solution for this problem, in part, in "making the socialized enterprises independent" so that it would be possible to "establish authentic workers' self-government" (ibid., 175, 182). Within Solidarity itself, the article said, "the self-governing factory organization" was to be "the basis of the whole union's operations" (ibid., 196).

Solidarity's interest in the broader social and economic dimensions of democracy was not idiosyncratic or unique, according to George Konrád: "For the most part, Eastern European social movements—especially workers' movements—have not demanded multiparty, parliamentary, representative democracy, but rather workplace self-management and direct democracy" (1984, 135). Konrád argued that the whole idea of any "delegated" authority was discredited. "It would seem more natural if authority and labor, administration and everyday life were to be separated as little as possible" (133).

Now this is not to say that transformative, strong, participatory, or radical democratic ideas predominated in the Eastern and Central European transitions. But they were clearly an important part of the anticommunist ideological mix. True, the new "democracies" of Eastern and Central Europe have not experimented with councils or with participatory or radical models of democracy. But as Geraint Parry and Michael Moran point out, this marks a strong contrast to "earlier revolutionary moments" in the region, including those in Hungary in 1956 and Czechoslovakia in 1968 (Parry and Moran 1994, 6). And it is surprising, they note, given the fact that for decades Central European intellectuals "reflected on the possibility of alternative political and economic orders to either the past authoritarianism of the communist bloc or to the liberal Western model" (ibid.). So the proper question is not why such ideas have had no influence on the democratization of Eastern and Central Europe. Rather, it is why such ideas have not come to fruition. Although this is not the place for a definitive answer, a number of possibilities seem apparent.

First, those who supported workplace and other radical visions of democracy tended to do so while proposing a kind of democratic socialism. But any conceptual version of socialism—indeed, even references to the working class or unions—were discredited for many Eastern Europeans by their use and deployment by Soviet communists (Michnik 1985, 333; Ost 1997, 21). David Ost argues that many Eastern European workers see even trade unions "as relics of communism": "Workers were supposed to be privileged then, and the discrediting of communism has meant the discrediting of all its key propositions. As workers' institutions, mandatory under the old regime, unions have become suspect" (Ost 1997, 21). The same argument would easily apply to workplace democracy. Second, there is the question of timing. The Eastern and Central European transitions took place at time that was hardly auspicious for experiments in economic democracy, in particular. The fall of communism coincided with the rise of neoconservatism and the predominance of the "Washington consensus" in international economic organizations—that is, trade liberalization, secure private property rights, fiscal austerity, privatization, and stringent marketizing (Waller 1994, 129). None of these is particularly conducive to workplace democracy, councils, and the like. Perhaps as a result, the so-called third-wave transitions to democracy have all been what some have called "dual" transitions; "new democratic governments have all felt compelled to pursue a similar, more or less 'orthodox' direction of [economic] reform" (Diamond and Plattner 1995, ix).

In stressing that democratic ideologies, democratic social movements, and the idea of a radical extension of democracy into social and economic spheres did play a role in these Eastern European transitions, I am not trying to replace liberal democratic triumphalism with complacency about the prospects of transformative democracy. Nor am I attempting to present my own causal theory of these transitions, or offering transformative democracy as a model for the explanation of transitions in general. It is apparent that the potentially transformative implications of democracy are not much noticed today. And any comprehensive attempt to understand how these transitions happened would have to examine a much wider range of factors than I have discussed here, including especially the chronic economic crises that plagued the communist countries and the signals Soviet president Mikhail Gorbachev sent, welcoming reform and indicating a reduced threat of Soviet intervention and invasion. Further, the transformative conception of democracy, as I have outlined it, presents a view of only those aspects of democracy that are most important. From this standpoint, it would be natural to stress certain problems and issues over others in analyzing democratization. Such emphases might well conflict with the emphases of well-known theories of democratization. But this does not make the transformative conception itself a causal model.

The kind of transformative conception of democracy whose contemporary relevance I would defend—one consciously redeployed, free of Schumpeter's prejudices—would contain an irreducible critical and normative aspect. Thus there is room to articulate, from the standpoint of a transformative conception, a critique of the type of democracy that has been achieved in the postcommunist transitions. In fact, one of the key reasons for reclaiming a transformative conception of democracy is to deploy it critically against liberal capitalist institutions and models, whether fully realized or not, and whether found in America, Western Europe, Eastern Europe, or elsewhere.

Such a critique would have to begin, as I think Schumpeter began, with a recognition of the power of democratic ideologies, or of democracy as ideology. When he was not mounting a tendentious attack on the straw man he created—"the classical doctrine of democracy"—

Schumpeter often conceded the great significance of democratic ideologies, or sets of democratic beliefs, values, and practices, linked together and tied to programs for political action ([1942] 1976, 264–268, 296–299). He thought that the European bourgeoisie's historic efforts to re-shape social and political institutions in their interests had relied on democratic ideologies (1920–21, 324; [1942] 1976, 297). But democratic ideologies, he thought, could also be deployed by workers in spreading the sphere of democratic politics to the organization of industry (1920–21, 337; [1942] 1976, 298–299). Today, we can imagine even broader applications.

Next, such a critique would have to recognize, as Schumpeter did, that democratic ideology often took on significance in a social world structured by a range of institutions, from those embodying relative equality and freedom to those embodying hierarchical, subservient social relations. As we saw in Chapters 2 and 3, Schumpeter argued that economic relations in capitalist societies, even liberal ones, remained starkly unequal and unfree—in his view, in fact, essentially feudal in character ([1941] 1991, 343, 359–360; [1942] 1976, 127, 135–136, 139–141, 157–161, 214; [1949] 1976, 417). In light of this complex and contradictory character of liberal capitalist society, and in light of his view that it was a transitional form of society, Schumpeter accorded no privileged status to the extent of democratization in liberal capitalism. Bourgeois democracy was not the only kind; it was a special case, he argued ([1942] 1976, 298–299; see also 1920–21, 324).

Finally, such a critique would have to emphasize that it is always possible for democratic ideologies to be deployed in the critique or active reconstruction of hierarchical social institutions. Indeed, Schumpeter saw evidence in both postwar Austria and New Deal America that this was taking place around him. Workers were seeking democratic representation in the areas that most materially affected them, and deploying democratic ideologies to challenge institutions that the bourgeoisie took for granted (1920–21, 330, 337–338; [1941] 1991, 343, 360; [1942] 1976, 298–299). At times Schumpeter expressed this fairly concrete idea in abstract terms, referring to the "rationalizing, leveling, mechanizing and democratizing" tendencies inherent to liberal capitalist societies that could eventually transform those societies into socialist ones (1939, 697). But concretely or abstractly stated, the point was the same.

Such a transformative conception need not be deterministic. Schumpeter himself regularly denied determinist readings of his views on the transformation from capitalism to socialism. "Analysis . . . never yields more than a statement about the tendencies present in an observable pattern," he wrote. "And these never tell us what *will* happen to the pattern but only what *would* happen if they continued to act as they have been acting in the time interval covered by our observation and if no other factors intruded" ([1942] 1976, 61). Today, having a transformative conception of democracy does not have to mean *defining* democracy or democratic ideology as transformative. Rather, recognizing democracy's transformative *potential* involves recognizing democracy as an ideology that can be deployed against undemocratic institutions. The meaning of democratic ideologies is not universal, fixed a priori by analytic fiat. Their meaning varies from one institutional and historical context to another. And it is an open question whether democratic ideologies will actually be deployed against hierarchic social and economic relations.

What, then, can a transformative conception of democracy offer us now? So long as democratic beliefs, values, and practices continue to inform some institutions and social realms and are there to be elicited and deployed—so long as democratic ideologies continue to motivate some groups in society—and so long as our society continues to be a complex set of institutions and structures, some formally democratic, egalitarian, and free, and some hierarchical, inegalitarian, and compulsory, a transformative conception of democracy will be relevant. More particularly, there are at least four aspects to the promise of a transformative conception.

A transformative conception of democracy focuses squarely on reshaping institutions and changing enduring social structures. Unlike Schumpeter's conception of democracy as method, a transformative conception does not assume that a fixed method or a fixed arrangement of institutions can satisfy the demands of democracy for all time. A transformative conception recognizes democratic ideologies as complex combinations of assumptions, beliefs about the world, customary habits of thought, and values that may enable political action. And it recognizes that one of the most important aspects of democratic ideologies has been their connection to movements for social reconstruction. Though not pleased by it, Schumpeter was forced to admit this fundamental role for democratic ideology in both the rise of bourgeois democracy and the spread of the council movement. The real significance of council democracy, he said, was its potential to reconfigure society.

A transformative conception of democracy embraces the economic and social implications of democratic ideologies and values—indeed, it embraces the potential application of democratic principles to the full range of social, economic, and political institutions. Unlike conceptions of democracy that are purely political—such as Schumpeter's own elite conception—a transformative conception acknowledges no such a priori limitations. And transformative democracy can certainly transcend Schumpeter's reluctant acknowledgment of this open-endedness. A commitment to the transformative implications of democracy may amount to the demand that more and more areas of social life be organized democratically. Bauer was committed to a form of "functional democracy" that "requires that the government in each branch of its activity should remain in constant touch with the citizens directly affected by this branch of government, organized according to their work places or their social and economic function" (Bauer [1925] 1970, 170). The corollary to such a demand would be the demand to examine an increasing range of problems from the standpoint of democratic principles such as equality, freedom, and human development.

A recognition of the transformative potential of democracy complements participatory and developmental arguments for democracy. Schumpeter, as we have seen, recognized the potentially transformative implications of democracy without ever favoring democratic transformation. But the way is always open for some to promote the transformative potential of democracy. Historically the democrats who have most often embraced the transformative potential of democracy have been those who argued that the spread of democratic practices could help individuals and groups develop their capacities for self-governance, deliberation, and social action (Bauer [1925] 1970; Cole 1920; Mill [1865] 1991; Pateman 1970; Rousseau 1967). Indeed, Schumpeter actually first formulated a transformative conception of democracy by incorporating in his own work the ideas of Austro-Marxists like Otto Bauer, who took such a position (see Chapter 3).

Bauer, in contrast to Schumpeter, united the elements of a transformative conception of democracy around a commitment to transforming not just institutions but also socialized humanity. Describing the ad hoc spread of councils and other democratic institutions in the early weeks of the first Austrian republic, Bauer wrote: "It is not too much to say that this social activity of the masses created a new type of manhood and womanhood . . . The transformation of political and social institutions is not an end in itself; for the development of peoples it has meaning only so far as it promotes the awakening, the inner change, and the upward movement of mankind" (Bauer 1925 [1970], 177–178). For Bauer, two transformations were intimately linked: the transformation of individual and group capacities, and the transformation of institutions. The goal was not merely the creation of democratic institutions in industry but also the corresponding development of society's capacity to manage the economy and all its common affairs democratically.

A transformative conception of democracy extends the values of equality and participation to the practice of theorizing itself. Schumpeter, Bauer, and Cole all offered their transformative conceptions of democracy as interpretations of existing demands for democracy. In Schumpeter's case, this is another way of saying he interpreted democratic transformation as a threat to the conservative institutions he valued. But not so for Cole and Bauer. They saw their role not as instructing or providing authoritative principles for political action but as voicing, systematizing, and thinking through real, practical demands for democracy. Bauer premised his democratic thought on existing demands for council democracy, and Cole likewise insisted that his book on functional democracy and guild socialism was "an attempt to explain the real character" of existing political demands and arose "essentially out of the actual historical situation in which we are placed at the present time" (Cole 1920, 2–3). This commitment meshed with a similar one to advancing the democratic claims of those who benefited the least from the existing extent of democracy. A present-day conception of transformative democracy could gain from both of these commitments—interpreting rather than just providing principles for the democratic claims of those who view their own struggles in terms of equality, participation, freedom, and self-governance.

These are promises rather than accomplishments of a transformative conception of democracy. There is nothing guaranteed about them. There is no "principle of transformation" that provides the single definitional or analytic key to a theory from which all of these advantages will follow with certainty. Rather, a transformative understanding of democracy and democratic theory provides a vantage point from which to view the connection between social transformation, democratic ideologies and beliefs, the development of social capacities, and an egalitarian approach to theorizing. Schumpeter himself recognized the transformative potential of democracy and democratic ideologies, but he did not leave us with work embodying a commitment to a democratic transformation of society. In all likelihood, each generation must provide that for itself.

Notes

1. Introduction

1. Schumpeter's *Theory of Economic Development* actually appeared in 1911, not 1912, as the title page of the original (German language) edition indicates. Throughout this book, when I refer to the English translation I give both the year of that edition, 1934, and the true original date of publication, 1911. In references to the German edition, however, I give the date listed on that title page, 1912.

2. Tory Democracy, Transformative Democracy

1. The letter (Bauer 1919) is in the Österreichisches Staatsarchiv in Vienna.
2. The Hungarian affair is discussed later in this chapter. For more on contacts with diplomatic representatives, see Allen, 1991, 1: 179; Low 1974, 207–208; März 1981, 171; and Swedberg 1991a, 62.
3. This matter is also discussed later in the chapter.
4. Ulrich Hedtke and Richard Swedberg have recently published evidence that Schumpeter's first official political position may have been as a member of a government commission studying the war economy and postwar economic transition (Schumpeter 2000, 219).
5. See also Schumpeter's aphorism quoted in Swedberg (1991a, 203).
6. Stolper is among a group of scholars who have uncovered some of the memos and other previously unknown and unpublished writings by Schumpeter that are essential to my interpretation here. Throughout this chapter, I present an argument that differs sharply from Stolper's, but all scholars interested in Schumpeter's work owe a debt to Stolper's painstaking scholarly efforts. It seems to me that this quotation embodies two mistakes. One is simply asserting, without providing substantial evidence, Schumpeter's commitment to tolerance. Another is making only a cursory reference to the historical context in question, and then only for the purpose of exculpation. The fact that the Habsburg monarchy was threatened by nationalist movements does not make proponents of the monarchy into

paragons of tolerance. In fact, the only strong political force in Austria-Hungary with a program for balancing political and cultural ethnic self-determination with mutual respect and cooperation among all nationalities was the Social Democratic Party, which favored a multinational democratic and federal republic, not an empire, as its model. Anyone who wishes to demonstrate that Schumpeter's monarchism was really an expression of his *tolerance* faces the difficulty of explaining why he did not join the Social Democrats in supporting such a platform.

7. This quotation is an exceptionally clear statement of a guiding assumption behind many people's work. Swedberg himself, however, does devote several pages to explicating Schumpeter's "political philosophy . . . from the First World War onwards," using a variety of sources, not just *Capitalism, Socialism, and Democracy* (1991a, 145–151).

8. Tom Bottomore does recognize that Schumpeter's essay "The Socialist Possibilities of Today" (1920–1921) includes reflections on the nature and significance of democracy, but he does not systematically relate this essay to Schumpeter's political activities during this period, nor does he link it to the passages on democracy in *Capitalism, Socialism, and Democracy* (Bottomore 1992, 37–38, 107–110).

9. However, this chapter is not an attempt at a political history of this period in Austria-Hungary or Austria. Just one example of why this is should make the point clear. Because of Schumpeter's interests and orientation, I emphasize here the leading *German*-Austrian political forces of the period and touch hardly at all on the substance of the positions taken by various non-German national parties and political organizations in the Habsburg empire. An analysis of these groups would constitute a crucial part of any political survey of the period.

10. Doubts about the Social Democrats' democratic credentials typically focus attention on the party's 1926 platform, which left open the possibility of taking up arms against the fascist militias (Heimwehr) that had begun to exert a strong influence in Austrian politics. But that platform endorsed the use of force only to defend democratic gains against avowedly antidemocratic forces in the country and did so in the context of broad support for the "democratic republic" and "all guarantees of democracy" (Gulick 1948, 1388–1393; Rabinbach 1985, 40, 82–83).

11. The complete Austro-Marxist theory of democracy cannot be developed adequately outside of the context of the party's efforts to achieve socialism and economic democracy—nor without reference to writings that appeared after the First World War. I will analyze this complete theory of democracy in the next section, as background for Schumpeter's own writings on socialization and democracy. But the utility of dealing with Schumpeter's early writings

chronologically and in two parts—roughly speaking, political democracy first, economic democracy second—imposes, unfortunately, an artificial distinction in presenting the SDP's stance.

12. The encouragement of popular, participatory cultural and political institutions in "Red Vienna" during the party's ascendancy in the capital should probably be included in the Austro-Marxist vision of a democratic political life. Andrew Arato uses the contemporary phrase "a democratic civil society" to refer to this entire democratic program (Rabinbach 1985, 135). The use of the term *civil society* in this context helps capture for us the meaning of the Austrian Social Democrats' manifold practical commitments to democratizing politics, but the German equivalent to the term, *die bürgerliche Gesellschaft,* would have had a different meaning for the Austro-Marxists, so I have avoided using that term here.

13. Most accounts agree these demonstrations were "huge" (Gulick 1948, 33). The figures here come from Rabinbach (1983, 12) and Johnston (1972, 100), respectively. Boyer seems to be alone in assessing the size of these demonstrations as relatively small; he estimates that there were 15,000 in the Vienna march (Boyer 1995, 75).

14. A recurring problem in some of the historical literature on the Austro-Hungarian empire is a failure to distinguish *universal* from *manhood* suffrage. For example, a number of writers, including Charles Gulick and Wolfgang Stolper, refer to the Austrian electoral reform of late 1906 as if it had established universal suffrage for parliamentary elections (Diamant 1960, 49; Gulick 1948, 33; Johnston 1972, 33; Stolper 1994, 175), when in fact it established only manhood suffrage (Gulick 1948, 61; Pauley 1972, 11; Rabinbach 1983, 13).

15. In particular, those in the left wing of the SDP believed that a genuine commitment to democracy required strenuous opposition or even revolt against the Habsburgs' war policy and dictatorship. Rudolph Hilferding, an economist and a member of this wing of the party, joined a conference of pacifist and internationalist dissidents from the German SDP, such as Karl Kautsky and Karl Liebknecht, at Zimmerwald in Switzerland in 1915; and during the war a cohesive group of left-wing antiwar members of the Austrian SDP began to gather around Friedrich Adler, the son of Viktor Adler, one of the party's founders (May 1966, 292; Rabinbach 1983, 18). Friedrich Adler argued that Social Democrats should be neutral on the war itself but resist both political and economic absolutism (Bauer 1925 [1970], 29). In October 1916, Count Stürgkh cut off one of the last legal avenues for even mild opposition by forbidding a simple meeting of university professors at which a parliamentary leader was to speak; the next day, the younger Adler shocked Austrian socialists by assassinating Stürgkh (Bauer 1925 [1970],

30; Gulick 1948, 38). Adler subsequently turned his own trial into a political forum to attack the Habsburg war dictatorship, and won many converts to the left wingers' cause (May 1966, 344; Rabinbach 1983, 18–19).

16. This problem was only exacerbated by the Social Democrats' position on language. As Eric Hobsbawm has pointed out, the choice of a language for public communication, a language for government and bureaucracy, was one of the most important stakes in many national struggles, especially as that controversy interested the classes that could aspire to clerical and bureaucratic jobs that required fluency in the official language of communication (Hobsbawm 1992, 117). But Social Democrats like Renner, with an airy cosmopolitanism, asserted that everyone should know a single common language in a multinational state, a view endorsed in the Brünn program's call for a language of communication; everyone knew and many people resented the fact that that language would almost surely end up being German (Hobsbawm 1992, 95; Rabinbach 1983, 15).

17. Since such a union of German Austria with Germany was forbidden by the Allies as a condition of peace, this became a moot point, until, of course, Hitler's troops marched into Austria in 1938.

18. Furthermore, late in life Schumpeter returned to Christian Social ideas in supporting a corporatist social organization. See below.

19. But the CSP's comparative strength in Vienna was really a fluke of incomplete democratization, and matters reversed after the war when peasant supporters of the CSP were enfranchised in the countryside for parliamentary elections, while working class supporters of the SDP were enfranchised for municipal elections in Vienna (Boyer 1995, 78; Gulick 1948, 2, 355; Rabinbach 1983, 22, 26–7).

20. In this respect, as we will see, they mirrored the views of the Social Democrats.

21. In light of this interpretation of the CSP's evolving position in 1905 and 1906, for which I rely, in part, on Boyer, it is difficult to understand what Boyer could mean when he asserts that the Christian Socials were strong supporters of democracy in this period (Boyer 1995, 462).

22. A number of scholars agree that the spirit of nationalist movements darkened considerably during the course of the nineteenth century (Hobsbawm 1992; Schorske 1980). Carl Schorske, in particular, has traced the evolution of the pan-German nationalism in Austria-Hungary, a movement which at the time of the 1848 revolution was liberal and democratic, into an anti-Semitic, anti-Slav campaign to unify German Austria with the German Reich (Schorske 1980, 122–133).

23. The letters and memos may be found in two volumes of Schumpeter's speeches, letters, and other writings, Schumpeter (1985) and Schumpeter (1992), both edited by Wolfgang Stolper and Christian Seidl.

24. The most comprehensive survey of the contents of the letters and memos is in Stolper (1994, 171–201). Schumpeter discussed in them such diverse matters as the position of the ethnic groups in the Hungarian half of the empire, the possibility of a coronation of the kaiser in Prague to convert the dual monarchy into a triple one, and the idea of Austria-Hungary leading a peace initiative. All these themes are interwoven with the main theme I discuss here: Tory democracy. In the interest of brevity, I give little attention to Schumpeter's reflections and advice concerning the nationalist forces that would indeed unmake the empire.

25. The complete German texts of the memoranda may be found in Schumpeter (1985), 251–310.

26. Certainly, Stolper's suggestions notwithstanding, Schumpeter never tried to provide a principled defense of monarchy on the basis of its supposed benefits for toleration (Stolper 1994, 196–197).

27. I am far from suggesting this is a unique weakness in Schumpeter's political thought. Rather, with Karl Mannheim, I would suggest it is characteristic of much political thinking (Mannheim 1985, 4).

28. The distinction I am making between what these memos *say* and what Schumpeter *was doing in writing them* is akin to (but not identical to) J. L. Austin's famous distinction between locutionary, illocutionary, and perlocutionary acts, in *How to Do Things with Words* (Austin 1962).

29. This term of address is functionally equivalent to "your Lordship."

30. The full German text of this letter may be found in Schumpeter (1992), 371–372.

31. Schumpeter was writing after the March but before the October phase of the Russian revolution (Schumpeter 1985, 289).

32. The full German text of this letter may be found in Schumpeter (1992), 371–372.

33. The full German text of this memorandum may be found in Schumpeter (1985), 251–272. The cited passage appears on 271.

34. The full German text of this letter may be found in Schumpeter (1992), 361–363.

35. The full German text of this letter may be found in ibid., 365–367.

36. See ibid.

37. See ibid.

38. It is true that historians have challenged this standard view, arguing that the radical democratic ideology of the Chartist period continued to motivate working-class political action in the later period, and that the success of Gladstonian liberalism can be explained by the liberals' embrace of that ideology and by the fact that some members of the working class believed the Gladstonian liberal program offered real solutions to their problems (Biagini 1992, 6–17; Biagini and Reid 1991, 1, 5–19; Finn 1993, 5–10).

39. The full German text of this memorandum may be found in Schumpeter 1985, 251–272. The cited passages appear on 271.

40. Wolfgang Stolper located Ellis Ashmead-Bartlett's somewhat obscure postwar narrative, the only source on Schumpeter's aristocratic counterrevolutionary activities. Ashmead-Bartlett's political commitments were somewhat fuzzy; he seems to have been a somewhat belated proponent of constitutional monarchy. He muses implausibly that the Austro-Hungarian empire might have survived had Franz Josef "given his country a Constitutional Government in time"; most of the counterrevolutionaries he conspired with were aristocrats, and the book is tinged with a hostility to both socialists and republicans and a notable sentimentality concerning the Habsburgs, including accounts of Kaiser Karl's attempts to regain the Hungarian throne (Ashmead-Bartlett 1923, 10–11, 27–31, 150, 151–152, 250–285).

41. Given this statement of opposition to republican government, it seems safe to assume that when Schumpeter said he supported a "moderate constitutional regime," he meant a constitutional monarchy—a decided step back from a democratic republic (Ashmead-Bartlett 1923, 159).

42. The chair of the German Socialization Commission was Karl Kautsky, the SDP's leading theorist. Other committee members included Rudolf Hilferding and Emil Lederer, both Marxists who had known Schumpeter since all three attended a seminar led by the economist Eugen von Böhm-Bawerk in 1905–1906 (Allen 1991, 1: 39).

43. Otto Bauer seems to have been Schumpeter's main sponsor for the finance ministry position. Bauer probably knew about his role on the German commission and was likely impressed by Schumpeter's "Crisis of the Tax State" and its advocacy of a wealth tax or capital levy, a controversial policy whose advocates promoted it for differing reasons; it is unlikely that Bauer or any other Social Democrats knew about Schumpeter's memos and letters on Tory democracy (März 1981, 166–167; Swedberg 1991a, 58–59).

44. In an intellectual biography there would of course be room to discuss at length the array of financial problems Austria faced at the end of the war and the plans Schumpeter drew up as finance minister for dealing with them, but my focus here must remain on the intertwined issues of socialization and democratization. In brief, Schumpeter thought that at the end of the war the Austrian economy suffered from at least two major economic problems brought on by the four-year conflict: inflation and a huge state budget deficit. In "The Crisis of the Tax State" and elsewhere, Schumpeter generally advocated the use of a "capital levy"—an in-kind tax on financial holdings, ultimately to be received by the state in the form of cash and war bonds—both to fight inflation and to reduce the state's deficit (Schumpeter 1918 [1991], 122–126). In Schumpeter's view, the levy would, on the one

hand, reduce the amount of money in the economy, and thus reduce infla-
tionary pressures; on the other (insofar as the levy was paid to the government in the form of war bonds), it would eliminate much of the state's war-
related indebtedness. Over time, his "finance plan" put less weight on the
capital levy and more weight on other measures he thought would restore the Austrian economy: stabilizing exchange rates, founding a new central bank, increasing indirect taxes, and restoring Austria's credit worthiness (März 1981, 167; Stolper 1985, 170, 171; Swedberg 1991a, 61).
Schumpeter's term in office was also marked by conflict with Bauer over
Anschluß, or union with Germany, and the Alpine-Montan-Gesellschaft affair. The latter I discuss briefly below. In general, my purpose here is not to
offer a complete overview of his tenure as finance minister. Such surveys
may be found in Allen 1991, 1: 165–180; März 1981; Stolper 1994, 217–
293; and Swedberg 1991a, 58–64.

45. I elaborate on this movement below.

46. Bauer's colleague the Austrian Social Democrat Karl Renner was somewhat
more influenced by Sidney and Beatrice Webb than by Cole (Rabinbach
1985, 138; Renner [1921] 1978).

47. This is a very important fact in assessing the nature of the council movement in western Europe. If the participants had believed, like Lenin, that
the essence of the council movement was the exclusion of the bourgeoisie
and the substitution of parliamentary democracy based on universal suffrage, with a state governed exclusively by the working class through councils, then a plausible case could be made that the council movement was far
from democratic. But historical evidence points to a different conclusion:
that participants in the council movement supported parliamentary democracy and regarded councils as a way of democratizing factories and the military.

48. Bauer's conception of democracy was certainly not limited to such a notion
of "assent," as should be clear from passages in which he wrote about the
need for "government in each branch of its activity" to remain "in constant
touch with the citizens," from his espousal of an extension of democratic
practices into the economy and society, and from his explication of a developmental theory of democracy, discussed below.

49. The full German text of this essay, "Der Weg zum Sozialismus," may be
found in Bauer [1919] 1976.

50. As we will see, Schumpeter later described the same process using the same
terms.

51. Cf. Bauer: "In modern capitalist society by the side of political democracy,
embodied in the democratic organization of the State and municipality, an
industrial democracy is developing" ([1925] 1970, 169).

52. See Bauer [1919] 1976, 108. Schumpeter argued in a quite Marxist way that full socialization would eradicate class distinctions, at least as they were known in liberal capitalist society (1920–21, 326). Thus his argument that the council movement would gradually lead to the unchallenged sovereignty of the workers within given plants does not imply the exclusion of any class from power in general—as, in his view, *mere* parliamentary democracy entailed the exclusion of the working class. It is important to note, moreover, that Schumpeter, like Bauer, rejected those syndicalist models that envisioned only worker control of factories and no representation for a broader public interest, and especially for consumers, in the management of whole industries.

53. It is worth noting that Schumpeter here made Tory democracy only a phase in a long process of political and social democratization. There is little sense here that he was confident that an elite-dominated Tory democracy could constitute a lasting settlement.

54. Zassenhaus is somewhat misleading in referring to Schumpeter's approving quotation of Georges Sorel (Zassenhaus 1981, 198). Schumpeter's citation of Sorel is in a footnote to a passage that argues that Lenin could not afford to use democratic means to bring about a premature transition to socialism (Schumpeter 1920–21, 328 and note). More on this below.

55. Cf. Bauer: "The example of Russia, where the democratic organization of industry which was attempted immediately after the October Revolution had quickly to give way to bureaucratic State capitalism, demonstrates that only bureaucratic State socialism, which merely replaces the despotism of the employer by the despotism of the bureaucrat, is possible so long as the workers are without the capacity for self-government in their labour process" (Bauer [1925] 1970, 144).

56. Workers' councils and factory councils should be distinguished. Workers' councils were intended as a mechanism for workers to seize direct political power, often to the exclusion of the bourgeoisie, as in Lenin's theory and in Soviet practice. Factory councils were conceived by Bauer and others as a means of achieving industrial democracy. Schumpeter emphasized the transformative significance of *factory* councils (see, for example, 1920–21, 338).

57. The minutes of the commission's confidential sessions may be found in the Bundesarchiv, Abteilungen Potsdam (see Sozialisierungskommission 1919a). Allen agrees that Schumpeter's emphasis during these sessions was on giving managers powers and incentives (1991, 1: 163–164).

58. The commission's full report may be found in the Bundesarchiv, Abteilungen Potsdam (see Sozialisierungskommission 1919b).

59. Schumpeter moved to the United States in 1932, leaving behind many of his

private papers. What he left behind in Germany was largely destroyed during World War II. As a result, what evidence exists about his anti-Semitism and pro-Hitler feelings is found largely in diaries dating from the time he lived in the United States, 1932 to 1950. The next chapter deals with Schumpeter's public writings during this American period. But the evidence of his pro-Nazi and anti-Semitic views is best handled in connection with his life and experiences in Europe.

60. This "laborite" period is discussed in Schumpeter's "Lowell Lectures" (Schumpeter [1941] 1991), in his "Wage and Tax Policy in Transitional States of Society" ([1948] 1991), in "English Economists and the State Managed Economy" ([1949] 1951b), in a talk he gave at the Institute of World Affairs in 1949 (1993, 249–254), and, most famously, throughout *Capitalism, Socialism, and Democracy* ([1942] 1976).

61. Allen was a graduate student of Schumpeter's—though not "an intimate nor one of his inner circle of students"—at Harvard in the late 1940s (Allen 1991, 1: xix).

62. Allen provides evidence that Schumpeter's anti-Bolshevism was partly due to his strong anti-Slav bias (1991 2: 91, 101, 113 n. 21).

63. Schumpeter made a similar comment, that Nazism could mean "catastrophe or glory" for Germany, in his farewell speech to students in Bonn in 1932, excerpted in Allen 1991, 1: 285. The full German text of the speech may be found in Schumpeter [1932] 1952.

64. Wolfgang Stolper, who studied with Schumpeter, recalls, however, that there was a whole list of ethnic slurs he never used (1994, 11 n. 13).

65. Stolper, citing conversations with Schumpeter, provides a version of the story that does not serve to indict Schumpeter with anti-Semitism. But Allen and Swedberg, who tell the version of the story reported here, cite an interview with a contemporary of Schumpeter's and two other secondary sources (Allen 1991 2: 112 n. 10; Stolper 1994, 12 n. 18; Swedberg 1991a, 272 nn. 8, 9, 10). A similar incident concerned a candidate applying to become a fellow of the Econometric Society. Interpretations of this incident also vary, but it is at least clear that, while denying that he was an anti-Semite and favoring the application, Schumpeter nevertheless took it for granted that Jews were clannish and that this was a legitimate topic of discussion in the application process (Schumpeter 2000, 228; and see Allen (1991) 2: 67, and Stolper [1994], 10–11).

66. Many letters in the Harvard University Archives, some of them collected in a volume of Schumpeter's letters (Schumpeter 2000), record this effort.

67. Claus-Dieter Krohn argues that Schumpeter's complaints about the Nazis' predecessors may have been oblique references to his belief that he had been denied a job for political reasons at the University of Berlin (Krohn 1993,

77). Schumpeter wrote in his *History of Economic Analysis* that, given the politicization of appointments at Berlin in the Weimar period, "the advent of National Socialism did not mean quite as great a break and did not cause all the damage that a foreign observer might expect" (1954b, 1155). But Schumpeter's sympathy for the Nazis seems to have run deeper than this.

68. Whatever "convictions" Schumpeter had that prevented him from condemning Hitler must have been "conservative" indeed. See the following review of the events of the spring of 1933, which illuminates precisely what it meant to refuse to censure Hitler at this time.

69. These efforts are also recorded in a number of letters in the Harvard University Archives. In one letter from 1939, Tisch expressed deep appreciation for Schumpeter's help, and described the waiting lists and policies that made emigration nearly impossible for her (Tisch 1939).

70. In a letter to Tisch written a few months earlier, Schumpeter agreed to send another affidavit in support of Tisch's emigration. That same letter, however, indicates that Tisch had asked or complained about previous, unanswered queries. Schumpeter wrote: "I do not know exactly the extent to which I have failed to respond to your appeals . . . I would not knowingly have left letters of you [*sic*] unanswered" (Schumpeter 2000, 335). As to the possibility that Schumpeter left earlier letters unanswered, it should be noted that the war may have prevented some mail from getting through. Regarding the fact that Schumpeter let at least one of Tisch's letters languish unopened in his possession, it is important to note that he professed at about the same time to another correspondent (though not in so many words) that he was depressed and that, as a result, his correspondence "accumulates in heaps and most of it I do not even open" (Schumpeter 2000, 337).

71. The full German text of the speech may be found in Schumpeter [1932] 1952.

72. Wolfgang Stolper, who was a student of Schumpeter's at Bonn and Harvard, and whose family maintained a long friendship with him, has told Richard Swedberg that Schumpeter advised Germans to stay in Germany, collaborate, but fight Hitler from within (Swedberg 1991a, 276 n. 73).

73. Dale L. Cramer and Charles G. Leathers are right to connect Schumpeter's theory of class, his emphasis on the role of the bourgeois family, and his scorn for "utilitarian" and "rationalist" philosophy to his corporatism, but the analysis cannot stop here. In Cramer and Leathers's case, however, it does because they adopt a peculiarly disembodied interpretive approach, which apparently involves "testing" the corporate economy that Schumpeter envisioned "against his economic theory" (Cramer and Leathers 1981, 753). They fail, furthermore, to read Schumpeter politically, in part because they *begin* with the assumption that he "never endorsed any

political philosophy and/or social ideals" and because they apparently be-lieve that "scholarly objectivity requires" an interpretive approach that rules out, a priori, "the false interpretation that he was advocating either fascism or neo-feudalism" (Cramer and Leathers 1981, 749).

3. The New Deal and Transformative Democracy

1. Of course, to say that labor democratized America is only to say that it moved America in the direction of greater democracy. That the process was nowhere near completed by labor in the 1930s is clear, given just one of many possible examples: the continuation of systematic political exclusion and social oppression of African Americans. This is worth pointing out, since, as Carole Pateman has argued, "political scientists tend to gloss over how hard it has been to consolidate . . . universal suffrage" for women and racial and ethnic minorities around the world (Pateman 1996, 11 n. 2).

2. Schumpeter's ties and debts to Weber are fairly well known (see, for exam-ple, Bottomore 1992, 13–14, n. 20; Swedberg 1991a, 2, 88–93; Swedberg 1991b, 45–46). But Schumpeter also knew Mannheim and his work well enough that, in 1933, he reported having been contacted by Mannheim, who was seeking to escape from Nazi Germany and find work in the United States (Schumpeter 1933). Schumpeter did subsequently write a few letters in support of Mannheim, and furthermore, in developing his own theory of science and ideology, he later argued for the indispensable role of a "soci-ology of knowledge" approach in developing any such theory, citing Mannheim as the best writer on the subject (2000, 244; 1954b, 33 n. 1; [1942] 1976, 11 n. 3).

3. Sorting out everything Schumpeter wrote about rationality is difficult, be-cause in addition to these uses of the term, he also used it in a narrower but more familiar sense, in connection with his writings on neoclassical eco-nomic theory and "methodological individualism," one tenet of which he sometimes referred to as the assumption of rationality. I do not wish to sug-gest that these different uses of rationality are entirely distinct from one an-other, yet it is important to see the differences among them. In particular it is important to note that although Schumpeter certainly was familiar with the use of rationality to mean the maximization of subjective utility, this was not the only meaning the term had for Schumpeter (1991, 316–338). This is worth emphasizing because of the extraordinary narrowing of the use of the term *rationality* in the social sciences in the past few decades.

4. Of these capitalist buttresses, I will take up only the bourgeois family below, in connection with Schumpeter's scattered comments on feminism.

5. Schumpeter's characterization of the political theorists that he groups to-

gether as proponents of "classical" democratic theory is highly mislead-ing. As Carole Pateman demonstrated, there is no classical theory of democ-racy uniting Bentham, the elder and younger Mills, and Rousseau (Pateman 1970). Furthermore, Schumpeter's characterization of Locke's political commitments, though no doubt on par for his time, would certainly today be regarded as misleading. The point here is not that Schumpeter was a sub-tle reader of others' political theory. Rather, the point is that what Schumpeter described as a process of "rationalization" was carried out by particular political movements, with varying ideologies and theories. Schumpeter's attempt to find unifying themes among these, insofar as it led him to posit the existence of a "classical doctrine," was misguided, but there is value in setting out a theory of the sociological and historical significance of democratization and democratic arguments in developing liberal capital-ist societies.

6. Schumpeter made, from a profoundly conservative standpoint, a somewhat contemporary-sounding critique of how the family dropped curiously out of view in neoclassical economics. "When we look more closely at their [the economists'] idea of the self-interest of entrepreneurs and capitalists," it be-comes clear that "consciously or unconsciously they analyzed the behavior of the man whose views and motives are shaped by such a home and who means to work and to save primarily for wife *and children,*" even though they never explicitly acknowledge this ([1942] 1976, 160). Of course, there was nothing of a critical or feminist edge to Schumpeter's observation.

4. Schumpeter's Elite Conception of Democracy as Method

1. Schumpeter argued earlier that democracy *is* a method. So his definition of the "democratic method" amounts to a definition of democracy.
2. It should be evident that the peculiarities of this sentence do not end with those I have just mentioned. Obviously it is no accident that in a passage ar-guing that in an "anti-feminist commonwealth," "sex" must be allowed to be a disqualification for voting, the "populus" that "must" be allowed to self-define is referred to with a masculine pronoun (1942 [1976] 244–245).
3. Logically, to be sure, it is one thing to rely on a set of "facts" in proposing a political program, and quite another to rely on a set of assumptions about human nature and elites. But to put too much weight on this logical distinc-tion is to risk missing the actual genesis of Schumpeter's thought.
4. For some indication of the way in which these theorists influenced each other, see Meisel 1962, 110, 169–189, 183–186; Michels [1915] 1962, 76, 343; Mommsen 1989, 95–100; Nye 1977, 22–23, 30.
5. Actually, Schumpeter admitted that utilitarians did not endow the com-

mon will with a "semi-mystic" status, but he argued that their arguments amounted to much the same thing ([1942] 1976, 252).

6. It should be pointed out that the opposition that this argument rests on is not persuasive even from Schumpeter's own standpoint. Schumpeter here opposes the kind of conception of the rational individual will that one might associate with methodological individualism with a pessimistic conception of pure irrationality and pure social determination of beliefs, desires, and the like. But as I will show in Chapter 5, Schumpeter himself provided a much more sophisticated critique of methodological individualism. In general, Schumpeter regarded a sophisticated analysis of historically varying social beliefs and practices as the alternative to the naive rationalism of methodological individualism. But Schumpeter's attack on the classical doctrine required a complete and categorical rejection of the idea of rationality; his own more nuanced critique of methodological individualism would not have served this purpose.

7. Schumpeter's definition of the democratic method suggests how he might have defined rule as well: to rule is to have "the power to decide" ([1942] 1976, 269).

8. For Rousseau's stark failure to include women in his analysis, see Okin 1979, 106–139.

9. Actually, Schumpeter also referred specifically to "housewives" as consumers. For discussion, see below.

10. The gendered language here cannot simply be attributed to Schumpeter's unthinking adherence to linguistic convention. Gender is deeply implicated in such questions as who, exactly, is an "active member" of a group—and in what way.

11. It seems fairly clear that part of Schumpeter's intention in citing "housewives" here is to diminish the apparent significance of the concessions he is making in this passage.

12. The point is that Schumpeter did not merely argue that democracy, "in reality," could serve to promote these ideals, and that some other way had to be found to promote them. Schumpeter's elite conception of democracy directly undermined arguments for these valued practices.

13. Contrary to Schumpeter's claim, this famous passage *assumed* that democracy was method but did not *prove* it. The substance of Schumpeter's argument in this passage was that democracy should not be considered an end in itself, or even assumed to include ideals that were ends in themselves, because democracy *conflicted* with "ultimate ideals and interests which the most ardent democrat will put above democracy" ([1942] 1976, 242). The mental experiment itself was actually quite brief, although the passage was filled out with several examples of religious persecution in supposedly

democratic societies. Schumpeter asked readers to imagine a "hypothetical country that, *in a democratic way,* practices the persecution of Christians, the burning of witches, and the slaughtering of Jews" (ibid., emphasis added). "The instance is not fanciful," he insisted, adding that "communities which most of us would recognize as democracies have burned heretics at the stake—the republic of Geneva did in Calvin's time—or otherwise persecuted them in a manner repulsive to our moral standards—colonial Massachusetts may serve as an example" (240–241). Given such a situation, he urged, a reasonable person would not approve of the persecution simply because it had been decided on democratically, but such a person *would* still approve of "the democratic constitution itself that produced such results" (242). For Schumpeter, this conflict between the ideals according to which one would reject persecution and the "democratic constitution" proved his point that democracy was method. The decisive moment of this mental experiment was contained in the very first step, where Schumpeter stipulated that the persecution was democratic because it took place "in a democratic way" (242). This first step entailed an identification of democracy with method, and it severed the definition of democracy from things with which it would ordinarily be connected, such as the protection of human rights. To support his point, he mentioned societies, nations, and instances most modern democrats would certainly not embrace as examples of democracies: Calvin's Geneva, colonial Massachusetts, ancient Rome, and so on. In fact, the coherence of the whole thought experiment, beginning with this first step, depended on agreement that democratic ideals and practices could be meaningfully distinguished from the democratic method.

14. Since democracy includes "freedom of discussion and association," Schumpeter really poses a "false dilemma," in Bachrach's view (1967, 19, 20).

15. All this suggests rather strongly that Held is too generous in assuming that Schumpeter's conception of democracy as method committed him to "freedom of discussion and speech" (Held 1987, 183). Bachrach, too, appears to have been too optimistic in arguing that Schumpeter sought to modify and qualify democracy "in the interest of . . . protecting liberty" (Bachrach 1967, 19).

16. It is not at all clear that definitively categorizing some governments as democracies is a high priority for democratic theory. In fact, if we take democratic theory to be critical, to embody a commitment to the moral and social development of individuals and groups, and in this sense to have implications for more than the organization of the state, there is no particularly strong reason to think that that democratic theory is best which helps us plug governments into a fixed typology. Still, democratic theory ought

to provide criteria for assessing *how democratic* particular institutions and practices are. And certainly any democratic theory ought to be able to provide the criteria by which to label as *undemocratic* some practices and institutions that are at odds with long-standing democratic commitments.

17. This is not the only place where Schumpeter reintroduces and uses for his own purposes the concept of the common will, whose coherence he elsewhere strongly denies.

18. It could be argued that these are simply flaws in the execution of Schumpeter's arguments, individual, subjective, and limited—that is, that the criterion is valid but that these contingent applications of the criterion are flawed. But I will argue below that these statements follow quite naturally from Schumpeter's assumptions about human nature in politics, and therefore from a straightforward explication of this criterion according to Schumpeter's own theory and definitions.

19. I am not suggesting that Rousseau cannot be faulted for attempting to find support in "nature" for his political preferences. But pointing to the best example of this does not help Schumpeter's cause. That example is Rousseau's assumption that women are naturally subordinate in the family (Okin 1979, 106–139).

20. Democratic theorists such as Bauer, too, have rejected it this option, treating these not as given qualities of human nature but as capacities or abilities that must be given substance and must be cultivated through appropriate practices and institutions.

21. This statement, of course, assumes that no theory of the limits, growth, and development of democratic capacities can claim to be uniquely determined by the "facts"—that is, it assumes acceptance of the idea that all such theories are underdetermined by the facts. Since theories partly determine the empirical field by which they are tested—observation is theory-laden—the choice of a theory and the test of its validity are not independent of each other. Recognition of this opens the door to an emphasis on *practice*. First, one's practical commitments—for example, to freedom and the development of capacities—will enter into the choice among theories. Second, the validity of a theory will be partly settled by the degree to which it serves those practical commitments. As Dewey put it, "*If* ideas, meanings, conceptions, notions, theories, systems are instrumental to an active reorganization of the given environment, to a removal of some specific trouble and perplexity, then the test of their validity and value lies in accomplishing this work" ([1920] 1950, 128).

22. Although the elite conception of democracy as a method was logically prior to the vision of democratic socialism, it is important to recognize that, in terms of Schumpeter's aims, one should say that his whole discussion of de-

mocracy in *Capitalism, Socialism, and Democracy* was explicitly directed toward preparing the way for a discussion of the role of "democracy in the socialist order."

23. Anticipating a potential objection, let me point out that it will not suffice to interpret this statement as merely an empirical observation about "responsible" socialists. Schumpeter wrote elsewhere in the same book: "*No responsible person* can view with equanimity the consequences of extending the democratic method, that is to say the sphere of 'politics,' to all economic affairs" ([1942] 1976, 299; emphasis added). Clearly it would be silly to argue that this is just a value-neutral empirical report about what "responsible" people say and do.

5. Schumpeter's Vision of Social Science

1. The "marginalist" or "neoclassical" revolution in economics was really as much the work of Carl von Menger and William Stanley Jevons as it was Walras's.

2. Shionoya argues, somewhat similarly, that Schumpeter's key works—*The Nature and Chief Subject Matter of Theoretical Economics* (1908), *The Theory of Economic Development* (1911), *Business Cycles* (1939), and *Capitalism, Socialism, and Democracy* (1942)—should all be seen be seen as part of one developing research program, and that *Economic Development* was a "midpoint" (1997, 31–33, 184–185, 191–192).

3. For the limits of pure theory for understanding the process of economic and social change as a whole, see chapter 7 of the original (1911) German edition of *A Theory of Economic Development (Theorie der wirtschaftlichen Entwicklung)*. Swedberg argues that Schumpeter omitted this chapter from subsequent editions, including the 1934 English edition, because he was annoyed to find that its inclusion led readers to think he had written a nontheoretical book of economic history (Swedberg 1991a, 37).

4. Please note that by "developing economy" I do not mean to point specifically to economies in what is sometimes termed the "developing world." Schumpeter considered that economic development was the essence of all capitalist economies. In this sense, a nondeveloping economy, for Schumpeter, was by definition not capitalistic. To flesh out what he meant by entrepreneurial activity, Schumpeter identified five different types of innovations. For more elaboration on the nature of entrepreneurial activity, see Schumpeter [1911] 1934, 66; Bottomore 1992, 31–32; Swedberg 1991a, 34. For a criticism of Schumpeter's typology of innovations, see Oakley 1990, 97–99.

5. Schumpeter never denied that outside disturbances, such as wars, could constitute part of an external explanation of booms or busts.

6. Thus Schumpeter linked his theory of business cycles to his theory of elites.

7. For evidence of the early roots of this view, see Schumpeter 1912, 463–548.

8. Schumpeter was still writing and revising his *History of Economic Analysis* (1954b) when he died. In the text of his opening chapter, he alludes to three fields—theory, statistics, and economic history—but goes on actually to list and discuss four, the field of economic sociology apparently constituting a later addition.

9. It is worth comparing these statements to Paul Sweezy's summary of the historical quality of Marx's thought. Sweezy wrote that Marx's method was "in its innermost essence historical," because, for Marx, "social reality is not so much a specified set of relations, still less a conglomeration of things. *It is rather the process of change inherent in a specified set of relations. In other words, social reality is the historical process,* a process which, in principle, knows no finality and no stopping places" (Sweezy 1942, 20; emphasis added). I do not quote this passage randomly. Sweezy was a friend and junior colleague of Schumpeter's at Harvard; his book on Marxist economics, from which this is excerpted, Schumpeter called "the best introduction to Marxist literature I know" (Schumpeter 1954b, 392).

10. Similarly, in *Cycles*, Schumpeter argued that the focus of his work was a process of change, so that particular methodological techniques were only ways of understanding that process: "Since what we are trying to understand is economic change in historic time, there is little exaggeration in saying that the ultimate goal is simply a reasoned (= conceptually clarified) history, not of crises only, nor of cycles or waves, but of the economic process in all its aspects and bearings to which theory merely supplies some of the tools and schemata, and statistics merely part of the material. It is obvious that only detailed historic knowledge can definitively answer most of the questions of individual causation and mechanism and that without it the study of time series must remain inconclusive, and theoretical analysis empty" (1939, 220).

11. Oakley is a notable exception (Oakley 1990, 49). And although Mitchell is interested in examining links between Schumpeter's work, including his methodological individualism, and public choice theory, he is careful to point out that *Capitalism, Socialism, and Democracy* cannot be understood as an exercise in this approach (Mitchell 1984, 71).

12. The rejection of this opposition is often a premise or an implication of arguments that the allegedly self-evident category of the individual is in the full sense of the term socially and historically constructed. Compare, for example, Marx and Engels 1978, 222–223 and Pateman 1988, 6, 14, 39–76.

13. It might be useful to consider here what Anthony Giddens refers to as the duality of structure and structuration (Giddens [1979] 1986). Social scientists who oppose agency to structure fail to grasp the duality of structure,

the sense in which social structure does not merely limit but also enables action; insofar as action is enabled by social structure, we can say action actually *presupposes* social structure. Such social scientists also fail to grasp what Giddens means by structuration, the sense in which social structures are created and re-created by action, as a language is maintained as a structure by those who continually speak it. Structuration then reveals the sense in which social structure *presupposes* agency.

14. I owe this terse distillation of what it means to offer a nonexplanation to Clifford Geertz (1973, 202).

15. Hilferding's criticism of Böhm-Bawerk, as well as Böhm-Bawerk's criticism of Marx, can be found in a volume edited by Schumpeter's junior colleague at Harvard, Paul Sweezy (Böhm-Bawerk 1975).

16. This, of course, is the core insight of any philosophy of science that attempts to incorporate a sociology of science, Kuhn's work being the best-known example (Kuhn 1970; Gunnell 1975). Schumpeter himself cited Karl Mannheim as the best starting point for a sociology of knowledge generally (Schumpeter [1942] 1976, 11 n. 3). It is important to bear in mind that acknowledging that science is unimaginable without a socially constituted and "transitive" dimension does not mean denying that science has an "intransitive" dimension, insofar as it is directed toward the study of enduring social structures. Roy Bhaskar argues that no theory of science can be adequate that does not take into account both of these dimensions (Bhaskar 1975). For the argument that Schumpeter also believed that science was or should be directed toward the study of such enduring social structures and mechanisms, see my section on scientific realism below.

17. This echoes a theme of one school in the logic and philosophy of science, at least as far back as John Dewey's "Thought and Its Subject Matter," which argued strongly for the context-dependency of thought (Dewey 1903). It is also a key component of contemporary arguments in the philosophy of science that advocate the relative methodological autonomy of different sciences and that are critical of behaviorism and logical positivism (Gunnell 1975; Kitcher 1989; Shapiro and Wendt 1992). Those who take this view are critics, of course, of philosophers like Carl Hempel, who saw the philosophy of science explicitly as an extension of the rules of logic to the realm of scientific procedure (Hempel 1942; Hempel 1970). In any case, Schumpeter tied his own enunciation of this sort of argument to similar ones by Dewey, as well as by William Whewell, John Stuart Mill, and Wilhelm Max Wundt (Schumpeter 1954b, 5).

18. Thus Oakley is right to say that "Schumpeter had an aversion to analysis that pursue methodological issues for their own sake or in which any attempt is made to defend substantive positions by means of some method-

ological premises," but he does not say enough about why this is so (Oakley 1990, 40).

19. Schumpeter argued elsewhere: "The historical or 'evolutionary' nature of the economic process unquestionably limits the scope of general concepts and of general relations between them ('economic laws') that we may be able to formulate . . . [I]t is true that 'economic laws' are much less stable than are the 'laws' of any physical science, that they work out differently in different [institutional] conditions, and that neglect of this fact has been responsible for many an aberration. It is also true that whenever we attempt to interpret human attitudes, especially attitudes of people far removed from us in time or culture, we risk misunderstanding them . . . All this is made much worse than it would be otherwise by the fact that the analyzing observer himself is the product of a given social environment—and of his particular location in that environment—that conditions him to see certain things rather than others, and to see them in a certain light" (Schumpeter 1954b, 34).

20. Note that the same starting point—the vision of the economy as a unique process in historic time—led Schumpeter to both economic sociology (the study of economic institutions and their development) and a sociology of economics.

21. It seems evident to me that this is an inadequate interpretation of Marx's theory of ideology. In particular it would be difficult to explain, from this standpoint, why Marx considered the work of Smith and Ricardo to be scientific, why he incorporated so much of it into his own work, and why he held them in higher esteem than the utopian (nonscientific) socialists. But this is not my focus here.

22. There is, of course, a similarity here to Weber's theory of ideal types, according to which the investigator necessarily began with a few matters of interest, taken out of the context of the chaotic social world, and then worked these up into a one-sided causal explanation (Weber 1949, 90–94). But Schumpeter was sharply critical of Weber's ambivalence about the relation of the resulting ideal types to social reality, and he was far less confident than Weber that science could escape its initial ideological conditioning and be made to serve any values at all. Indeed, he found uninteresting the whole distinction between statements of facts and statements of values.

6. Democracy and Equilibrium

1. Many critiques of rational choice theory doubt that the model of a human agent as a rational maximizer is adequate for social science or philosophy. This chapter does not provide such a critique of rational choice theory. Such

criticisms typically focus on the importance of the meaningful and communicative dimensions of conduct, on "commitment," altruistic behavior, and norm- or value-governed behavior. The contributions to this discussion are too numerous to cite. But for some basic statements and the way in which such critiques have been viewed, answered, and incorporated by some rational choice theorists, see Jon Elster, "Selfishness and Altruism," in Jane J. Mansbridge, ed., *Beyond Self-Interest* (Chicago: University of Chicago Press, 1990); John Ferejohn, "Rationality and Interpretation: Parliamentary Elections in Early Stuart England," in Kristen Renwick Monroe, ed., *The Economic Approach to Politics: A Critical Reassessment of the Theory of Rational Action* (New York: Harper Collins, 1991); Jürgen Habermas, *The Theory of Communicative Action,* vol. 1: *Reason and the Rationalization of Society* (Boston: Beacon Press, 1984), esp. 75–101; Mansbridge, "The Rise and Fall of Self-Interest in the Explanation of Public Life," in Mansbridge, ed., *Beyond Self-Interest;* Amartya K. Sen, "Rational Fools: A Critique of the Behavioural Foundations of Economic Theory," in Frank Hahn and Martin Hollis, eds., *Philosophy and Economic Theory* (Oxford: Oxford University Press, 1979); Charles Taylor, "Interpretation and the Sciences of Man," in Paul Rabinow and William M. Sullivan, eds., *Interpretive Social Science: A Reader* (Berkeley and Los Angeles: University of California Press, 1979); Albert S. Yee, "Thick Rationality and the Missing 'Brute Fact': The Limits of Rationalist Incorporations of Norms and Ideas," *Journal of Politics* 59, no. 4 (November 1997): 1001–1039. A different approach, reviewing the track record of rational choice approaches, is taken by Donald P. Green and Ian Shapiro, *Pathologies of Rational Choice Theory: A Critique of Applications in Political Science* (New Haven: Yale University Press, 1993).

2. Schumpeter regarded the physiocrats' *"tableau économique"* as an equilibrium vision of the economy (1954b, 242–243). Likewise, functionalist explanations have many characteristics of equilibrium models. Given these examples, I disagree with Riker, who argues that rational choice models are the only equilibrium models in social science (Riker 1990, 175).

3. This, of course, invites criticisms that Schumpeter's elite conception of democracy is not very democratic. But that is not my point here.

4. The conception presented here draws on Schumpeter's work cited above and several other sources: Clifford Geertz (1973), Karl Mannheim ([1936] 1985), and Karl Marx and Friedrich Engels (1978). Scholarly discussion of these sources, especially Marx and Mannheim, all too often focuses on whether any precinct of thought can be saved from the "ideological" label, and on the problem of whether a particular conception of ideology commits one to a self-undermining admission that even one's own perspective

is ideological. Generally speaking, I am convinced, like Schumpeter, that the problems of uncertainty, perspective, and the social conditioning of thought—usually associated with ideology—are endemic to all forms of knowledge and investigation, including those we deem (more or less justifiably) scientific. With this in mind, my conception of ideology also draws on a number of sources that would normally be considered contributions not to the theory of ideology but to epistemology, the theory of language, and the philosophy of science. These include: Austin 1962, Bernstein 1983, Bhaskar 1975, Dewey [1920] 1950, Feyerabend 1988, Gunnell 1975, Kuhn 1970, Lakatos 1970, and Quine 1990.

5. For those who wish to pursue the point, my argument here is analogous to Quine's portrayal of knowledge as a "man-made fabric" or a "field" so "underdetermined" by experience "that there is much latitude of choice as to what statement to reevaluate in the light of any single contrary experience" (1990, 37).

6. Galileo, for example, did not refute Aristotelian astronomical ideas merely with facts; he did so with telescopic observations, which in turn rested on a theory of optics (Lakatos 1970, 98).

7. In fact, Downs twice quotes Schumpeter's summary argument from *Capitalism, Socialism, and Democracy*, 282.

8. Downs clearly equated information with data or facts (Downs 1957, 79 and 83).

9. Cf. Mannheim ([1936] 1985, 29), quoted above.

10. Standing on purely terminological grounds, one might acquit Downs of the charge of contradiction by pointing out that "universal suffrage" and "manhood suffrage" have often been used synonymously. But the overall point would be the same. Downs's failure to recognize the real, practical, and principled contradiction between universal suffrage and the exclusion of women and "resident aliens" from voting was emblematic of his larger failure to make the establishment of democracy and battles about the meaning of democracy part of his supposedly comprehensive theory of democracy.

11. In one article, Weingast's language slips, without explanation, between several different formulations of what he is attempting to explain: the establishment of "democracy," "democratic stability," or "the stability of limited government," and the protection of a "set of economic and political rights [that] are compatible with economic prosperity" (1997, 245–247). And in another, which rather tendentiously associates "limited government" with a state that does not "confiscate wealth," he presents the rise of a form of limited-government "federalism" that protects business interests in terms vir-

tually identical to his account of the establishment of "democracy" (1995, 1). Neither article explains how he distinguishes between "democracy," "limited government," "federalism," and the protection of business interests.

12. He poses the problem similarly elsewhere (Przeworski 1999, 46 and 49), as part of a broader argument in favor of what he terms a "Schumpeterian conception of democracy" (ibid., 23).

13. See, for example, Przeworski 1991, 27.

14. It was only after decades of Jim Crow oppression that many Americans recognized even the most blatant transgressions of African Americans' democratic rights (see, for example, McAdam 1982, 109). There were at least two intertwined aspects to the ideological shift brought about by African American insurgency. McAdam refers to one of these as "cognitive liberation," the process by which some African Americans themselves came to recognize what Weingast would call "transgressions" as problems they could challenge by collective action. As McAdam points out (35), "structural inequities may be constant, but the collective perception of the legitimacy *and* mutability of those conditions is likely to vary a great deal over time." The other aspect was the shift in the ideological response of "other groups to blacks," which McAdam largely attributes to a sense of legitimacy won by the civil rights movement through the tactic of forcing the federal government to intervene on its behalf (108, 163–166, 169–172).

15. Weingast argues (1997, 253) that although democracy rests, in a sense, on "a set of political institutions and rights of citizens that define limits on the state, and a shared set of beliefs among the citizenry that those limits are appropriate and worth defending," political scientists should look not to norms as the explanation for such agreements on democratic institutions but to the experience of reaching an agreement about what constitutes transgression of democracy (see Weingast 1997, 245, 253, 254, 262). Weingast thus attempts to avoid simply making stable democracy dependent on the existence of "norms." But since he begins with the assumption that individuals can recognize transgressions of democracy, and this enters into his analysis of how they can reach agreement about violations, Weingast does not really escape resting his analysis on the existence of beliefs and practices external to his model.

16. At the same time, however, he argues that some recognition of both the "strategic pursuit of interests" and "norms" is generally necessary to understand "the world around us" (Przeworski 1991, 24). He simply sets out to demonstrate that norms are not necessary to explain the establishment of democratic institutions.

7. Conclusion

1. As R. J. Crampton puts it, "That the demand for free trade unions should become a national liberation movement was a product of the communist system. A trade union cannot function without the population being free to join it without fear; the population cannot do that if it does not live in an open, democratic society" (1994, 368). That was not how Solidarity originally saw things. It attempted throughout 1980 and 1981 to define its goals in terms of antipolitics and a lack of desire to take on the state (Ost 1990, 1–6, 75–148).

References

Addleson, Mark. 1995. *Equilibrium versus Understanding: Toward the Restoration of Economics as Social Theory.* London: Routledge.

Alexander, Jeffrey C. 1983. *The Classical Attempt at Synthesis: Max Weber,* vol. 3: *Theoretical Logic in Sociology.* Berkeley and Los Angeles: University of California Press.

Allen, Robert Loring. 1991. *Opening Doors: The Life and Work of Joseph Schumpeter.* 2 vols. New Brunswick, N.J.: Transaction Publishers.

Almond, Gabriel A. 1980. "The Intellectual History of the Civic Culture Concept." In *The Civic Culture Revisited,* ed. G. A. Almond and S. Verba. Boston: Little, Brown.

Alter, Max. 1990. *Carl Menger and the Origins of Austrian Economics.* Studies in the History, Methods, and Boundaries of Economics. Boulder, Colo.: Westview Press.

Anderson, P. R. 1970. "Gustav von Schmoller (1838–1917)." In *Essays in Modern European Historiography,* ed. S. W. Halperin. Chicago: University of Chicago Press.

Arrow, Kenneth. 1968. "Economic Equilibrium." In *International Encyclopedia of the Social Sciences,* ed. D. L. Sills. New York: Macmillan.

Ashcraft, Richard. 1975. "On the Problem of Methodology and the Nature of Political Theory." *Political Theory* 3: 5–25.

———. 1984. "One Step Backward, Two Steps Forward: Reflections upon Contemporary Political Theory." In *What Should Political Theory Be Now?* ed. J. S. Nelson. Albany: State University of New York Press.

———. 1986. *Revolutionary Politics and Locke's Two Treatises of Government.* Princeton, N.J.: Princeton University Press.

———. 1989. "Class Conflict and Constitutionalism in J. S. Mill's Thought." In *Liberalism and the Moral Life,* ed. N. L. Rosenblum. Cambridge, Mass.: Harvard University Press.

———. 1995. "Joseph Schumpeter and the Problem of Democracy." Department of Political Science, University of California, Los Angeles. Photocopy.

Ashmead-Bartlett, Ellis. 1923. *The Tragedy of Central Europe*. London: Thornton Butterworth.

Austin, J. L. 1962. *How to Do Things with Words*. Oxford: Clarendon Press.

Bachhofer, Ludwig, James Franck, and Hans Goffron. 1945. "An Appeal" [with handwritten notation by Joseph A. Schumpeter]. In Harvard University Archives, HUG (FP) 4.7 Box 1. Courtesy of the Harvard University Archives.

Bachrach, Peter. 1967. *The Theory of Democratic Elitism: A Critique*. Basic Studies in Politics, ed. S. S. Wolin. Boston: Little, Brown.

Balabkins, Nicholas. 1988. *Not by Theory Alone: The Economics of Gustav von Schmoller and Its Legacy to America, Volkswirtschaftliche Schriften*. Berlin: Duncker and Humbolt.

Bauer, Otto. [1907] 1978. "Socialism and the Principle of Nationality" [from "Die Nationalitätenfrage und die Sozialdemokratie"]. In *Austro-Marxism*, ed. T. Bottomore and P. Goode. Oxford: Clarendon Press.

———. 1919. Letter to Karl Renner, 31 May 1919. In Österreichisches Staatsarchiv/Archiv der Republik, Neues Politisches Archiv-Präsidium, Nachlaß Bauer. Vienna.

———. [1919] 1976. "Der Weg zum Sozialismus." In *Otto Bauer: Werkausgabe*, ed. H. Pepper. Vienna: Europaverlag.

———. [1919] 1978. "Political and Social Revolution" [from "Der Weg zum Sozialismus"]. In *Austro-Marxism*, ed. T. Bottomore and P. Goode. Oxford: Clarendon Press.

———. [1925] 1970. *The Austrian Revolution*, trans. H. J. Stenning. Research and Source Works Series, Selected Essays in History, Economics and Social Science. New York: Burt Franklin.

Beetham, David. 1985. *Max Weber and the Theory of Modern Politics*, 2nd ed. Cambridge: Polity Press.

Bellamy, Richard. 1991. "Schumpeter and the Transformation of Capitalism, Liberalism, and Democracy." *Government and Opposition* 26: 500–519.

Berelson, Bernard, Paul F. Lazarsfeld, and William N. McPhee. 1954. *Voting: A Study of Opinion Formation in a Presidential Campaign*. Chicago: University of Chicago Press.

Bernstein, Richard. 1983. *Beyond Objectivism and Relativism: Science, Hermeneutics and Praxis*. Philadelphia: University of Pennsylvania Press.

Bhaskar, Roy. 1975. *A Realist Theory of Science*. Leeds, England: Leeds Books.

Biagini, Eugenio F. 1992. *Liberty, Retrenchment and Reform*. Cambridge: Cambridge University Press.

Biagini, Eugenio F., and Alastair J. Reid, eds. 1991. *Currents of Radicalism: Popular Radicalism, Organised Labour, and Party Politics in Britain, 1850–1914*. Cambridge: Cambridge University Press.

Boehm, Stephan. 1990. "The Austrian Tradition: Schumpeter and Mises." In

Neoclassical Economic Theory, 1870–1930, ed. K. Hennings and W. J. Samuels. Boston: Kluwer Academic Publishers.

Böhm-Bawerk, Eugen von. 1975. *Karl Marx and the Close of His System, by Eugen von Böhm-Bawerk, and Böhm-Bawerk's Criticism of Marx, by Rudolf Hilferding,* trans. Paul M. Sweezy. Reprints of Economic Classics. Clifton, N.J.: A. M. Kelley.

Bosanquet, Nick. 1983. *After the New Right.* London: Heinemann.

Bottomore, Tom. 1964. *Elites and Society.* New York: Basic Books.

——. 1992. *Between Marginalism and Marxism: The Economic Sociology of J. A. Schumpeter.* New York: St. Martin's Press.

Bottomore, Tom, and Patrick Goode, eds. 1978. *Austro-Marxism.* Oxford: Clarendon Press.

Boyer, John W. 1981. *Political Radicalism in Late Imperial Vienna: Origins of the Christian Social Movement, 1848–1897.* Chicago: University of Chicago Press.

——. 1995. *Culture and Political Crisis in Vienna: Christian Socialism in Power, 1897–1918.* Chicago: University of Chicago Press.

Breiner, Peter. 1996. *Max Weber and Democratic Politics.* Ithaca, N.Y.: Cornell University Press.

Breitman, Richard. 1981. *German Socialism and Weimar Democracy.* Chapel Hill: University of North Carolina Press.

Brown, Douglas V., et al. 1934. *The Economics of the Recovery Program.* New York and London: Whittlesey House, McGraw-Hill.

Caldwell, Bruce J., ed. 1990. *Carl Menger and His Legacy in Economics,* annual supplement to vol. 22, *History of Political Economy.* Durham, N.C.: Duke University Press.

Calvert, Randall L. 1995. "Rational Actors, Equilibrium, and Social Institutions." In *Explaining Social Institutions,* ed. J. Knight and I. Sened. Ann Arbor: University of Michigan Press.

Carmon, Arye. 1976. "The Impact of the Nazi Racial Decrees on the University of Heidelberg: A Case Study." *Yad Vashem Studies* 11: 131–163.

Catephores. 1994. "The Imperious Austrian: Schumpeter as Bourgeois Marxist." *New Left Review* 205 (May/June): 3–30.

Cole, G. D. H. 1915. *The World of Labour: A Discussion of the Present and Future of Trade Unionism,* 2nd ed. London: G. Bell and Sons.

——. 1920. *Guild Socialism: A Plan for Economic Democracy.* New York: Frederick A. Stokes Co.

Cooke, Morris Llewellyn, and Philip Murray. 1940. *Organized Labor and Production: Next Steps in Industrial Democracy.* New York: Harper and Brothers.

Craig, Gordon A. 1978. *Germany, 1866–1945.* Oxford: Oxford University Press.

Cramer, Dale L., and Charles G. Leathers. 1981. "Schumpeter's Corporatist Views: Links among his Social Theory, Quadragesimo Anno, and Moral Reform." *History of Political Economy* 13 (4): 745–771.

Crampton, R. J. 1994. *Eastern Europe in the Twentieth Century.* London: Routledge.

Daal, Jan van, and Albert Jolink. 1993. *The Equilibrium Economics of Leon Walras.* London: Routledge.

Dahl, Robert A. 1956. *A Preface to Democratic Theory.* Chicago: University of Chicago Press.

Davies, Morton R. 1972. "J. A. Schumpeter and the Methodology of the Social Sciences." *Political Science Review* 11 (2/3): 105–123.

Dewey, John. [1920] 1950. *Reconstruction in Philosophy.* New York: Mentor.

———. 1935. *Liberalism and Social Action.* New York: G. P. Putnam's Sons.

Dewey, John, ed. 1903. *Studies in Logical Theory.* The Decennial Publications, vol. 11. Chicago: University of Chicago Press.

Diamant, Alfred. 1960. *Austrian Catholics and the First Republic: Democracy, Capitalism, and the Social Order, 1918–1934.* Princeton, N.J.: Princeton University Press.

Diamond, Larry, and Marc F. Plattner. 1995. "Introduction." In *Economic Reform and Democracy,* ed. L. Diamond and M. F. Plattner. Baltimore: Johns Hopkins University Press.

Dobb, M. 1973. *Theories of Value and Distribution since Adam Smith: Ideology and Economic Theory.* Cambridge: Cambridge University Press.

Downs, Anthony. 1957. *An Economic Theory of Democracy.* New York: HarperCollins.

Elliott, J. E. 1994. "Joseph A. Schumpeter and the Theory of Democracy." *Review of Social Economy* 54 (4): 280–300.

Elster, Jon. 1986. "Introduction." In *Rational Choice,* ed. J. Elster. New York: New York University Press.

———. 1990. "Selfishness and Altruism." In *Beyond Self-Interest,* ed. J. Mansbridge. Chicago: University of Chicago Press.

Endres, A. M. 1991. "Menger, Wieser, Böhm-Bawerk, and the Analysis of Economizing Behavior." *History of Political Economy* 23 (2): 279–299.

Ferejohn, John. 1991. "Rationality and Interpretation: Parliamentary Elections in Early Stuart England." In *The Economic Approach to Politics: A Critical Reassessment of the Theory of Rational Action,* ed. K. R. Monroe. New York: HarperCollins.

Feyerabend, Paul. 1988. *Against Method,* rev. ed. London: Verso.

Finn, Margot C. 1993. *After Chartism: Class and Nation in English Radical Politics, 1848–1874.* Cambridge: Cambridge University Press.

Foner, Philip S. 1965. *The Industrial Workers of the World, 1905–1917,* vol. 4:

History of the Labor Movement in the United States. New York: International Publishers.

Fraser, Steve. 1989. "The 'Labor Question.'" In *The Rise and Fall of the New Deal Order, 1930–1980,* ed. S. Fraser and G. Gerstle. Princeton, New Jersey: Princeton University Press.

Freeman, Joshua, et al. 1992. *Who Built America? Working People and the Nation's Economy, Politics, Culture and Society,* ed. S. Brier. 2 vols. Vol. 2: *From the Gilded Age to the Present.* American Social History Project. New York: Pantheon Books.

Frey, Bruno S. 1982. "Schumpeter, Political Economist." In *Schumpeterian Economics,* ed. H. Frisch. Eastbourne, England: Praeger.

Friedländer, Saul. 1997. *Nazi Germany and the Jews,* vol. 1: *The Years of Persecution, 1933–1939.* New York: HarperPerennial.

Frisch, Helmut, ed. 1981. *Schumpeterian Economics.* Praeger Special Studies. Eastbourne, England: Praeger.

Fukuyama, Francis. 1989. "The End of History?" *The National Interest* 16 (Summer): 3–18.

Fusfeld, Daniel R. 1987. "Methodenstreit." In *The New Palgrave: A Dictionary of Economics,* ed. J. Eatwell, M. Milgate, and P. Newman. London: Macmillan.

Geertz, Clifford. 1973. *The Interpretation of Cultures.* New York: Basic Books.

Gerlich, Rudolf. 1980. *Die Gescheiterte Alternative.* Vienna: Wilhelm Braumueller.

Giddens, Anthony. [1979] 1986. *Central Problems in Social Theory: Action, Structure and Contradiction in Social Analysis.* Berkeley and Los Angeles: University of California Press.

Goldhagen, Daniel Jonah. 1996. *Hitler's Willing Executioners: Ordinary Germans and the Holocaust.* New York: Alfred A. Knopf.

Goldscheid, Rudolf. 1958. "A Sociological Approach to the Problems of Public Finance." In *Classics in the Theory of Public Finance,* ed. R. A. Musgrave and A. T. Peacock. London: Macmillan.

Goode, Patrick. 1991. "Councils." In *A Dictionary of Marxist Thought,* ed. T. Bottomore. Oxford: Blackwell.

Green, Donald P., and Ian Shapiro. 1994. *Pathologies of Rational Choice Theory: A Critique of Applications in Political Science.* New Haven, Conn.: Yale University Press.

Gulick, Charles A. 1948. *Austria from Habsburg to Hitler.* 2 vols. Berkeley and Los Angeles: University of California Press.

Gunnell, John G. 1975. *Philosophy, Science, and Political Inquiry.* Morristown, N.J.: General Learning Press.

Haberler, Gottfried. 1950. "Joseph Alois Schumpeter, 1883–1950." *Quarterly Journal of Economics* 64 (3): 333–384.

Havel, Václav. 1991. "The Power of the Powerless." In *Open Letters, Selected Prose, 1965–1990*, ed. P. Wilson. London: Faber and Faber.

Hayek, Friedrich A. von. 1939. *Freedom and the Economic System*, ed. H. D. Gideonse. Public Policy Pamphlet No. 29. Chicago: University of Chicago Press.

———. 1944. *The Road to Serfdom*. Chicago: University of Chicago Press.

Hayek, Friedrich A. von, ed. 1935. *Collectivist Economic Planning: Critical Studies on the Possibilities of Socialism*. London: George Routledge and Sons.

Heertje, Arnold, ed. 1981. *Schumpeter's Vision: Capitalism, Socialism and Democracy after Forty Years*. Praeger Special Studies. Eastbourne, England: Praeger.

Heilbroner, Robert L. 1988. *Behind the Veil of Economics: Essays in the Worldly Philosophy*. New York: Norton.

Held, David. 1987. *Models of Democracy*. Stanford, Calif.: Stanford University Press.

Hempel, Carl. 1942. "The Function of General Laws in History." *Journal of Philosophy* 39: 35–48.

———. 1970. "On the 'Standard Conception' of Scientific Theories." In *Analyses of Theories and Methods of Physics*, ed. M. Radner and S. Winokur. Minneapolis: University of Minnesota Press.

Hilferding, Rudolf. 1910 [1981]. *Finance Capital: A Study of the Latest Phase of Capitalist Development,* trans. Morris Watnick and Sam Gordon. London: Routledge and Kegan Paul.

———. 1975. "Böhm-Bawerk's Criticism of Marx." In *Karl Marx and the Close of His System, by Eugen von Böhm-Bawerk and Böhm-Bawerk's Criticism of Marx, by Rudolf Hilferding*, ed. P. M. Sweezy. Clifton, N.J.: Augustus M. Kelley.

Hobsbawm, Eric J. 1992. *Nations and Nationalism since 1789: Programme, Myth, Reality,* 2nd ed. Cambridge: Cambridge University Press, Canto.

———. 1994. *The Age of Extremes: A History of the World, 1914–1991*. New York: Vintage.

Huntington, Samuel P. 1984. "Will More Countries Become Democratic?" *Political Science Quarterly* 99 (Summer): 193–218.

Isaac, Jeffrey C. 1987a. "Beyond the Three Faces of Power: A Realist Critique." *Polity* 20: 4–31.

———. 1987b. *Power and Marxist Theory: A Realist View*. Ithaca, N.Y.: Cornell University Press.

———. 1998. *Democracy in Dark Times*. Ithaca, N.Y.: Cornell University Press.

Jensen, Hans E. 1987. "New Lights on J. A. Schumpeter's Theory of the History of Economics?" *Research in the History of Economic Thought and Methodology* 5: 117–148.

Johnston, William M. 1972. *The Austrian Mind: An Intellectual and Social History, 1848–1938*. Berkeley and Los Angeles: University of California Press.

Keohane, Nannerl O. 1978. "'The Masterpiece of Policy in Our Century': Rousseau on the Morality of the Enlightenment." *Political Theory* 6, 4 (November): 457–484.

Kershaw, Ian, ed. 1990. *Weimar: Why Did German Democracy Fail? Debates in Modern History.* New York: St. Martin's Press.

Kitcher, Philip. 1989. "Explanatory Unification and the Causal Structure of the World." In *Scientific Explanation,* ed. P. Kitcher and W. Salmon. Minneapolis: University of Minnesota Press.

Kolb, Eberhard. 1988. *The Weimar Republic,* trans. P. S. Falla. London: Unwin Hyman.

Konrád, George. 1984. *Antipolitics: An Essay,* trans. Richard E. Allen. San Diego: Harcourt Brace Jovanovich.

Krohn, Claus-Dieter. 1993. *Intellectuals in Exile: Refugee Scholars and the New School for Social Research,* trans. Rita Kimball and Robert Kimball. Amherst: University of Massachusetts Press.

Kuenne, Robert E. 1971. *Eugen von Böhm-Bawerk.* Columbia Essays on Great Economists. New York: Columbia University Press.

Kuhn, Thomas. 1970. "Logic of Discovery or Psychology of Research?" In *Criticism and the Growth of Knowledge,* ed. I. Lakatos and A. Musgrave. Cambridge: Cambridge University Press.

Laclau, Ernesto, and Chantal Mouffe. 1985. *Hegemony and Socialist Strategy: Towards a Radical Democratic Politics.* London: Verso.

Lakatos, Imre. 1970. "Falsification and the Methodology of Scientific Research Programs." In *Criticism and the Growth of Knowledge,* ed. I. Lakatos and A. Musgrave. Cambridge: Cambridge University Press.

Lange, Oskar, and Fred M. Taylor. 1938. *On the Economic Theory of Socialism,* ed. B. E. Lippincott. 2 vols. Vol. 2: *Government Control of the Economic Order.* Minneapolis: University of Minnesota Press.

Le Bon, Gustave. [1895] 1981. *The Crowd: A Study of the Popular Mind.* New York: Penguin.

Lenin, V. I. 1975. *The Lenin Anthology,* ed. R. C. Tucker. New York: W. W. Norton.

Lichtman, Richard. 1969. "The Facade of Equality in Liberal Democratic Theory." *Inquiry* 12. 170–208.

Lipset, Seymour Martin. 1959. "Some Social Requisites of Democracy. Economic Development and Political Legitimacy." *American Political Science Review* 53 (1): 69–105.

———. 1960. *Political Man: The Social Bases of Politics.* Garden City, N.Y.: Doubleday.

Little, Daniel. 1991. *Varieties of Social Explanation: An Introduction to the Philosophy of Social Science.* Boulder, Colo.: Westview Press.

Low, Alfred D. 1974. *The Anschluss Movement, 1918–19, and the Paris Peace Conference*. Philadelphia: American Philosophical Society.

Lukes, Steven. 1977. *Essays in Social Theory*. London: Macmillan.

Macdonald, Ronan. 1965. "Schumpeter and Max Weber: Central Visions and Social Theories." *Quarterly Journal of Economics* 79: 373–396.

Machlup, Fritz. 1951. "Schumpeter's Economic Methodology." In *Schumpeter: Social Scientist*, ed. S. E. Harris. Freeport, N.Y.: Books for Libraries Press.

Macpherson, C. B. 1977. *The Life and Times of Liberal Democracy*. Oxford: Oxford University Press.

Maier, Charles S. 1975. *Recasting Bourgeois Europe: Stabilization in France, Germany and Italy in the Decade after World War I*. Princeton, N.J.: Princeton University Press.

Manicas, Peter. 1987. *A History and Philosophy of the Social Sciences*. London: Basil Blackwell.

Mannheim, Karl. [1936] 1985. *Ideology and Utopia: An Introduction to the Sociology of Knowledge*, trans. Louis Wirth and Edward Shils. San Diego: Harcourt Brace Jovanovich.

Mansbridge, Jane. 1990. "The Rise and Fall of Self-Interest in the Explanation of Public Life." In *Beyond Self-Interest*, ed. J. Mansbridge. Chicago: University of Chicago Press.

März, Eduard. 1981. "Joseph A. Schumpeter as Minister of Finance of the First Republic of Austria, March 1919–October 1919." In *Schumpeterian Economics*, ed. H. Frisch. Eastbourne, England: Praeger.

———. 1991. *Joseph Schumpeter: Scholar, Teacher and Politician*. New Haven, Conn.: Yale University Press.

Marx, Karl, and Friedrich Engels. 1978. *The Marx-Engels Reader*, ed. R. C. Tucker. New York: W. W. Norton.

May, Arthur J. 1966. *The Passing of the Hapsburg Monarchy, 1914–1918*. 2 vols. Philadelphia: University of Pennsylvania Press.

McAdam, Doug. 1982. *Political Process and the Development of Black Insurgency, 1930–1970*. Chicago: University of Chicago Press.

McAdam, Doug, John D. McCarthy, and Mayer N. Zald. 1996. "Introduction: Opportunities, Mobilizing Structures, and Framing Processes—Toward a Synthetic, Comparative Perspective on Social Movements." In *Comparative Perspectives on Social Movements: Political Opportunities, Mobilizing Structures, and Cultural Framings*, ed. D. McAdam, J. D. McCarthy, and M. N. Zald. Cambridge: Cambridge University Press.

McMullin, Ernan. 1984. "Two Ideals of Explanation in Natural Science." In *Causation and Causal Theories*, ed. P. A. French, T. E. Uehling, and H. K. Wettstein. Minneapolis: University of Minnesota Press.

Meek, R. L. 1967. *Economics and Ideology and Other Essays: Studies in the Development of Economic Thought.* London: Chapman and Hall.

Meisel, James H. 1962. *The Myth of the Ruling Class: Gaetano Mosca and the 'Elite.'* Ann Arbor: University of Michigan Press.

Michels, Robert. [1915] 1962. *Political Parties: A Sociological Study of the Tendencies of Modern Democracy,* trans. Eden Paul and Cedar Paul. New York: Free Press.

Michnik, Adam. 1985. "Conversation in the Citadel." In *Letters from Prison and Other Essays.* Berkeley and Los Angeles: University of California Press.

Mill, John Stuart. [1835] 1973. "Tocqueville on Democracy in America, Vol. I." In *Essays on Politics and Culture,* ed. G. Himmelfarb. Reprint. Gloucester, Mass.: Peter Smith.

———. [1865] 1991. *Considerations on Representative Government.* Buffalo, N.Y.: Prometheus.

———. [1873] 1989. *Autobiography.* London: Penguin.

Miller, David. 1983. "The Competitive Model of Democracy." In *Democratic Theory and Practice,* ed. G. Duncan. Cambridge: Cambridge University Press.

Mitchell, William C. 1984a. "Schumpeter and Public Choice, Part I: Precursor to Public Choice?" *Public Choice* 42: 73–88.

———. 1984b. "Schumpeter and Public Choice, Part II: Democracy and the Demise of Capitalism: The Missing Chapter in Schumpeter." *Public Choice* 42: 161–174.

Mommsen, Wolfgang J. 1989. *The Political and Social Theory of Max Weber: Collected Essays.* Cambridge: Polity Press.

Mosca, Gaetano. 1967. *The Ruling Class,* trans. Hannah D. Kahn. New York: McGraw-Hill.

Mukherji, Anjan. 1990. *Walrasian and Non-Walrasian Equilibria: An Introduction to General Equilibrium Analysis.* Oxford: Clarendon Press.

Nye, Robert A. 1977. *The Anti-Democratic Sources of Elite Theory: Pareto, Mosca, Michels.* Beverly Hills: Sage Publications.

Oakley, Allen. 1990. *Schumpeter's Theory of Capitalist Motion: A Critical Exposition and Reassessment.* Hants, England: Edward Elgar.

Oberschall, Anthony. 1996. "Opportunities and Framing in the Eastern European Revolts of 1989." In *Comparative Perspectives on Social Movements: Political Opportunities, Mobilizing Structures, and Cultural Framings,* ed. D. McAdam, J. D. McCarthy, and M. N. Zald. Cambridge: Cambridge University Press.

Okin, Susan Moller. 1979. *Women in Western Political Thought.* Princeton, N.J.: Princeton University Press.

Ordeshook, Peter C. 1982. "Political Disequilibrium and Scientific Inquiry: A Comment on William Riker's 'Implications for the Disequilibrium of Majority Rule for the Study of Institutions.'" In *Political Equilibrium*, ed. P. C. Ordeshook and K. A. Shepsle. Boston: Kluwer-Nijhoff.

———. 1986. "Preface." In *Game Theory and Political Theory*, ed. P. C. Ordeshook. Cambridge: Cambridge University Press.

———. 1992. "Constitutional Stability." *Constitutional Political Economy* 3 (Spring/Summer): 137–175.

Orren, Karen. 1991. *Belated Feudalism: Labor, the Law, and Liberal Development in the United States.* Cambridge: Cambridge University Press.

Ost, David. 1990. *Solidarity and the Politics of Anti-Politics: Opposition and Reform in Poland since 1968.* Philadelphia: Temple University Press.

———. 1997. "Can Unions Survive Communism?" *Dissent* 44, 1 (Winter): 21–27.

Osterhammel, Jurgen. 1987. "Varieties of Social Economics: Joseph A. Schumpeter and Max Weber." In *Max Weber and His Contemporaries*, ed. W. J. Mommsen and J. Osterhammel. London: Allen and Unwin.

O'Toole, Laurence J., Jr. 1977. "Schumpeter's 'Democracy': A Critical View." *Polity* 4: 446–462.

Pareto, Vilfredo. 1966. *Sociological Writings*, trans. Derick Mirfin, ed. S. E. Finer. London: Pall Mall Press.

Parry, Geraint. 1969. *Political Elites.* Studies in Political Science. London: George Allen and Unwin.

Parry, Geraint, and Michael Moran. 1994. "Introduction: Problems of Democracy and Democratization." In *Democracy and Democratization*, ed. G. Parry and M. Moran. London: Routledge.

Pateman, Carole. 1970. *Participation and Democratic Theory.* Cambridge: Cambridge University Press.

———. 1974. "Criticising Empirical Theorists of Democracy: A Comment on Skinner." *Political Theory* 2 (2): 215–218.

———. 1979. *The Problem of Political Obligation: A Critical Analysis of Liberal Theory.* Chichester, England: John Wiley and Sons.

———. 1983. "Feminism and Democracy." In *Democratic Theory and Practice*, ed. G. Duncan. Cambridge: Cambridge University Press.

———. 1988. *The Sexual Contract.* Stanford, Calif.: Stanford University Press.

———. 1996. "Democracy and Democratization, Presidential Address, 16th World Congress, IPSA." *International Political Science Review* 17 (1): 5–12.

Pauley, Bruce F. 1972. *The Habsburg Legacy, 1867–1939.* New York: Holt, Rinehart and Winston.

———. 1992. *From Prejudice to Persecution: A History of Austrian Anti-Semitism.* Chapel Hill: University of North Carolina Press.

Phillips, Anne. 1991. *Engendering Democracy.* University Park, Pa.: Pennsylvania State University Press.

Plamenatz, John P. 1973. "Schumpeter and Free Competition for Power." In *Democracy and Illusion: An Examination of Certain Aspects of Modern Democratic Theory.* London: Longman.

Plattner, Marc F. 1996. "The Democratic Moment." In *The Global Resurgence of Democracy,* ed. L. D. and M. F. Plattner. Baltimore: Johns Hopkins University Press.

Plotke, David. 1989. "The Wagner Act, Again: Politics and Labor, 1935–1937." *Studies in American Political Development* 3: 105–156.

Przeworski, Adam. 1991. *Democracy and the Market.* Cambridge: Cambridge University Press.

———. 1999. "Minimalist Conception of Democracy: A Defense." In *Democracy's Value,* ed. I. Shapiro and C. Hacker-Cordon. Cambridge: Cambridge University Press.

Pulzer, Peter. 1988. *The Rise of Political Anti-Semitism in Germany and Austria,* rev. ed. Cambridge, Mass.: Harvard University Press.

Putnam, Robert D. 1993. *Making Democracy Work: Civic Traditions in Modern Italy.* Princeton, N.J.: Princeton University Press.

Quine, W. V. O. 1990. "Two Dogmas of Empiricism." In *The Philosophy of Language,* ed. A. P. Martinich. New York: Oxford University Press.

Rabinbach, Anson. 1983. *The Crisis of Austrian Socialism: From Red Vienna to Civil War, 1927–1934.* Chicago: University of Chicago Press.

Rabinbach, Anson, ed. 1985. *The Austrian Socialist Experiment: Social Democracy and Austromarxism, 1918–1934.* Westview Special Studies in West European Politics and Society. Boulder, Colo.: Westview Press.

Raina, Peter. 1985. *Poland 1981: Toward Social Renewal.* London: George Allen and Unwin.

Rapaport, E. 1982. "Is Democracy Possible?" *American Philosophical Quarterly* 19: 355–363.

Redlich, Josef. 1954. *Das Politische Tagebuch Josef Redlichs.* Graz, Austria: Verlag Hermann Boehlaus.

Renner, Karl. [1921] 1978. "Democracy and the Council System" [from "Demokratie und Rätesystem"]. In *Austro-Marxism,* ed. T. Bottomore and P. Goode. Oxford: Clarendon Press.

Ricci, David M. 1970. "Democracy Attenuated: Schumpeter, the Process Theory, and American Democratic Thought." *Journal of Politics* 32 (1970): 348–352.

Riker, William H. 1980. "Implications of the Disequilibrium of Majority Rule for the Study of Institutions." *American Political Science Review* 74: 432–446.

———. 1990. "Political Science and Rational Choice." In *Perspectives on Posi-*

tive Political Economy, ed. J. E. Alt and K. A. Shepsle. Cambridge: Cambridge University Press.

Rousseau, Jean-Jacques. 1967. *The Social Contract and the Discourse on the Origin of Inequality*, ed. Lester G. Crocker. New York: Washington Square Press.

Rutkoff, Peter M., and William B. Scott. 1986. *New School: A History of the New School for Social Research*. New York: Free Press.

Sale, Kirkpatrick. 1973. *SDS*. New York: Vintage Books.

Salvadori, Massimo. 1979. *Karl Kautsky and the Socialist Revolution, 1880–1938*, trans. Jon Rothschild. London: NLB.

Santarelli, Enrico, and Enzo Pesciarelli. 1990. "The Emergence of a Vision: The Development of Schumpeter's Theory of Entrepreneurship." *History of Political Economy* 22 (4): 677–696.

Santoro, Emilio. 1993. "Democratic Theory and Individual Autonomy: An Interpretation of Schumpeter's Doctrine of Autonomy." *European Journal of Political Research* 23: 121–143.

Sarle, Charles F. 1935. Letter to Joseph A. Schumpeter. In Harvard University Archives, HUG (FP) 4.7 Box 3. Courtesy of the Harvard University Archives.

Satz, Debra, and John Ferejohn. 1994. "Rational Choice and Social Theory." *The Journal of Philosophy* 91: 71–87.

Schefold, B. 1987. "Gustav von Schmoller." In *The New Palgrave: A Dictionary of Economics*, ed. J. Eatwell, M. Milgate, and P. Newman. London: Macmillan.

Schmitter, Phillippe C., and Terry Lynn Karl. 1996. "What Democracy Is . . . and Is Not." In *The Global Resurgence of Democracy*, ed. L. Diamond and M. F. Plattner. Baltimore: Johns Hopkins University Press.

Schneider, Erich. 1951. "Schumpeter's Early German Work, 1906–1917." In *Schumpeter, Social Scientist*, ed. S. E. Harris. Cambridge, Mass.: Harvard University Press.

Schorske, Carl E. 1980. *Fin-de-Siecle Vienna: Politics and Culture*. New York: Alfred A. Knopf.

Schumpeter, Joseph A. 1908. *Das Wesen und der Hauptinhalt der theoretischen Nationalökonomie*. Leipzig: Duncker and Humbolt.

———. [1911] 1934. *The Theory of Economic Development: An Inquiry into Profits, Capital, Credit, Interest, and the Business Cycle*, trans. Redvers Opie. Harvard Economic Studies 46. Cambridge, Mass.: Harvard University Press.

———. 1912. *Theorie der wirtschaftlichen Entwicklung*. Leipzig: Duncker and Humbolt.

———. [1918] 1991. "The Crisis of the Tax State." In *The Economics and Sociology of Capitalism*, ed. R. Swedberg. Princeton, N.J.: Princeton University.

———. [1918–19] 1991. "The Sociology of Imperialisms." In *The Economics and Sociology of Capitalism*, ed. R. Swedberg. Princeton, N.J.: Princeton University Press.

————. 1920–21. "Sozialistische Möglichkeiten von heute." *Archiv für Sozial-wissenschaft und Sozialpolitik* 48: 305–360.

————. [1924] 1952. "Der Sozialismus in England und bei uns." In *Aufsätze zur Ökonomischen Theorie*, ed. E. Schneider and A. Spietoff. Tübingen: J. C. B. Mohr.

————. [1927] 1991. "Social Classes in an Ethnically Homogenous Environment." In *The Economics and Sociology of Capitalism*, ed. R. Swedberg. Princeton, N.J.: Princeton University Press.

————. [1928] 1951. "The Instability of Capitalism." In *Essays of J. A. Schumpeter*, ed. R. V. Clemence. Cambridge, Mass.: Addison-Wesley.

————. [1932] 1952. "Das Woher und Wohin unserer Wissenschaft." In *Aufsätze zur Ökonomischen Theorie*, ed. E. Schneider and A. Spiethoff. Tübingen: J. C. B. Mohr.

————. 1933. Letter to Beatrice Löwe, 19 May 1933. In Harvard University Archives, HUG (FP) 4.7 Box 6. Courtesy of the Harvard University Archives.

————. [1936] 1951. "Review of Keynes's General Theory." In *Essays of J. A. Schumpeter*, ed. R. V. Clemence. Cambridge, Mass.: Addison-Wesley.

————. [1936] 1991. "Can Capitalism Survive?" In *The Economics and Sociology of Capitalism*, ed. R. Swedberg. Princeton, N.J.: Princeton University Press.

————. [1937] 1951. "Preface to the Japanese Edition of 'Theorie der Wirtshaftlichen Entwicklung.'" In *Essays of J. A. Schumpeter*, ed. R. V. Clemence. Cambridge, Mass.: Addison-Wesley.

————. 1939. *Business Cycles: A Theoretical, Historical and Statistical Analysis of the Capitalist Process*. 2 vols. New York: McGraw-Hill.

————. [1940] 1991. "The Meaning of Rationality in the Social Sciences." In *The Economics and Sociology of Capitalism*, ed. R. Swedberg. Princeton, N.J.: Princeton University Press.

————. [1941] 1991. "An Economic Interpretation of Our Time: The Lowell Lectures." In *The Economics and Sociology of Capitalism*, ed. R. Swedberg. Princeton, N.J.: Princeton University Press.

————. [1942] 1947. *Capitalism, Socialism, and Democracy*, 2nd ed. New York: Harper and Brothers.

————. [1942] 1976. *Capitalism, Socialism, and Democracy*, 3rd ed. New York: Harper Torchbooks.

————. 1946. "Review: The Road to Serfdom, Friedrich A. Hayek." *Journal of Political Economy* 54 (3): 269–270.

————. [1946] 1991. "The Future of Private Enterprise in the Face of Modern Socialistic Enterprises." In *The Economics and Sociology of Capitalism*, ed. R. Swedberg. Princeton, N.J.: Princeton University Press.

————. [1948] 1991. "Wage and Tax Policy in Transitional States of Society." In

The Economics and Sociology of Capitalism, ed. R. Swedberg. Princeton, N.J.: Princeton University Press.

———. 1949. "Vilfredo Pareto (1848–1923)." *Quarterly Journal of Economics* 63 (2): 147–173.

———. [1949] 1951a. "The Communist Manifesto in Sociology and Economics." In *Essays of J. A. Schumpeter,* ed. R. V. Clemence. Cambridge, Mass.: Addison-Wesley.

———. [1949] 1951b. "English Economists and the State-Managed Economy." In *Essays of J. A. Schumpeter,* ed. R. V. Clemence. Cambridge, Mass.: Addison-Wesley.

———. [1949] 1951c. "Science and Ideology." In *Essays of J. A. Schumpeter,* ed. R. V. Clemence. Cambridge, Mass.: Addison-Wesley.

———. [1949] 1976. "The March into Socialism." In *Capitalism, Socialism, and Democracy.* New York: Harper Torchbooks.

———. 1951a. *Essays of J. A. Schumpeter,* ed. R. V. Clemence. Cambridge, Mass.: Addison-Wesley.

———. 1951b. *Ten Great Economists: From Marx to Keynes.* New York: Oxford University Press.

———. 1952. *Aufsätze zur ökonomischen Theorie.* Tübingen: J. C. B. Mohr.

———. 1953. *Aufsätze zur Soziologie.* Tübingen: J. C. B. Mohr.

———. 1954a. *Economic Doctrine and Method: An Historical Sketch,* trans. R. Aris. Oxford: Oxford University Press.

———. 1954b. *History of Economic Analysis.* New York: Oxford University Press.

———. 1985. *Aufsätze zur Wirtschaftspolitik,* ed. W. F. Stolper and C. Seidl. Tübingen: J. C. B. Mohr.

———. 1987. "Some Questions of Principle." *Research in the History of Economic Thought and Methodology* 5: 93–116.

———. 1991. *The Economics and Sociology of Capitalism,* ed. R. Swedberg. Princeton, N.J.: Princeton University Press.

———. 1992. *Politische Reden,* ed. C. Seidl and W. F. Stolper. Tübingen: J. C. B. Mohr.

———. 1993. *Aufsätze zur Tagespolitik,* ed. C. Seidl and W. F. Stolper. Tübingen: J. C. B. Mohr.

———. 2000. *Briefe/Letters,* ed. U. Hedtke and R. Swedberg. Tübingen: Mohr Siebeck.

Semmel, Bernard. 1992. "Schumpeter's Curious Politics." *The Public Interest* 106 (Winter): 3–16.

Sen, Amartya K. 1979. "Rational Fools: A Critique of the Behavioural Foundations of Economic Theory." In *Philosophy and Economic Theory,* ed. F. Hahn and M. Hollis. Oxford: Oxford University Press.

Shapiro, Ian. 1982. "Realism in the Study of the History of Ideas." *History of Political Thought* 3, 3 (November): 535–577.

———. 1994. "Three Ways to Be a Democrat." *Political Theory* 22 (1): 124–151.

Shapiro, Ian, and Alexander Wendt. 1992. "The Difference that Realism Makes: Social Science and the Politics of Consent." *Politics and Society* 20 (2): 197–223.

Sheehan, Thomas. 1988. "Heidegger and the Nazis." Review of *Heidegger et le Nazisme,* by Victor Farias. *New York Review of Books* 35.

Shionoya, Yuichi. 1990a. "Instrumentalism in Schumpeter's Economic Methodology." *History of Political Economy* 22 (2): 187–222.

———. 1990b. "The Origin of the Schumpeterian Research Program: A Chapter Omitted from Schumpeter's Theory of Economic Development." *Journal of Institutional and Theoretical Economics* 146 (2): 314–327.

———. 1991. "Schumpeter on Schmoller and Weber: A Methodology of Economic Sociology." *History of Political Economy* 23 (2): 193–219.

———. 1997. *Schumpeter and the Idea of Social Science: A Metatheoretical Study.* Historical Perspectives on Modern Economics, ed. C. D. Goodwin. Cambridge: Cambridge University Press.

Simpson, David. 1983. "Joseph Schumpeter and the Austrian School of Economics." *Journal of Economic Studies* 10 (4): 15–28.

Sinclair, Upton. 1970. "The Industrial Republic." In *Socialism in America, From the Shakers to the Third International: A Documentary History,* ed. A. Fried. Garden City, N.Y.: Doubleday.

Skinner, Quentin. 1973. "The Empirical Theorists of Democracy and Their Critics: A Plague on Both Their Houses." *Political Theory* 1 (3): 287–306.

———. 1988. "Meaning and Understanding in the History of Ideas." In *Meaning and Context: Quentin Skinner and His Critics,* ed. J. Tully. Princeton, N.J.: Princeton University Press.

Sorel, Georges. 1976. *From Georges Sorel: Essays in Socialism and Philosophy,* trans. John Stanley and Charlotte Stanley, ed. J. L. Stanley. New York: Oxford University Press.

Sozialisierungskommission. 1919a. Protokolle der vertraulichen Sitzungen der Sozialisierungskommission. In Bundesarchiv, Abteilungen Potsdam, 31.05.

———. 1919b. Vorläufiger Bericht der Sozialisierungskommission über die Frage der Sozialisierung des Kohlenbergbaus. In Bundesarchiv, Abteilungen Potsdam, 31.05.

Steenson, Gary P. 1978. *Karl Kautsky, 1854–1938: Marxism in the Classical Years.* Pittsburgh: University of Pittsburgh Press.

Stolper, Wolgang F. 1985. "Schumpeter and the German and Austrian Socialization Attempts of 1918–1919." *Research in the History of Economic Thought and Methodology* 3: 161–185.

————. 1994. *Joseph Alois Schumpeter: The Public Life of a Private Man.* Princeton, N.J.: Princeton University Press.

Streissler, Eric. 1983. "Schumpeter and Hayek: On Some Similarities in Their Thought." In *Reflections on a Troubled World Economy,* ed. F. Machlup, G. Fels, and H. Miller-Groeling. London: Macmillan.

Struve, Walter. 1973. *Elites against Democracy: Leadership Ideals in Bourgeois Political Thought in Germany, 1890–1933.* Princeton, N.J.: Princeton University Press.

Swedberg, Richard. 1989. "Joseph A. Schumpeter and the Tradition of Economic Sociology." *Journal of Institutional and Theoretical Economics* 145: 508–524.

————. 1991a. *Joseph A. Schumpeter: His Life and Work.* Cambridge: Polity Press.

————. 1991b. "The Man and His Work." In *The Economics and Sociology of Capitalism,* ed. R. Swedberg. Princeton, N.J.: Princeton University Press.

Sweezy, Paul M. 1942. *The Theory of Capitalist Development: Principles of Marxian Political Economy.* New York: Oxford University Press.

Taylor, Charles. 1979. "Interpretation and the Sciences of Man." In *Interpretive Social Science: A Reader,* ed. P. Rabinow and W. M. Sullivan. Berkeley and Los Angeles: University of California Press.

Thomas, Norman. 1938. *Socialism on the Defensive.* New York: Harper and Brothers Publishers.

Thompson, E. P. 1963. *The Making of the English Working Class.* New York: Vintage Books.

Tisch, Kläre. 1939. Letter to Joseph A. Schumpeter. In Harvard University Archives, HUG (FP) 4.7.5. Courtesy of the Harvard University Archives.

Tocqueville, Alexis de. [1835] 1945. *Democracy in America,* trans. Henry Reeve. Vol. 1. New York: Alfred A. Knopf.

————. [1840] 1945. *Democracy in America,* trans. Henry Reeve. Vol. 2. New York: Vintage Books.

Turner, Stephen P., and Regis A. Factor. 1984. *Max Weber and the Dispute over Reason and Value: A Study in Philosophy, Ethics and Politics.* London: Routledge and Kegan Paul.

Vaughan, Karen I. 1987. "Carl Menger." In *The New Palgrave: A Dictionary of Economics,* ed. J. Eatwell, M. Milgate, and P. Newman. London: Macmillan.

Vogelstein, Theodor M. 1950. "Joseph A. Schumpeter and the Sozialisierungskommission: An Annotation to Gottfried Haberler's Memoir of Schumpeter." In Harvard University Archives, HUG (FP) 4.7 Box 3. Courtesy of the Harvard University Archives.

Walker, Jack L. 1966. "A Critique of the Elitist Theory of Democracy." *American Political Science Review* 60, 2 (June): 285–305.

Wallas, Graham. 1981. *Human Nature in Politics*. New Brunswick, N.J.: Transaction Books.

Waller, Michael. 1994. "Voice, Choice, and Loyalty: Democratization in Eastern Europe." In *Democracy and Democratization*, ed. G. Parry and M. Moran. London: Routledge.

Warriner, Doreen. 1931. "Schumpeter and the Conception of Static Equilibrium." *The Economic Journal* 41 (161): 38–50.

Weber, Max. [1919] 1946. "Politics as a Vocation." In *From Max Weber: Essays in Sociology*, ed. H. H. Gerth and C. W. Mills. New York: Oxford University Press.

———. 1946. "Science as a Vocation." In *From Max Weber: Essays in Sociology*, ed. H. H. Gerth and C. W. Mills. New York: Oxford University Press.

———. 1949. *The Methodology of the Social Sciences*, trans. Edward A. Shils and Henry A. Finch. New York: Free Press.

———. 1978. *Economy and Society: An Outline of Interpretive Sociology*, trans. Ephraim Fischoff et al., ed. G. Roth and C. Wittich. 2 vols. Berkeley and Los Angeles: University of California Press.

Weingast, Barry R. 1995. "The Economic Role of Political Institutions: Federalism, Markets, and Economic Development." *Journal of Law, Economics, and Organization* 11 (April): 1–31.

———. 1997. "The Political Foundations of Democracy and the Rule of Law." *American Political Science Review* 91, 2 (June): 245–263.

Wilentz, Sean. 1988. "Many Democracies: On Tocqueville and Jacksonian America." In *Reconsidering Tocqueville's Democracy in America*, ed. A. S. Eisenstadt. New Brunswick, N.J.: Rutgers University Press.

Wood, Ellen Meiksins. 1983. "The State and Popular Sovereignty in French Political Thought: A Genealogy of Rousseau's 'General Will.'" *History of Political Thought* 4, 2 (Summer): 281–315.

Wright, David M. 1951. "Schumpeter's Political Philosophy." In *Schumpeter, Social Scientist*, ed. S. E. Harris. Cambridge, Mass.: Harvard University Press.

Xenos, Nicholas. 1981. "Democracy as Method: Joseph A. Schumpeter." *Democracy* 1 (4): 110–123.

Yee, Albert S. 1997. "Thick Rationality and the Missing 'Brute Fact': The Limits of Rationalist Incorporations of Norms and Ideas." *Journal of Politics* 59, 4 (November): 1001–1039.

Young, Iris Marion. 1990. *Justice and the Politics of Difference*. Princeton, N.J.: Princeton University Press.

Zassenhaus, Herbert K. 1981. "The 'Vision' and the 'Theories.'" In *Schumpeter's Vision: Capitalism, Socialism, and Democracy after Forty Years*, ed. A. Heertje. Eastbourne, England: Praeger.

Index

Administration and democracy, 105

Allen, Robert Loring, 223n61; on Schumpeter's political theory, 10, 11; use of Schumpeter's diaries, 12; on Schumpeter's political activities, 21; on Schumpeter's Nazi sympathies, 21–22, 69, 75; on Schumpeter as member of the German Socialization Commission, 66; on science and ideology, 167; on Schumpeter's anti-Bolshevism, 223n62; on Schumpeter's anti-Semitism, 223n65

Almond, Gabriel, 10

Alpine-Montan-Gesellschaft, 65, 67

Antipolitics, 201–202

Anti-Semitism, 71. *See also* Schumpeter, Joseph A.

Arato, Andrew, 217n12

Aristocracy, 39. *See also* Tory democracy

Ashmead-Bartlett, Ellis, 220n40

Austerlitz, Friedrich, 25

Austin, J. L., 219n28

Austrian civil war, 76

Austrian Social Democratic Party, 22; Schumpeter's response to, 23; and freedom of expression, 24; protest actions by, 24; and universal suffrage, 24–25; opposition to kaiser, 25; and establishment of republic, 26, 27; and nationalism, 27, 28; and Brünn program, 27; and integration with Germany, 28; and Christian Social Party, 30; decline in strength of, 80

Austrian Socialization Commission, 48, 56

Austro-Marxists, 22, 23. *See also* Austrian Social Democratic Party; Bauer, Otto; Hilferding, Rudolf; Renner, Karl

Autocracy, 128

Bachrach, Peter, 144, 228n14, 228n15

Bauer, Otto, 22; as foreign minister of Austria, 19; on establishment of a democratic republic, 26; on nationalism, 27, 56; influence on Schumpeter, 48, 58, 135; on socialization, 48–49; transformative conception of democracy, 51–57, 210–211; G. D. H. Cole's influence on, 54; and functional democracy, 54, 210; on political and social revolution, 54–55; on Bolshevik revolution, 55; as president of Austrian Socialization Commission, 56; and Alpine-Montan-Gesellschaft, 67; on developmental aspects of democracy, 118, 131–132, 229n20; Schumpeter in seminar with, 169; and Schumpeter as finance minister, 220n43; and syndicalism, 222n52

Bentham, Jeremy, 114–115

Berelson, Bernard R., 2

Bhaskar, Roy, 232n16

Böhm-Bawerk, Eugen von, 169, 232n15

Bolshevism/Bolshevik revolution, 55, 58, 64, 137, 138

Bottomore, Tom, 12, 141, 216n8

Bourgeois family, 86, 89–90

Boyer, John W., 217n13, 218n21

Business cycles, 151, 152

Capitalist motion, 83

Capitalist order, 83, 84–88, 153

Capitalist system, 83–84, 153

Capital levy, 220n44

Catholics, Austrian, 41. *See also* Christian Social Party

Christian Social Party, 22; ideology of, 29; on

Elite theory and theorists: critique of democracy, 4, 7–8; Schumpeter's turn toward, 107, 113; political aims, 107–108; and social structure, 108–109; and elite capabilities, 110; and circulation of elites, 110–111; and democracy, 111–112; and innovation, 182

Entrepreneurs: and economic development, 59, 81; and capitalist decline, 81; and rational action, 84, 163–164; and economic sociology, 157; politicians as, 180

Equilibrium, 152

Equilibrium analysis, 9, 177–199; and Walras, 145–149; and determinacy, 146; main features, 146; in Schumpeter's work, 146–147, 178; limits of, 147–149, 170, 177, 182–199; external and internal sources of change, 148; Schumpeter's main criticisms of, 148–149, 186; and elite conception of democracy, 179–182; and ideology, 185–186; and economic sociology, 193–195; different approaches to, 196

Facts: and values, 167, 174–175; and scientific method, 174; and ideology, 183, 184, 191

Feminism, 89–90

Ferejohn, John, 190

Franz Josef I, 24, 25, 43–44

Freedom of expression, 124–126

Friedländer, Saul, 7

Fukuyama, Francis, 200

Functional democracy, 50, 54, 131, 210

Geertz, Clifford, 184, 185, 232n14

Gender and democracy, 122–124

General will. *See* Common will

German Social Democratic Party, 65

German Socialization Commission, 47, 65, 66

Giddens, Anthony, 231n13

Gladstone, William E., 41, 42

Guild socialism, 50

Gulick, Charles, 67

Gunnell, John, 143

Haberler, Gottfried, 65

Habsburg empire: electoral system of, 24;

collapse of, 26, 28, 31–32; and Christian Social Party, 31–32; endangered by democracy, 38; war economy of, 64

Harrach, Count Otto, 33, 37, 40

Havel, Václav, 202

Hayek, Friedrich A. von, 102–104

Hedtke, Ulrich, 215n4

Heidegger, Martin, 68

Held, David, 10, 11, 168, 228n15

Hempel, Carl, 232n17

Hilferding, Rudolf: on finance capital, 49; influence on other Austro-Marxists, 49; Schumpeter in seminar with, 169; critique of marginalism, 169, 223n15; possible influence on Schumpeter, 169–170; pacifism, 217n15; and German Socialization Commission, 220n42

Historical perspective in social science, 154, 176

Hobsbawm, Eric J., 218n16

Human nature, 118–119, 121, 126–127

Hungarian soviet, 45

Huntington, Samuel, 2, 10

Ideology: political theory as, 13; and science, 14, 167–176, 183; Marxist theory of, 172; Schumpeter's view of, 182–183; elements of a conception of, 183–186; and equilibrium analysis, 185–186; and developmental aspects of democracy, 188; and Anthony Downs, 191–193; and social agreements, 197; and fall of communism, 201–203. *See also* Democracy

Individualism. *See* Methodological individualism; Political individualism; Sociological individualism

Individual will, 117

Industrial democracy. *See* Economic democracy

Innovation: and economic development, 59, 150–151, 164, 186; and rational action, 163–164; individual and group, 165; versus invention, 165; and ideology, 178, 201–203; and transformative conception of democracy, 178, 186–187; and elite conception of democracy, 181–182

Intellectuals, 94

Interests, 185

Interpretive methodology, 13–15